Treasures for Scholars Worldwide

浙江省档案馆藏
中国旧海关瓯海关税务司与
海关总税务司署往来机要函

Semi-official Correspondence Between Wenchow Commissioners and the Inspectorate General of Customs in Zhejiang Provincial Archives

主　　编｜赵　伐　周彩英

本册编译｜何习尧

1

广西师范大学出版社

·桂林·

浙江省档案馆藏中国旧海关瓯海关税务司与海关总税务司署往来机要函（1—5册）
ZHEJIANGSHENG DANG'ANGUAN CANG ZHONGGUO JIUHAIGUAN OUHAIGUAN SHUIWUSI YU HAIGUANZONGSHUIWUSISHU WANGLAI JIYAOHAN

图书在版编目（CIP）数据

浙江省档案馆藏中国旧海关瓯海关税务司与海关总税务司署往来机要函. 1—5册 / 赵伐，周彩英主编.
桂林 : 广西师范大学出版社，2024.12. -- ISBN 978-7-5598-7397-2

Ⅰ. F752.55

中国国家版本馆 CIP 数据核字第 2024B2H461 号

广西师范大学出版社出版发行

（广西桂林市五里店路9号　邮政编码：541004
　网址：http://www.bbtpress.com ）

出版人：黄轩庄
全国新华书店经销
广西广大印务有限责任公司印刷
（桂林市临桂区秧塘工业园西城大道北侧广西师范大学出版社集团
有限公司创意产业园内　邮政编码：541199）
开本：880 mm × 1 240 mm　1/16
印张：168.75　　　字数：2 700 千
2024 年 12 月第 1 版　　2024 年 12 月第 1 次印刷
定价：4600.00 元（1—5 册）

如发现印装质量问题，影响阅读，请与出版社发行部门联系调换。

浙江省文化研究工程指导委员会

主　　任　王　浩
副　主　任　刘　捷　彭佳学　邱启文　赵　承
　　　　　　胡　伟　任少波
成　　员　高浩杰　朱卫江　梁　群　来颖杰
　　　　　陈柳裕　杜旭亮　陈春雷　尹学群
　　　　　吴伟斌　陈广胜　王四清　郭华巍
　　　　　盛世豪　程为民　蔡袁强　蒋云良
　　　　　陈　浩　陈　伟　施惠芳　朱重烈
　　　　　高　屹　何中伟　李跃旗　吴舜泽

《浙江省档案馆藏中国旧海关
瓯海关税务司与海关总税务司署往来机要函》编委会
（1—5册）

编委会主任　胡元潮　赵　伐
编　　委　　何秋琴　周彩英　何习尧　肖奇民
主　　编　　赵　伐　周彩英

浙江文化研究工程成果文库总序

　　有人将文化比作一条来自老祖宗而又流向未来的河，这是说文化的传统，通过纵向传承和横向传递，生生不息地影响和引领着人们的生存与发展；有人说文化是人类的思想、智慧、信仰、情感和生活的载体、方式和方法，这是将文化作为人们代代相传的生活方式的整体。我们说，文化为群体生活提供规范、方式与环境，文化通过传承为社会进步发挥基础作用，文化会促进或制约经济乃至整个社会的发展。文化的力量，已经深深熔铸在民族的生命力、创造力和凝聚力之中。

　　在人类文化演化的进程中，各种文化都在其内部生成众多的元素、层次与类型，由此决定了文化的多样性与复杂性。

　　中国文化的博大精深，来源于其内部生成的多姿多彩；中国文化的历久弥新，取决于其变迁过程中各种元素、层次、类型在内容和结构上通过碰撞、解构、融合而产生的革故鼎新的强大动力。

　　中国土地广袤、疆域辽阔，不同区域间因自然环境、经济环境、社会环境等诸多方面的差异，建构了不同的区域文化。区域文化如同百川归海，共同汇聚成中国文化的大传统，这种大传统如同春风化雨，渗透于各种区域文化之中。在这个过程中，区域文化如同清溪山泉潺潺不息，在中国文化的共同价值取向下，以自己的独特个性支撑着、引领着本地经济社会的发展。

　　从区域文化入手，对一地文化的历史与现状展开全面、系统、扎实、有序的研究，一方面可以藉此梳理和弘扬当地的历史传统和文化资源，繁荣和丰富当代的先进文化建设活动，规划和指导未来的文化发展蓝图，增强文化软实力，为全面建设小康社会、加快推进社会主义现代化提供思想保证、精神动力、智力支持和舆论力量；另一方面，这也是深入了解中国文化、研究中国文化、发展中国文化、创新中国文化的重要途径之一。如今，区域文化研究日益受到各地重视，成为我国文化研究走向深入的一个重要标志。我们今天实施浙江文化研究工程,其目的和意义也在于此。

千百年来,浙江人民积淀和传承了一个底蕴深厚的文化传统。这种文化传统的独特性,正在于它令人惊叹的富于创造力的智慧和力量。

浙江文化中富于创造力的基因,早早地出现在其历史的源头。在浙江新石器时代最为著名的跨湖桥、河姆渡、马家浜和良渚的考古文化中,浙江先民们都以不同凡响的作为,在中华民族的文明之源留下了创造和进步的印记。

浙江人民在与时俱进的历史轨迹上一路走来,秉承富于创造力的文化传统,这深深地融汇在一代代浙江人民的血液中,体现在浙江人民的行为上,也在浙江历史上众多杰出人物身上得到充分展示。从大禹的因势利导、敬业治水,到勾践的卧薪尝胆、励精图治;从钱氏的保境安民、纳土归宋,到胡则的为官一任、造福一方;从岳飞、于谦的精忠报国、清白一生,到方孝孺、张苍水的刚正不阿、以身殉国;从沈括的博学多识、精研深究,到竺可桢的科学救国、求是一生;无论是陈亮、叶适的经世致用,还是黄宗羲的工商皆本;无论是王充、王阳明的批判、自觉,还是龚自珍、蔡元培的开明、开放,等等,都展示了浙江深厚的文化底蕴,凝聚了浙江人民求真务实的创造精神。

代代相传的文化创造的作为和精神,从观念、态度、行为方式和价值取向上,孕育、形成和发展了渊源有自的浙江地域文化传统和与时俱进的浙江文化精神,她滋育着浙江的生命力、催生着浙江的凝聚力、激发着浙江的创造力、培植着浙江的竞争力,激励着浙江人民永不自满、永不停息,在各个不同的历史时期不断地超越自我、创业奋进。

悠久深厚、意韵丰富的浙江文化传统,是历史赐予我们的宝贵财富,也是我们开拓未来的丰富资源和不竭动力。党的十六大以来推进浙江新发展的实践,使我们越来越深刻地认识到,与国家实施改革开放大政方针相伴随的浙江经济社会持续快速健康发展的深层原因,就在于浙江深厚的文化底蕴和文化传统与当今时代精神的有机结合,就在于发展先进生产力与发展先进文化的有机结合。今后一个时期浙江能否在全面建设小康社会、加快社会主义现代化建设进程中继续走在前列,很大程度上取决于我们对文化力量的深刻认识、对发展先进文化的高度自觉和对加快建设文化大省的工作力度。我们应该看到,文化的力量最终可以转化为物质的力量,文化的软实力最终可以转化为经济的硬实力。文化要素是综合竞争力的核心要素,文化资源是经济社会发展的重要资源,文化素质是领导者和劳动者的首要素质。因此,研究浙江文化的历史与现状,增强文化软实力,为浙江的现代化建设服务,是浙江人民的共同事业,也是浙江各级党委、政府的重要使命和责任。

2005年7月召开的中共浙江省委十一届八次全会,作出《关于加快建设文化大省的决定》,提出要从增强先进文化凝聚力、解放和发展生产力、增强社会公共服务能力入手,大力实施文明素质工程、文化精品工程、文化研究工程、文化保护工程、文化产业促进工程、文化阵地工程、文化传播工程、文化人才工程等"八项工程",实施科教兴国和人才强国战略,加快建设教育、科技、卫生、体育等"四个强省"。作为文化建设"八项工程"之一的文化研究工程,其任务就是系统研究浙江文化的历史成就和当代发展,深入挖掘浙江文化底蕴、研究浙江现象、总结浙江经验、指导浙江未来的发展。

浙江文化研究工程将重点研究"今、古、人、文"四个方面,即围绕浙江当代发展问题研究、浙江历史文化专题研究、浙江名人研究、浙江历史文献整理四大板块,开展系统研究,出版系列丛书。在研究内容上,深入挖掘浙江文化底蕴,系统梳理和分析浙江历史文化的内部结构、变化规律和地域特色,坚持和发展浙江精神;研究浙江文化与其他地域文化的异同,厘清浙江文化在中国文化中的地位和相互影响的关系;围绕浙江生动的当代实践,深入解读浙江现象,总结浙江经验,指导浙江发展。在研究力量上,通过课题组织、出版资助、重点研究基地建设、加强省内外大院名校合作、整合各地各部门力量等途径,形成上下联动、学界互动的整体合力。在成果运用上,注重研究成果的学术价值和应用价值,充分发挥其认识世界、传承文明、创新理论、咨政育人、服务社会的重要作用。

我们希望通过实施浙江文化研究工程,努力用浙江历史教育浙江人民、用浙江文化熏陶浙江人民、用浙江精神鼓舞浙江人民、用浙江经验引领浙江人民,进一步激发浙江人民的无穷智慧和伟大创造能力,推动浙江实现又快又好发展。

今天,我们踏着来自历史的河流,受着一方百姓的期许,理应负起使命,至诚奉献,让我们的文化绵延不绝,让我们的创造生生不息。

2006年5月30日于杭州

前　言

中国旧海关又称中国近代海关。浙江近代海关有浙海关、瓯海关、杭州关。

清康熙二十四年(1685)，清政府在今温州前街设立浙海关温州口，由浙海关统辖。1861年温州口改为常关，归浙常关管理。1876年温州作为通商口岸开放，1877年4月正式成立温海关，后改名为"瓯海关"，管辖温台沿海一带税务，与原设温州常关分别征收进出口岸的洋式船舶和本国木帆船及所载货物的关税和常税。1931年常关被裁撤。抗战时期，瓯海关曾迁至瑞安、平阳等处办公。1945年迁回温州，恢复稽征。1949年温州解放后，瓯海关由温州市军管会接管。

外籍税务司管理下的瓯海关形成了一批海关档案，现存于浙江省档案馆，包括海关出版物、海关人物档案、外交档案和海关内部档案四大类。海关内部档案除在税收、缉私、检疫、海务、关务和人事管理等业务过程中的日常记录、报表、通知、账簿、备忘外，还包括海关总税务司署总税务司、副总税务司、各科税务司与瓯海关税务司，瓯海关税务司与海关监督和所辖分关、分卡、分所负责人及关员，瓯海关税务司与当地军、政、商、学、民各界人士之间的往来函件和业务文书。

中国近代海关文书的种类较多，主要文种有：

1. 由总税务司遍发各关的"通令"(I. G. Circulars)；

2. 由副总税务司遍发各关的"通函"(D.I.G. Circulars, Printed Notes, or Circular Memoranda)；

3. 由总税务司或副总税务司遍发各关的"机要通令"(S/O Circulars)；

4. 由总税务司署各科税务司遍发各关或单独发给某个或某几个海关的"通启"(Inspectorate Secretaries' Circular Notes or Memoranda)；

5. 由总税务司署总务科税务司发给各关或单独发给某个或某几个海关的"总务科税务司令"

(Chief Secretary's Orders);

6.由各海关税务司发给所辖分关、分卡、分所的"税务司令"(Commissioner's Orders);

7.由总税务司发给各关或某个或某几个海关的"指令或训令"(Despatches from I.G. to Districts);

8.由各关税务司呈送总税务司的"呈文"(Despatches from Districts to I.G.);

9.由总税务司发给各关的"手令"(S/O or Circular S/O from I.G. to Districts);

10.由各关税务司呈送总税务司的"函呈"(S/O from Districts to I.G.);

11.由总税务司发给各关的"密令"(IGS or Circular IGS from I.G. to Districts);

12.由各关税务司呈送总税务司的"密呈"(IGS from Districts to I.G.);

13.总税务司署各科税务司与各关税务司之间的"笺函"(Memoranda between Inspectorate Secretaries and District Commissioners)。

除上述文种外,近代海关文书还包括各关之间,各关与分关、分卡、分所之间,各关与当地政府和社会各界之间往来的电报、电函、公函、笺函、半官函和私函等。上述"机要通令""手令""函呈""密令"和"密呈",统称为"机要函(密函)"(亦译半官函)(S/O Letter或IGS/Letter)。

机要函(密函)因其情报性质和功能成为近代海关独特的函件类型。近代海关总税务司署通令第15号(1874年)规定:"作为呈文之补充,税务司须每隔两周以机要函或密函向总税务司报告所驻在口岸或其附近发生之令人关注或重要事件,而不宜以正式公文上报者。……任何非海关事务,凡涉及洋人或当地华人,须上达北京者或可能招致北京官员干预者,或发生之事件有益或有损于当地利益者,或对他处利益有特殊影响者,以及任何个人之言行,为海关利益计总税务司应知晓者,均可成为机要函之内容。……用机要函方法传递此类消息,与办理海关日常公事同为税务司职责所在。"此后,在通令第874号(1899年)、第958号(1900年)、第1213号(1905年)、第1983号(1912年)、第2633号(1917年)、第2911号(1919年)、第3165号(1921年)、第3426号(1923年)、第123号和第5047号(1935年),以及副总税务司通启第12号(1900年)中,又对机要函(密函)的内容、性质、格式和建档做了重申和要求,强调各关"须每两周一次定期呈报,其间如有特殊情况发生亦可随时提交"(1917年通令第2633号),重申机要函(密函)"应作为申呈之补充而非取代申呈",其内容须为当地重要或有影响的事件(1935年通令第5047号和第123号)。至于各关如何保存、处置机要函(密函),1912年第1983号通令也有规定:"机要函属税务司档案,应建档并移交下任,各口岸海关税务司离任和就任报告中须包括机要函移交和接收的内容。总税务司署的机要函须登记并存入总税务司机要函机密档案(Inspector General's confidential semi-official archives)。"可见,各口岸海关税务司在工作中所形成和保存的机要函(密函),其内容涉及对当地局势的陈述及看法,当地发生的气象、地质、瘟疫、天灾、人祸等灾害及影响,与地方政府机构、军队、警察、商会、海关监督、国外使领馆及洋商洋人等之间的关系,对当地官员及施政的评价,以及对海关税收、港务、关产、财务、人事等事务的评价,内容丰富,信息敏感,是极为宝贵的海关史料,对了解各海关驻在地当时的政治、经济、社会、文化、商情、社情、民情等具有独特的史料价值,是研究口岸所在地历史的珍贵文献。

本书编译的瓯海关机要函(密函)始于1914年,止于1949年,既有涉及"不宜以正式公文上报"之非海关事务的内容,如当地政情、军情、商情、民情等,又有涉及海关业务处理、申请拨款、处置关产,与海关监督和常关关系,以及海关各项制度和规定在当地执行时的困难、差异和变通等细节内容。这些都可成为研究海关驻在地地方史和中国近代海关内部运行和效能的独特资料。比如,从1921年—1922年瓯海关税务司阿拉巴德和代理税务司威立师先后与总税务司安格联的密函中,可详细了解浙江省宪自治运动期间温州当地局势、浙江督军卢永祥与当地道尹的关系和对选举中央政府的态度、永嘉筹金赎路会开展向日本赎回胶州铁路的游行、温州抵制日货运动、海关官员对当地局势、当地政府效能和海关监督机构的评价、外商在当地建造储油设施、赈灾济贫情况等。这些记载从外籍税务司的观察和思考出发,带有明显的"他者观点",为考证和分析浙江地方近代社会提供了多维视角。再如,在近代海关制度设计中,海关监督原本作为清政府在某一地区行使海关主权的名义首长,"各口税务司……系帮同各监督办事"(何桂清复华约翰照会,《吴煦档案选编》第4辑),但为控制征税权力,实现关政统一,"把关税行政完全从地方当局手中取出"(赫德和威妥玛密商语),总税务司赫德有意混淆海关监督和税务司的职责界限,称"在税务司和监督之间设置一条固定的分界线是不可能的"(《总税务司通札》第1辑1861—1875),指示各口税务司利用巧妙手法,窃夺海关监督权力,形成"税务司为事实上之监督官。海关监督仅为名义上之监督官而已"(高柳松一郎《中国关税制度论》,2015)之现状。海关监督与税务司的这种畸形关系导致其在实际工作中龃龉不断,前者被后者逐步架空,而这一演变过程在瓯海关各个时期的机要函(密函)中得以生动展现,可为研究中国近代海关内部运行机制和实况提供个案。

本书采用编年方式对机要函(密函)进行整理和编译,以"形成时间""发文者""受文者""事由"为关键要素编译信函标题。选取的信函种类包括:总税务司或副总税务司发给瓯海关税务司的手令、密令、密函和机要通令,瓯海关税务司呈送总税务司或副总税务司的函呈、密呈、密函,以及瓯海关税务司与总署各科税务司往来的半官函,统称为机要函(密函)。这些档案文献与近代海关内部出版物不同,是瓯海关税务司及关员在其工作中直接形成的档案,既具有原始性,也具独特性。同时,因旧海关档案以英文为主,之前整理未细化到文件级目录,更没有中文目录,瓯海关档案的具体内容鲜为人知,浙江省档案馆对外未有全文公布,本次整理出版也属首次编译出版。

据剑桥大学东亚研究所中国现代史教授方德万(Hans Van De Ven)在其著作《潮来潮去:海关与中国现代性的全球起源》(姚永超、蔡维屏译,山西人民出版社,2017)中介绍,机要函(密函)是半官函性质的文书,外籍税务司在离职时,偶有带走,故它们散落在世界各地,但依然有大部分散存于各地馆藏的13万卷旧海关档案中。不过,由于这些档案现分散存于各地档案馆或图书馆,很难全面、系统地从中整理出属于机要函(密函)这一类文书,因此留世的旧海关半官函究竟有多少难以考证。因编者精力有限,本次整理的机要函(密函)以浙江省档案馆藏近代海关档案为基础,未到其他档案馆进行挖掘、考证、补充。受馆藏的局限,所选信函难免不够齐全、完整,敬请谅解。

赵　伐　周彩英
2023年4月8日
于小和山寻语山下

凡　例

一、《浙江省档案馆藏中国旧海关瓯海关税务司与海关总税务司署往来机要函》(1—15册)收录1914年至1949年瓯海关与海关总税务司署之间往来的机要函(密函)，由浙江省档案馆藏瓯海关全宗(L060)的原件复制整理、翻译编目而成。

二、本书采用编年方式，分年代对原始档案进行整理，以机要函形成的年、月、日为编排顺序。

三、各分册内容包括：提要、分册目录、函件原件。各分册目录列信函标题、页码两项。标题内容包含了信函形成时间，责任者与受文者、事由、信函原编码、档号等要素。

1.函件形成时间指该函件正式发出时间，该函件附件形成的时间不列出。如原件中出现多个时间，如函件起草时间、正式发出时间、函件整理归档时间，以函件正式发出时间为准。无正式发出时间的，采用起草时间，前两者均无的函件，采用整理归档时间。

2.函件标题的发文者、受文者中文译名使用中国海关出版社2004年出版的孙修福编译的《中国近代海关高级职员年表》中的译名。其中涉及的海关名、职衔名、机构名、税种名、货品名、地名、舰艇名、币种名、度量衡单位等使用中国海关出版社2002年出版的陈诗启和孙修福主编的《中国近代海关常用语英汉对照宝典》中的译名。

3.函件标题中，信函发文者与受文者之间用了"致"或"与"连接，"×××致×××"表示发文者给受文者单向的信函，"×××与×××"表示发文者与受文者之间往来的双向信函。

4.档号为函件原件在浙江省档案馆藏档案的编号，由"瓯海关"档案全宗号、分类目录号、档案案卷号及案内档案件号组成，档案号形式为"全宗号(L060)+目录号(001)+案卷号(××××)+案卷内件号(×××)"，例：L060-001-0001-0005。

5.函件标题中表示并列事由的标点符号使用顿号或逗号,括弧使用圆括号,引号使用双引号。

6.函件标题中的年、月、日使用公元纪年。中文信函中如有"民国××年",改写成公元纪年,如:1936年。

7.函件标题中的数字,如"第一二九号文""二千五百元"等使用阿拉伯数字"第129号""2500元"表示。

8.同一事由的多个文件如在上下条视文件的内容的具体情形有组合成一个条目,也有分别列出的,未完全统一;正文与附件用正文标题作为本件标题,转发文与被转发文用转发文名作本件标题。

四、本书收录的是海关总税务司署与瓯海关税务司之间的往来机要函,其他与本主题无关的信函均未包括在内,如瓯海关税务司与海关监督、与所辖分关分卡人员、与其他海关税务司、与当地军、政、商、学、民各界人士的来往信函等。

五、本次整理的原始档案以浙江省档案馆馆藏的中国近代海关档案为基础。受原始档案存档的局限,本主题的档案不一定齐全。

赵 伐　周彩英
2023年4月8日
于小和山浙江外国语学院寻语山下

提　要

　　本册收录了浙江省档案馆藏1914年至1917年瓯海关税务司与海关总税务司署总税务司及铨叙科、秘书科、总务科等税务司的往来机要函(亦称半官函)。信函如包含有附件,则用符号( )将附件名称列在该信函标题之后。为简化每封信函的标题起见,信函的责任者与受文人只写人名的中文译名,其英文原名、职务、供职单位集中在下表中列出。

姓名	职务
安格联(F. A. Aglen)	海关总税务司署总税务司
包罗(C. A. V. Bowra)	海关总税务司署总务科税务司
桑德克(L. Sandercock)	海关总税务司署铨叙科襄办副税务司兼秘书科襄办副税务司
阿其荪(G. F. H. Acheson)	海关总税务司署铨叙科署税务司兼秘书科副税务司
李家森(J. W. Richardson)	海关总税务司署总税务司秘书副税务司
易纳士(A. H. Edwardes)	海关总税务司署署襄办秘书科副税务司
伟博德(W. H. C. Weippert)	海关总税务司署秘书科副税务司
阿歧森(J. Acheson)	瓯海关税务司
谭安(C. E. Tanant)	瓯海关税务司

Contents
目　录

1914 年

4月27日，阿岐森致安格联：汇报自己已于24日就任、对新职务的适应情况及对温州的初步印象（S/O 1）（L060-001-0182-001） ……………………………………………………… 3

5月9日，李家森致阿岐森：收到其第1号半官函（S/O）（L060-001-0182-002） ………… 5

5月16日，阿岐森致安格联：汇报准备制作书箱以便更好地保存档案、修订英文版常关税则、地图和章程的进展、与领事馆沟通租用其房产等（S/O 2）（L060-001-0182-004） ………… 6

5月19日，安格联致阿岐森：希望其改善当地常关状况（S/O）（L060-001-0182-003） … 8

5月25日，李家森致阿岐森：收到其第2号半官函（S/O）（L060-001-0182-005） ………… 9

6月3日，阿岐森致安格联：申请购买打字机、新增浮标收效甚好、阴雨天气下难以精准绘制常关地图、当地政府对出口木材征收厘金遭商人抵制等（S/O 3）（L060-001-0182-006） …………………………………………………………………………………………………… 10

6月10日，阿岐森致安格联：就温州民船载木材出口于吴淞被税所征税一事建议此后向船主发放完税收据、一名常关录事被指控敲诈、制定常关关税章程和地图的进展、盐务署由杭州派员前来调查为何浙南盐税仅有浙北的一半等（S/O 4）（L060-001-0182-008） ………………… 12

6月16日，安格联致阿岐森：希望当地政府与商人就木材厘金征收达成的妥协不会导致常关税收减少（S/O）（L060-001-0182-007） ……………………………………………………… 15

6月23日，安格联致阿岐森：就温州民船于吴淞被税所征税一事询问该船在瓯海关通关时的归类情况（S/O）（L060-001-0182-009） ……………………………………………………… 16

6月24日，阿岐森致安格联：汇报厘金局对木材征税的情况、常关章程和地图绘制的进展、气温状况、政府复设道尹一职等（S/O 5）（L060-001-0182-010） ……………………… 17

7月4日，阿岐森致安格联：汇报夹板船 Chin Pao Fa 因在税务司处登记故在洋关通关、政府加征厘金暂未对常关税收造成影响、天气状况等（S/O 6）（L060-001-0182-012） ………… 21

7月7日，李家森致阿岐森：收到其第5号半官函（S/O）（L060-001-0182-011） ……… 23

7月14日，李家森致阿岐森：收到其第6号半官函（S/O）（L060-001-0182-013） ……… 24

7月21日，阿岐森致安格联：汇报推行新税则的进展、监督收到税务处的指示后对海关作调查及自己的应对、天气状况等（S/O 7）（L060-001-0182-014） …………………………… 25

8月12日，阿岐森致安格联：汇报制定常关章程和地图的进展、预计在欧洲的战争将带来的影响、天气状况等（S/O 8）（L060-001-0182-015） ……………………………………………… 31

8月25日，李家森致阿岐森：收到其第8号半官函（S/O）（L060-001-0182-016） ……… 33

8月26日，阿岐森致安格联：说明已就邮包处理问题提交呈文、汇报一名常关验货员逝世、常关职员的工作情况、道尹因贪污被解职及新任道尹情况、天气状况等（S/O 9）（L060-001-0182-017） ……………………………………………………………………………………………… 34

9月1日，李家森致阿岐森：收到其第9号半官函（S/O）（L060-001-0182-018） ……… 36

9月17日，阿岐森致安格联：汇报民船船员的私人交易现象、租用温州英国领事馆房屋的进展、缙云地区匪患猖獗、贸易及税收下降、天气状况等（S/O 10）（L060-001-0182-019） … 37

9月29日，李家森致阿岐森：收到其第10号半官函（S/O）（L060-001-0182-020） …… 39

10月6日，阿岐森致安格联：汇报派外籍钤子手调查常关支关税收及验货的工作情况、钤子手 Lee 表现良好、海关及常关税收情况、天气状况、与新设的中国银行温州支行沟通业务等（S/O 11）（L060-001-0182-021） ………………………………………………………………… 40

10月12日，阿岐森致安格联：汇报缴获德国乘客所携左轮手枪的详情（S/O 12）（L060-001-0182-023） ……………………………………………………………………………………… 43

10月20日，安格联致阿岐森：表明对支关工作除进行频繁检查外亦需变更职员（S/O）（L060-001-0182-022） ……………………………………………………………………………… 45

10月20日，安格联致阿岐森：要求就缴获左轮手枪一案以公文汇报、枪支应由税务司移交当局（S/O）（L060-001-0182-024） …………………………………………………………… 46

10月24日，阿岐森致安格联：汇报实施新税则并预估其对税收的影响、缴获的左轮手枪仍由超等总巡司第芬保管、天气状况等（S/O 13）（L060-001-0182-025） ……………………… 47

10月28日，阿岐森致安格联：汇报更换常关支关巡役及派遣钤子手 Lee 检查民船、监督对海关工作干预较少等（S/O 14）（L060-001-0182-027） ……………………………………… 49

11月3日，安格联致阿岐森：告知缴获的左轮手枪须交给监督（S/O）（L060-001-0182-026） ……………………………………………………………………………………………………… 51

11月10日，李家森致阿岐森：收到其第14号半官函（S/O）（L060-001-0182-028）…… 52

11月18日，阿岐森致安格联：详述德国人携带枪械的原因及处理情况（S/O 15）（L060-001-0182-029）……………………………………………………………………………………… 53

11月28日，阿岐森致安格联：汇报已将左轮手枪交给监督、阐述常关章程中的民船锚地界限及特别许可证相关条款、汇报道尹没收由福建民船运入的大米、天气状况等（S/O 16）（L060-001-0182-031）……………………………………………………………………………… 56

12月1日，安格联致阿岐森：认为缴获的左轮手枪不该由海关职员保存（S/O）（L060-001-0182-030）…………………………………………………………………………………… 59

12月8日，安格联致阿岐森：告知大米进口的管理不在道尹的权限范围内若道尹持续介入则要求监督上报税务处（S/O）（L060-001-0182-032）……………………………………… 60

12月19日，阿岐森致安格联：认为海关监督不可能将道尹干涉海关工作上报税务处并详细解释该案件、将办公室的保险柜和打字机送到常关使用、就棺材进口采用琼海关办法等（S/O 17）（L060-001-0182-033）………………………………………………………………… 61

12月29日，李家森致阿岐森：收到其第17号半官函（S/O）（L060-001-0182-034）…… 65

1915 年

1月4日，阿岐森致安格联：就进口大米一案说明监督暗中支持道尹、汇报司秤 Yen Po-chuang 受到不实指控、就新税则作说明、职员薪金及工作状况、外籍职员短缺、天气状况等（S/O 18）（L060-001-0182-035）…………………………………………………………………… 69

1月9日，阿岐森致安格联：汇报监督对舱单上交时间的调查（S/O 19）（L060-001-0182-037）…………………………………………………………………………………………… 79

1月19日，安格联致阿岐森：建议就进口大米一案顺其自然不再过问（S/O）（L060-001-0182-036）…………………………………………………………………………………… 80

1月19日，李家森致阿岐森：收到其第19号半官函（S/O）（L060-001-0182-038）…… 81

1月23日，安格联致阿岐森：告知就进口大米一案仍应保持行动（S/O）（L060-001-0182-039）……………………………………………………………………………………… 82

2月3日，阿岐森致安格联：汇报已按指示对进口大米一案采取行动、道尹将调离、夹板船改名事宜、与中国银行温州支行的协议基本达成、英领事希望建造用于停靠轮船的码头等（S/O 20）（L060-001-0182-040）…………………………………………………………… 83

2月17日，安格联致阿岐森：认为后续仍需修改与中国银行的协议及询问除鹰洋外在温州流通的货币（S/O）（L060-001-0182-041）……………………………………………………… 87

2月26日，阿岐森致安格联：汇报道尹拒绝归还没收的大米、道尹即将调任江苏、请示与保结相关的通令是否适用于常关录事、帮办调动事宜、温州流通的货币情况、拒绝使用监督推荐的新完税收据等（S/O 21）（L060-001-0182-042） ……………………………………… 88

3月9日，安格联致阿岐森：询问若以日本货币、湖北货币、广东货币、江南货币纳税时的汇率情况（S/O）（L060-001-0182-043） ………………………………………………………… 91

3月11日，阿岐森致安格联：汇报海关两及库平银之间汇率、关员无明显酗酒现象、天气状况、前道尹设立的稽查处被废止等（S/O 22）（L060-001-0182-044） …………………… 92

3月23日，李家森致阿岐森：收到其第22号半官函（S/O）（L060-001-0182-045） …… 94

3月23日，阿岐森致安格联：申请为常关职员升薪、汇报帮办调动情况、已要求常关职员提交保结，汇报日本货币、北洋货币、湖北货币、江南货币、广东货币的汇率等（S/O 23）（L060-001-0182-046） ………………………………………………………………………… 95

3月26日，阿岐森致安格联：汇报帮办会田常夫申请调往大连、寄出超等总巡司第芬巡视从宁波到温州内河航线的报告、5月1日起由中国银行代征税收、常关二等验货胡廷干逝世等（S/O 24）（L060-001-0182-048） …………………………………………………………… 97

3月30日，李家森致阿岐森：收到其第23号半官函（S/O）（L060-001-0182-047） …… 99

4月6日，安格联致阿岐森：说明大连关暂无职位空缺只能将会田常夫调任至其他港口、要求将司第芬的报告发送给海务巡工司（S/O）（L060-001-0182-049） ………………………… 100

4月17日，阿岐森致安格联：汇报将寄出海关两及库平银之间汇率的回复、铃子手Lee对升职表示感谢、另一名常关验货逝世但暂不打算补缺、由监督派往常关的录事因渎职被解职、批准超等总巡司第芬请假赴沪参加女儿婚礼等（S/O 25）（L060-001-0182-050） …………… 101

4月27日，安格联致阿岐森：告知可参考监督对职员的推荐但监督无任命权（S/O）（L060-001-0182-051） ……………………………………………………………………………… 104

5月6日，阿岐森致安格联：汇报因监督提出的新完税收据会导致工作量增加而拒绝该提议、就此前录取监督推荐的录事作说明、4月常关税收下降、对铃子手Lee将调任表示不舍等（S/O 26）（L060-001-0182-052） ……………………………………………………………… 105

5月18日，阿其荪致阿岐森：收到其第26号半官函（S/O）（L060-001-0182-053） …… 108

5月24日，阿岐森致安格联：汇报已将税款转移至中国银行、由于常关税收微薄申请补发款等（S/O 27）（L060-001-0182-054） ……………………………………………………… 109

6月8日，阿其荪致阿岐森：收到其第27号半官函（S/O）（L060-001-0182-055） ……… 111

6月12日，阿岐森致安格联：阐述解雇录事的原因、汇报5月和6月常关税收及贸易状况、监督就道尹没收大米一案表态、所有支关每10天将收据交至银行、监督请求让职员购买内债等（S/O 28）（L060-001-0182-056） ……………………………………………………… 112

6月29日，安格联致阿岐森：告诫税务司不应干涉职员的私人投资（S/O）（L060-001-0182-057） ……………………………………………………………………………………… 116

7月5日，阿岐森致安格联：汇报民船不上交文书的现象、4艘汽艇在无登记证书的情况下行驶、铃子手Stocks工作表现良好、暂不发放罚没罂粟花头的奖金、常关税收状况转好等（S/O 29）（L060-001-0182-058） ……………………………………………………………… 117

7月20日，安格联致阿岐森：告诫税务司对于载货民船只需索取货物申报单并依照关税章程征税（S/O）（L060-001-0182-059） …………………………………………………………………… 122

7月29日，阿岐森致安格联：就进口鱼类征税提出建议、竹子出口商就验货及税率向监督及财政部请愿、建议给民船发放结关文书并收取出口文书、关员调任情况等（S/O 30）（L060-001-0182-060） ……………………………………………………………………………………… 124

8月14日，阿其荪致阿岐森：收到其第30号半官函（S/O）（L060-001-0182-061） …… 131

8月19日，阿岐森致安格联：就油桶标识提出建议、建议为文案和常关委员加薪、关员从事引水工作所得报酬微薄、改进常关工作流程以减少验货员勒索商人的机会、浙江巡按使屈映光到访温州、常关工作备忘录草案已完成但地图尚未完成等（S/O 31）（L060-001-0182-062） … 132

8月31日，阿其荪致阿岐森：询问职员是否能兼顾海关与引水工作、拒绝为常关委员加薪、建议外籍铃子手定期检查验货员工作等（S/O）（L060-001-0182-063） ……………………… 137

9月10日，阿岐森致安格联：汇报将统计林氏兄弟引水所得报酬、就改进常关工作流程作进一步说明、未经总税务司授权放行硝石、天气及农作物状况等（S/O 32）（L060-001-0182-064） ……………………………………………………………………………………………………… 139

9月20日，阿其荪致阿岐森：收到其第32号半官函（S/O）（L060-001-0182-065） …… 142

9月28日，阿岐森致安格联：汇报林氏兄弟引水所得报酬情况、因职员薪金上调常关开支有所增加、监督对华班帮办不满等（S/O 33）（L060-001-0182-066） ……………………… 143

10月5日，桑德克致阿岐森：收到其第33号半官函（S/O）（L060-001-0182-067） …… 146

10月12日，阿岐森致安格联：汇报常关工作仍需改善、当地官员没收大米干涉海关工作、辞退两名关员、与监督就验货员被竹商指控一事的沟通情况、对职员林慈源的调离表示不舍、超等总巡司第芬患病等（S/O 34）（L060-001-0182-068） ……………………………… 147

10月26日，安格联致阿岐森：说明不能接受海关管辖下的货物被其他部门没收、要求就四联完税收据以正式公文汇报、告知征税不属于二等验货职责（S/O）（L060-001-0182-069） ……………………………………………………………………………………………………… 155

11月6日，阿岐森致安格联：汇报对鱼类的征税情况、缴获硫磺事宜、尚未收到监督就四联完税收据的消息、说明此前案件中警察未扣押乘客货物、常关税收情况、新职员到任、修改并寄出年度统计表等（S/O 35）（L060-001-0182-070） ……………………………………… 157

11月23日，阿其荪致阿岐森：收到其第35号半官函（S/O）（L060-001-0182-071） … 163

11月26日，阿岐森致安格联：汇报当地发现天然气的详情、本月鱼类税收微薄、暂未收到监督就完税收据的通知等（S/O 36）（L060-001-0182-072） ………………………………… 164

12月14日，阿其苏致阿岐森：收到其第36号半官函（S/O）（L060-001-0182-073） … 166

12月22日，阿岐森致安格联：汇报道尹令警察检查乘客有无携带违禁品、监督派委员搜查乘客有无携带革命信件、由于天气原因鱼类税收减少、为部分华员申请加薪、天气状况等（S/O 37）（L060-001-0182-074） … 167

1916年

1月10日，阿岐森致安格联：汇报因银行与海关记录每月税收的方式不同导致税收报表有误、1915年常关税收减少、鱼类税收增加、下游支关税收增加、部分关员购买内债后未收到凭证及息票等（S/O 38）（L060-001-0182-076） … 173

1月11日，安格联致阿岐森：说明警察可以在岸上检查乘客是否携带违禁品（S/O）（L060-001-0182-075） … 177

1月25日，安格联致阿岐森：告知应向代理机构索要息票并询问是否通过银行购买内债（S/O）（L060-001-0182-077） … 178

2月8日，阿岐森致安格联：汇报就内债息票问题的处理情况、目前关务较闲（S/O 39）（L060-001-0182-078） … 179

2月22日，阿其苏致阿岐森：收到其第39号半官函（S/O）（L060-001-0182-079） … 181

2月22日，阿岐森致安格联：汇报常关工作备忘录及运河地图的完善情况、商人不满货物运单的新规、因交通局未发行注册凭单导致轮船在内河无证运行、收到内债息票等（S/O 40）（L060-001-0182-080） … 182

2月26日，阿岐森致安格联：汇报寄出海关关产情况并说明常关关产情况将随后寄出、监督按财政部要求填报的统计表有小差错、天气状况等（S/O 41）（L060-001-0182-082） … 185

3月6日，阿岐森致安格联：汇报在道尹要求下警察归还误扣的大米、警察及关员奖金分发事宜、内河轮船公司开始搭建码头及仓库、对土货征税存在的不合理之处、发放内河轮船证明书时扣留其国籍登记证等（S/O 42）（L060-001-0182-084） … 187

3月7日，安格联致阿岐森：告知机制洋式货物运单的新规有待重新考虑、要求请监督将无内河行轮证书轮船的航行问题告知交通局（S/O）（L060-001-0182-081） … 192

3月14日，阿其苏致阿岐森：收到其第41号半官函（S/O）（L060-001-0182-083） … 194

3月21日，安格联致阿岐森：就内河轮船的征税事宜提出建议（S/O）（L060-001-0182-085） … 195

4月8日，阿岐森致安格联：汇报3月大量明矾出口、收到就内河轮船征税的建议并将着手处理、华商对持子口税票的洋货被征落地税表示不满、天气状况、出口的烟草被要求支付烟草专卖税等（S/O 43）（L060-001-0182-086） … 198

4月17日，阿岐森致安格联：请示浙江省宣布独立后将税款存于中国银行是否安全、内河轮船收到注册凭单及证书、放行一批军用硝石、道尹要求禁止金银出口、天气状况等（S/O 44）（L060-001-0182-088） ……… 200

4月18日，阿其苏致阿岐森：收到其第43号半官函（S/O）（L060-001-0182-087） …… 202

4月24日，阿岐森致安格联：汇报流感对海关工作造成影响、因电报局不配合故委托监督代发电报、邮政局信件失踪、天气状况等（S/O 45）（L060-001-0182-090） ……… 203

4月25日，安格联致阿岐森：认为只要外籍人士不受影响当地禁止金银出口的命令能够得以执行（S/O）（L060-001-0182-089） ……… 205

5月2日，阿其苏致阿岐森：收到其第45号半官函（S/O）（L060-001-0182-091） …… 206

5月10日，阿岐森致安格联：汇报超等总巡司第芬已完成温州河道地图并将其寄往上海、常关巡役Ma Paohing被指控袭击一名女性后请求辞职、浙江省处于军管中、认为金银的出口难以完全禁绝等（S/O 46）（L060-001-0182-092） ……… 207

5月23日，安格联致阿岐森：说明对巡役Ma Paoching的指控应由地方长官调查判处（S/O）（L060-001-0182-093） ……… 210

5月31日，阿岐森致安格联：说明自己与监督对常关人员任命的流程、对未悬挂新旗帜的水警轮船不做处理、道尹一职被裁撤、铃子手Stocks中文学习的进展、天气状况等（S/O 47）（L060-001-0182-094） ……… 211

6月20日，阿其苏致阿岐森：收到其第47号半官函（S/O）（L060-001-0182-095） …… 213

6月20日，阿岐森致安格联：汇报在袁世凯逝世后悼念问题上采取的措施、未接收监督准备移交的印花税票、英领事馆地产即将出售、因税务司公馆租约即将到期希望续租或另寻适宜场所等（S/O 48）（L060-001-0182-096） ……… 214

7月4日，安格联致阿岐森：赞同在袁世凯逝世后悼念问题上采取的措施（S/O）（L060-001-0182-097） ……… 217

7月7日，阿岐森致安格联：汇报袁世凯悼念期结束后用红色公印盖章寄出报表、对内河轮船的通商口岸贸易加强管理、常关在对茶叶征税上存在的误差、认为包税制存在问题（S/O 49）（L060-001-0182-098） ……… 218

7月18日，阿其苏致阿岐森：收到其第49号半官函（S/O）（L060-001-0182-099） …… 223

8月7日，阿岐森致安格联：汇报常关铃子手Stocks因被控渎职而辞职、收到第2533号通令并即将寄出回复、收到第2527号通令但由于监督已填报相关数据故未采取行动（S/O 50）（L060-001-0182-100） ……… 224

8月12日，阿岐森致包罗：寄送修订后的第3146号和第3154号呈文（L060-001-0182-119） ……… 227

8月14日，阿岐森致安格联：汇报Stocks被控渎职的详情、得到的相关证据、对其余涉事人员的处置、为便于监管下游支关工作申请配置汽艇等（S/O 51）（L060-001-0182-102） … 228

8月15日，安格联致阿岐森：告知在未证实Stocks的指控前应报告此事而非令其辞职（S/O）（L060-001-0182-101） ··· 237

8月16日，阿岐森致安格联：建议对常关职员加强监管、汇报下月将对巡役进行调整、怀疑Stocks可能受诽谤、监督就其职位事宜前往北京、天气状况等（S/O 52）（L060-001-0182-104） ··· 238

8月25日，易纳士致阿岐森：收到其第51号半官函（S/O）（L060-001-0182-103） ······ 241

8月31日，安格联致阿岐森：建议派洋员对各支关加强巡视检查（S/O）（L060-001-0182-105） ··· 242

9月3日，阿岐森致安格联：希望总税务司告知在北京的瓯海关监督对海关工作及Stocks事件的看法、在常关给帮办金子四郎安排隔间作办公用、帮办黄厚诚请假等（S/O 53）（L060-001-0182-106） ··· 243

9月9日，阿岐森致安格联：汇报铃子手Power刚到任即辞职并请求继任者（S/O 54）（L060-001-0182-108） ··· 246

9月14日，阿岐森致包罗：希望告知继任税务司的相关信息以便提前做好相关安排（L060-001-0182-120） ··· 247

9月19日，阿其荪致阿岐森：收到其第53号半官函（S/O）（L060-001-0182-107） ······ 248

9月26日，阿其荪致阿岐森：收到其第54号半官函（S/O）（L060-001-0182-109） ······ 249

9月27日，阿岐森致安格联：汇报温州范围内出现霍乱、根据目前人手及设备情况无法实施防疫章程、三等同文供事正后班Ko Yuping工作表现良好、Kabbert尚未达到温州等（S/O 55）（L060-001-0182-110） ··· 250

10月11日，阿其荪致阿岐森：收到其第55号半官函（S/O）（L060-001-0182-111） ··· 254

10月14日，阿岐森致安格联：汇报关员工作情况、过去3个月税收上涨、得知谭安将接任瓯海关税务司、就驻扎在温州的军队即将转移请示其携带武器离境等事宜（S/O 56）（L060-001-0182-112） ··· 255

10月21日，阿岐森致安格联：建议上海对土纱做标记以便验货、汇报安装电灯的开销、常关工作顺利开展（S/O 57）（L060-001-0182-114） ··· 258

10月24日，安格联致阿岐森：认为超等总巡应该提早发现Stocks的工作表现无问题、得知金子四郎工作表现良好（S/O）（L060-001-0182-113） ··· 260

10月31日，安格联致阿岐森：同意对土纱做标记以避免税收损失（S/O）（L060-001-0182-115） ··· 261

11月1日，阿岐森致安格联：汇报Kabbert因居住条件受限申请辞职、超等总巡难以对常关作全面管理、常关职员工作由相关帮办负责监督、希望接任税务司谭安尽快到达（S/O 58）（L060-001-0182-116） ··· 263

11月8日，阿岐森致安格联：汇报已将职权移交给谭安及表达对海关祝福（S/O 59）（L060-001-0182-118） ··· 266

11月14日，安格联致谭安：告知可能让日籍职员接替Kabbert（S/O）（L060-001-0182-117） ······ 267

11月18日，谭安致安格联：汇报已就任瓯海关税务司、监督由北京返回（S/O 60）（L060-001-0182-121） ······ 268

12月7日，谭安致安格联：汇报一条新夹板船的注册、建议海关及交通注册局统一注册费用和章程、关员任命及调任事宜等（S/O 61）（L060-001-0182-123） ······ 269

12月9日，谭安致安格联：请示是否对装橘子用的木桶征税（S/O 62）（L060-001-0182-125） ······ 271

12月11日，谭安致安格联：请示是否停止新年期间与当地官员互赠礼物（S/O 63）（L060-001-0182-127） ······ 272

12月12日，阿其荪致谭安：收到其第60号半官函（S/O）（L060-001-0182-122） ······ 273

12月18日，阿其荪致谭安：收到其第61号半官函（S/O）（L060-001-0182-124） ······ 274

12月18日，安格联致谭安：要求就装橘子用的桶征税事宜查询过往的相似案例并以正式公文请示（S/O）（L060-001-0182-126） ······ 275

12月27日，安格联致谭安：表明可自行决定是否停止新年期间与当地官员互赠礼物（S/O）（L060-001-0182-128） ······ 276

1917年

1月9日，谭安致安格联：就凭子口税票进口的煤油在温州的分装事宜作请示、汇报美孚石油公司的货物运输情况、员工工作情况及动向、英国领事馆给验货员Verner寄送征兵函等（S/O 64）（L060-001-0182-129） ······ 279

1月16日，谭安致安格联：汇报宁村支关的公文被盗案件及对涉事的常关二等验货Feng Chenhai的调查情况（S/O 65）（L060-001-0182-131） ······ 284

1月22日，安格联致谭安：告知持有子口税票进口的煤油无须在瓯海关交税可直接通关前往目的地（S/O）（L060-001-0182-130） ······ 287

1月25日，谭安致安格联：汇报常关二等验货Wu Chita接受建议并辞职、任命巡役Tung Chiu为二等验货、任命Wu Chita的儿子为巡役、建议以后从巡役中提拔验货员等（S/O 66）（L060-001-0182-133） ······ 288

1月27日，谭安致安格联：汇报监督试图对坎门的鱼类征税并建议设法阻止（1914-1916年各支关鱼类税收明细）（S/O 67）（L060-001-0182-135） ······ 291

1月30日，安格联致谭安：强调必须公正处理宁村支关公文被盗案件（S/O）（L060-001-0182-132） ······ 297

2月5日，谭安致安格联：汇报美孚石油公司煤油运输目的地的详情、将有走私嫌疑的邮包移交给邮务长、工人拆卸武器时发生的爆炸事件等（附邮务长给瓯海关税务司的信函）（S/O 68）（L060-001-0182-137） 298

2月10日，谭安致安格联：汇报宁村支关公文被盗案件已解决及对Feng Chenhai采取扣除一部分工资的处罚、三等验货员Verner患病、天气状况等（S/O 69）（L060-001-0182-139） 307

2月14日，安格联致谭安：要求就是否将"二等验货"改称为"司事"提交意见并详述其地位和职责（S/O）（L060-001-0182-134） 308

2月14日，安格联致谭安：要求就美孚石油公司煤油运输目的地一事提交附地图的公函、告知不该在半官函中添加附件（S/O）（L060-001-0182-138） 309

2月16日，谭安致安格联：汇报内河轮船所载通商口岸货物的纳税问题、进口货物较少对轮船航行带来影响、轮船招商局的代理抵达温州等（S/O 70）（L060-001-0182-141） 310

2月19日，谭安致安格联：汇报已与监督联合张贴布告通知新辅币的流通并要求不得拒收（S/O 71）（L060-001-0182-143） 313

2月27日，阿其荪致谭安：收到其第67号半官函（S/O）（L060-001-0182-136） 314

2月27日，阿其荪致谭安：收到其第70号半官函（S/O）（L060-001-0182-142） 315

2月27日，阿其荪致谭安：收到其第71号半官函（S/O）（L060-001-0182-144） 316

3月9日，阿其荪致谭安：收到其第69号半官函（S/O）（L060-001-0182-140） 317

3月12日，谭安致安格联：建议采取宁波的制度以解决鹰洋兑海关两的汇率问题、监督对坎门鱼类征税的计划被阻止但税务处允许其在瑞安征收该税、抗议监督在灵昆私自征税、由杭州前来调查监督受指控一案的专员已离开（S/O 72）（L060-001-0182-145） 318

3月20日，安格联致谭安：告知税务处允许监督在瑞安征收鱼税在其预料之中（S/O）（L060-001-0182-146） 321

3月30日，谭安致安格联：汇报因海门常关开具的四联单所录重量与实际不符而对轮船公司罚款、建议向税务处汇报海门委员的渎职行为、新道尹到达温州、验货员Verner病后复职等（S/O 73）（L060-001-0182-147） 322

4月3日，谭安致安格联：建议由警察确认外国乘客国籍或予以足够的权力要求外国乘客出示护照、拒绝监督阻留德国传教士所乘轮船的要求、建议将Verner调往北部港口等（S/O 74）（L060-001-0182-149） 324

4月10日，阿其荪致谭安：收到其第73号半官函（S/O）（L060-001-0182-148） 327

4月10日，安格联致谭安：认为在温州确认外国乘客的国籍并非难事（S/O）（L060-001-0182-150） 328

4月11日，谭安致安格联：汇报政府炮舰超武在温州巡弋、帮办金子四郎的轿夫被逮捕判刑、就海关两兑国币汇率提高寻求监督的帮助及相关工作（S/O 75）（L060-001-0182-151） 329

4月19日，谭安致安格联：汇报商会反对汇率调整并建议采取标准汇率（S/O 76）（L060-001-0182-153） ……………………………………………………………………………… 332

4月24日，安格联致谭安：要求暂时不对炮舰超武采取行动（S/O）（L060-001-0182-152） ……………………………………………………………………………………………… 334

4月25日，谭安致安格联：汇报商会、监督、商人和银行对标准税率的态度、建议汇率数值等（S/O 77）（L060-001-0182-154） …………………………………………………… 335

5月1日，安格联致谭安：要求稳步推进使用标准税率、不采取折中措施（S/O）（L060-001-0182-155） …………………………………………………………………………………… 338

5月4日，谭安致安格联：汇报已通知相关方延迟调整汇率、已为持分运单的内河航行货船办理退税、夹板船 Chin Yung-fu 被定海海警扣留、超武实为警察巡逻艇、Verner 再次患病等（S/O 78）（L060-001-0182-156） ………………………………………………………… 339

5月15日，阿其荪致谭安：收到其第78号半官函（S/O）（L060-001-0182-157） ……… 344

5月23日，谭安致安格联：汇报对当地货币现状进行的调查、与中国银行就货币现状及宁波制度应用的讨论、银行要员延迟新协议实行等（S/O 79）（L060-001-0182-159） ………… 345

5月25日，谭安致安格联：汇报未收到监督冒广生就允许大米和小麦等谷物出口的回复、商会建议允许出口5000担小麦等（S/O 80）（L060-001-0182-161） ……………………… 349

6月4日，谭安致安格联：汇报缴获鸦片并逮捕涉事人员、谷物出口禁令继续、海关税收减少常关税收增加、洋广局对出口猪油征税、地方长官宣布浙江独立、监督的家眷离开温州、员工调任事宜等（S/O 81）（L060-001-0182-164） ……………………………………… 351

6月5日，安格联致谭安：说明若汇率以上海为基准中国银行在执行上应无困难（S/O）（L060-001-0182-160） …………………………………………………………………………… 355

6月5日，安格联致谭安：说明在有中央政府指令的情况下可强制解除各类谷物的出口禁令（S/O）（L060-001-0182-162） ……………………………………………………………… 356

6月9日，谭安致安格联：反对宁波的汇率实施方案在温州实行、请求就汇率问题的指示、汇报即将汇出税款（S/O 82）（L060-001-0182-166） ……………………………………… 357

6月19日，安格联致谭安：认为日本国民无权凭其政府颁发的鸦片吸食许可证将鸦片带入中国（S/O）（L060-001-0182-165） ……………………………………………………………… 360

6月19日，安格联致谭安：建议采用宁波的汇率实施方案及告知无需担心海关的权威受威胁（S/O）（L060-001-0182-167） ……………………………………………………………… 361

6月28日，谭安致安格联：汇报拒绝向银行支付额外费用、新汇率将于7月1日推行、总营造司狄克来温州实地查勘关产、6月税收状况良好等（S/O 83）（L060-001-0182-168） … 362

7月5日，谭安致安格联：汇报二等验货后班 Singer 仍处于患病状态并建议替换该职员、得知张勋复辟的消息、6月总税收状况良好、500名士兵到达温州等（S/O 84）（L060-001-0182-170） ……………………………………………………………………………… 364

7月10日，安格联致谭安：很高兴得知与银行就税收的协议已修改及汇率已提高、要求验货员H. Singer上交医生证明（S/O）（L060-001-0182-169） ………… 367

7月17日，阿其荪致阿岐森：收到其第84号半官函（S/O）（L060-001-0182-171） …… 368

7月17日，谭安致安格联：询问在海关对旅客携带现金的限制是否不适用于常关、缴获劣币及移交监督情况、驻温州军队前往处州平乱、验货员Singer仍患病由署理头等总巡雷达代替其工作、台风尚未对关产造成损失等（S/O 85）（L060-001-0182-172） …………… 369

7月21日，谭安致安格联：汇报验货员Singer申请假期、职员的住房安排及其原因、台风即将来临等（S/O 86）（L060-001-0182-174） …………………………………………… 371

7月24日，安格联致谭安：告知劣币等违禁品只能通过固定程序而不能通过贩卖来处理（S/O）（L060-001-0182-173） …………………………………………………………… 372

7月31日，阿其荪致谭安：收到其第86号半官函（S/O）（L060-001-0182-175） …… 373

8月4日，谭安致安格联：汇报监督的委员越权给货物开收税单、贸易状况不佳、海关税收减少但常关税收增加、商办轮船招商局对货运的需求少、邮政服务紊乱等（S/O 87）（L060-001-0182-176） …………………………………………………………………………… 374

8月7日，谭安致安格联：汇报给监督发放许可证以搜查乘客是否携带反动文件（S/O 88）（L060-001-0182-178） …………………………………………………………………… 379

8月9日，谭安致安格联：汇报警察擅自放行无护照大米并请求当局处罚警察违规行为（S/O 89）（L060-001-0182-180） …………………………………………………………… 380

8月14日，安格联致谭安：就监督的委员违规征税一事指示对相关货物继续征收常关税以使商人提出抗议并告知难以依靠税务处解决该问题（S/O）（L060-001-0182-177） ……… 381

8月14日，阿其荪致谭安：收到其第88号半官函（S/O）（L060-001-0182-179） ……… 382

8月21日，阿其荪致谭安：收到其第89号半官函（S/O）（L060-001-0182-181） ……… 383

8月23日，谭安致安格联：汇报就红单与监督的交涉、已就警察随委员上船搜查乘客行李提出抗议、当地长官为大米出口发放护照、当地邮件电报受限、关员调任情况等（S/O 90）（L060-001-0182-182） …………………………………………………………………… 384

9月5日，阿其荪致谭安：收到其第90号半官函（S/O）（L060-001-0182-183） ……… 389

9月10日，谭安致安格联：汇报邮局的搬迁计划并希望将邮包处保留在海关附近、申请授权提高租赁给邮局房间的租金、员工安置情况、建议不许被派往常关的司秤使用轿子等（S/O 91）（L060-001-0182-184） …………………………………………………………………… 390

9月13日，谭安致安格联：汇报商办轮船招商局的轮船上存在走私现象并建议对船员罚款、自己与总巡在缉私问题上的分歧、8月税收不佳（S/O 92）（L060-001-0182-186） ……… 395

9月15日，谭安致安格联：汇报与监督在常关税则问题上的争议、与监督的委员就番薯片出口禁令的沟通情况、新验货员Ehtman目前患病但工作表现较佳（S/O 93）（L060-001-0182-189） ……………………………………………………………………………………… 397

9月18日，谭安致安格联：汇报监督及其委员设法截留海关税收的详情并希望其呈告税务处（S/O 94） ······ 399

9月22日，谭安致安格联：汇报警察协助大米私自出口一案的处理进展、与监督就解除番薯片出口禁令、委员截留咸鱼税收、预购地产之价格、调查民船锚地等事宜的沟通情况（S/O 95）（L060-001-0182-191） ······ 404

9月26日，安格联致谭安：就温州邮局搬迁一事表明邮局需将包裹送至海关接受检查、同意禁止司秤使用轿子（S/O）（L060-001-0182-185） ······ 410

9月26日，安格联致谭安：就商办轮船招商局船员涉嫌走私一事要求寻求监督配合逮捕涉案船员（S/O）（L060-001-0182-187） ······ 411

9月26日，阿其荪致谭安：告知收到其第93号半官函（S/O）（L060-001-0182-188） ······ 412

10月1日，谭安致安格联：汇报批准验货Ehtman3周假期赴沪治病、请示在紧急情况下应将权限移交给谁、就港口条例修改作沟通、就"厘金"号检查港口一事申请预付款（S/O 96）（L060-001-0182-194） ······ 413

10月2日，谭安致安格联：汇报与监督及其委员在税收问题上的交锋、委员因征税超额被捕并被解雇、请其向税务处争取鱼类征税权、海关和常关的税收状况等（S/O 97）（L060-001-0182-196） ······ 416

10月3日，安格联致谭安：就海关税收被截留一事询问能否取得此前的相关布告、税务处在此事上支持监督、同意其认为四联税单不合适的意见但表明谭安的前任已赞同此事（S/O）（L060-001-0182-190） ······ 419

10月3日，安格联致谭安：建议与监督搞好关系而不是通过总税务司及税务处解决问题、认为番薯片的出口禁令应尽快撤销（S/O）（L060-001-0182-193） ······ 420

10月8日，谭安致安格联：汇报监督的委员被解雇、希望在与监督争夺征税权一事上获取总税务司的支持（S/O 98）（L060-001-0182-198） ······ 421

10月11日，谭安致安格联：汇报监督可能被解职、希望向税务处重提蒲岐的咸鱼征税、番薯片出口禁令和在瑞安的征税权等（S/O 99）（L060-001-0182-201） ······ 426

10月16日，安格联致谭安：告知若发生紧急情况将另派员接管瓯海关、就勘查瓯海关港口的费用开销一事要求先与巡工司沟通（S/O）（L060-001-0182-195） ······ 430

10月16日，阿其荪致谭安：收到其第97号半官函（S/O）（L060-001-0182-197） ······ 431

10月16日，谭安致安格联：汇报前任税务司阿岐森并未赞同使用四联税单、认为监督被免职是向税务处重提其截留海关税收的好时机、与上海的邮件往来不畅等（S/O 100）（L060-001-0182-203） ······ 432

10月23日，安格联致谭安：告知新监督就任后可以尝试解决蒲岐支关征税权问题（S/O）（L060-001-0182-199） ······ 436

10月25日，谭安致安格联：汇报终于收到委员寄来的前征税布告、就私自出口大米的商人尚未提交罚金一事已通过监督知会地方长官要求处理（S/O 101）（L060-001-0182-205） …… 437

10月26日，谭安致安格联：汇报所收到布告中涉及征税权的内容、二等验货Ehtman已康复等（S/O 102）（L060-001-0182-207） …… 440

10月30日，阿其荪致谭安：收到其第99号半官函（S/O）（L060-001-0182-202） …… 442

10月30日，安格联致谭安：告知税务处在下决定前往往只听从一方的意见（S/O）（L060-001-0182-204） …… 443

11月3日，谭安致安格联：汇报银行拒绝按所标面值接受新国币、商人请愿要求解除小麦出口禁令、二等验货Ehtman已复职、申请任用一名二等验货及一名铃子手等（S/O 103）（L060-001-0182-209） …… 444

11月6日，安格联致谭安：赞同将监督关于征税问题的相关文件记录在案（S/O）（L060-001-0182-206） …… 448

11月6日，阿其荪致谭安：收到其第102号半官函（S/O）（L060-001-0182-208） …… 449

11月12日，谭安致安格联：汇报美孚石油公司在未知会海关的情况下修建储油池的情况、关产购置的进展、私自出口大米的商人仍未提交罚金等（S/O 104）（L060-001-0182-211） …… 450

11月13日，安格联致谭安：就银行拒绝按所标面值接受新国币一事表明海关只在其含银量足值的情况下接受政府当局所铸货币（S/O）（L060-001-0182-210） …… 453

11月19日，谭安致安格联：汇报商办轮船招商局所运一件货物被盗并请示税收处理的方式、浙江邮政司来温州考察设立邮局用地并与税务司就邮包检查交换意见等（S/O 105）（L060-001-0182-213） …… 454

11月22日，谭安致安格联：汇报监督的职务交接未完成、就条例中修改后的港口界限与总税务司署记录不一致作解释、宁波民船的锚地问题仍未解决等（S/O 106）（L060-001-0182-215） …… 458

11月28日，包罗致谭安：就商办轮船招商局所运一件货物被盗一案说明江海关税务司有权对虚报货物的船主进行罚款（S/O）（L060-001-0182-214） …… 463

11月29日，伟博德致谭安：收到其第106号半官函（S/O）（L060-001-0182-216） …… 464

12月1日，谭安致安格联：汇报温州正式宣告独立、新政府在中国银行安置警卫以防止官员取款潜逃、目前海关在资金方面并无困难、监督冒广生潜逃、新任监督徐锡麒上任等（S/O 107）（L060-001-0182-217） …… 465

12月4日，谭安致安格联：汇报省政府恢复对温州的控制、当地放松小麦出口禁令等（S/O 108）（L060-001-0182-219） …… 467

12月11日，包罗致谭安：希望温州的独立不会对征税事宜产生干扰（S/O）（L060-001-0182-218） …… 470

12月13日，谭安致安格联：建议通知浙海关及江海关免税放行赈灾物品、省政府派员调查温州的独立事件、就获许出口小麦的护照及证书采取的措施、询问是否根据袋子数量对小麦征税等（S/O 109）（L060-001-0182-221） ········· 471

12月14日，安格联致谭安：告知在地方当局正式批准美孚石油公司设立储油池之前海关不用采取任何行动（S/O）（L060-001-0182-212） ········· 474

12月18日，伟博德致谭安：收到其第108号半官函（S/O）（L060-001-0182-220） ······ 475

12月20日，谭安致安格联：就规章中的港口界限问题请示意见、汇报江海关税务司关于商办轮船招商局所运货物被盗一案的处理意见、当地政局趋稳但贸易不振等（S/O 110）（L060-001-0182-224） ········· 476

12月26日，安格联致谭安：告知在原则上小麦出口禁令"部分"取消的说法不成立、要求就护照的印花税票执行指令（S/O）（L060-001-0182-222） ········· 479

12月29日，安格联致谭安：告知已指示江海关免税放行赈灾物品（S/O）（L060-001-0182-223） ········· 480

12月31日，安格联致谭安：就商办轮船招商局所运货物被盗一案告知船长有权在一定时限内修改舱单、海关只需核对舱单不用过问偷窃案（S/O）（L060-001-0182-225） ········· 481

1914 年

S/O NO.1.

Custom House,
Wenchow, 27th April, 1914.

DEAR MR AGLEN,

Arrival,
Charge taken.

I arrived here on the 24th and, in accordance with your telegram, took over charge from Mr Bowring to-day. I was in Wenchow for six weeks in 1893 and liked my short experience of it. I think I shall enjoy life in the place just as well this time. As I have been in the port only three days, I know as yet very little about present conditions. After a while, when I have read up the correspondence and got hold of the office routine and become acquainted with the people, I shall have more to say. The impression one gets of the country and the city in coming up the river is that both are prosperous and flurishing. The crops look good and the houses well built. And the number of ships going and coming would seem to indicate quite a large trade, also a bigger revenue than we collect. No doubt in time business will increase. But, until political conditions are more settled and inland communications more up to date, we can hardly look for any great improvement.

Weather.

Weather getting warm, but still cool at

(2)

night.

  Hoping this will find you quite well,

    I remain

  Yours faithfully,

[-42]

S/O Inspectorate General of Customs,

PEKING, 9th May, 1914.

Dear Sir,

I am directed by the Inspector General to acknowledge receipt on the 8th May of your S/O No.1 dated 27th April.

Yours truly,

Richardson
Private Secretary.

J. Acheson, Esquire,

WENCHOW.

S/O NO.2

Custom House,

Wenchow, 16 May, 1914.

DEAR MR AGLEN,

Work.
   Mr Bowring left everything here in very good order and I have no difficulty in getting hold of the

Archives.
work. But a fire which took place near the Custom House on the day I took over charge directed my attention to the way in which our archives are kept and I find that this might be made more safe. We keep all our ~~books~~ correspondence and publications in book cases with glass doors and, if we had to move them, it would necessary to take them all ~~out~~ of their shelves ~~cases~~ and pack them into boxes or baskets. The result would be that insecure binding would give way and loose leaves would fly out and get lost or into the hands of people for whom they were not intended. So I am going to ~~intend~~ doing what I did at Pakhoi, i.e., get the carpenter to make some boxes in the style of the Globe-Wernicke bookcases into which I shall keep all the correspondence, past and present as well as the Customs publications of the Service, ~~and following Series~~ Ofice and Inspectorate Series. These would be locked up at the end of each day and will be furnished with brass handles, so that they will be easily removed. The cost will be small.

Native Customs.
   I have your despatch re Native Customs. I am getting the tariff turned into English and also trying to get

(2)

on with the map. Stevens has got it fairly complete, but it does not include enough of the surrounding country and I am on the look out for additional sources of information to enable me to enlarge the area of it. The regulations you wish drawn up I will take in hand in a day or two, as soon as the tariff is finished and will also see what can be done in the way of reducing expenditure and simplifying methods ~~as soon as~~ when I know more about the details of existing procedure.

Consulate.

I am preparing a form of lease for the renting of the Consulate and will send it to the Consul in Ningpo for his approval as soon as finished. It is, mutatis mutandis, the same as the lease of the Commissioner's house here. I am hurrying up with it, as Pearson, the Consul, who has just been here on a visit, has told me that the Standard Oil people want to buy ~~it~~ the house.

Weather.

Weather warmer than when I last wrote, but we are not into white clothes yet.

I remain
Yours faithfully,

INSPECTORATE GENERAL OF CUSTOMS.

S/O

PEKING, 19th May, 1914.

Dear Mr. Acheson,

I have duly received your S/O No.1 of 27th April.

I hope that you will devote your energies to improving Native Customs procedure and administration.

Yours truly,

[signature]

. Acheson, Esquire,
    WENCHOW.

42]

S/O Inspectorate General of Customs,

PEKING, 25th May, 1914.

Dear Sir,

I am directed by the Inspector General to acknowledge receipt on the 24th May of your S/O No. 2 dated 16th May.

Yours truly,

A. R. Richardson
Private Secretary.

J. Acheson, Esquire,

WENCHOW.

S/O NO.3.   Custom House,
                        Wenchow, 3rd June, 1914.

DEAR MR AGLEN,

Typewriter.   I trust you will allow the Underwood
Typewriter I have applied for in despatch No.3009. I
am willing to take the trouble to teach typewriting to
as many of the staff as possible. But the Underwood
is my machine; the Hammond has various defects which
unsuit it for doing perfectly satisfactory work.

Buoy.   The buoy Stevens has put down, and which has
been reported in my despatch No.3008, is appreciated
by the Captains navigating the river here, one or
two of them having already acknowledged its usefulness.

Native Customs.   I have been making trips on the canals
during the last few days to get some knowledge of
the trade channels and fix the positions of the
Native Customs stations accurately on the map which
is in preparation. It is now the rainy season and
most of the time the prominent marks on the surrounding hills are obscured by mist and observations
difficult to make. But in time we shall have the
map all right; I go afloat very often to see how
the junks' cargoes are dealt with. I am not certain
if the examination shed recommended in Mr Assistant
Huang's Memo. would be worth the cost. A great many

(2)

of our imports come from Ningpo under hung tan and ~~and~~ no strict examination of them is called for, pay us no duty at all, ~~and~~ the timber exported, which yields ~~more duty~~ about 50 % of the total duties, could not ~~be able to come to~~ be brought to an examination shed. But later on I shall come to a decided opinion on the matter. An export likin, or Tungchüan, as it has been renamed, has been imposed on timber from the 1st of this month. The levy amounts to about as much as the Customs export duty. It is objected to by the merchants, who have ceased pro tem from exporting timber. I dare say a compromise will be arrived at. The government must have more money and is not strong enough to obtain it otherwise than by imposts on goods.

Weather kept cool by the rain; no white clothes or punkahs as yet.

I remain
Yours faithfully,

S/O.
6.4

Custom House,
Wenchow, 10th June, 1914.

DEAR MR AGLEN,

orcha and
axing sta-
tion.

In my Non-Urgent Correspondence for May you will notice the case of the junk Chin Pao Fa which was made to pay $51 by a taxing station at Wusung, where she had temporarily anchored on her way up the Yangtse to T'ungchow. Perhaps this office should have issued, in addition to the Cargo Certificate, the Duty Receipt mentioned in Circular No.27, Second Series, Paragraph 2, sub-paragraph 2. In this case the shipper of the timber would have had a document to show which would have told exactly what kind of duty he had paid. But the practice here has been only to issue the Cargo Certificate. No doubt the station had the right to board the junk, but should not have made the charge before referring the matter either to the Foreign Customs at Wusung or to this office. The Weiyuan in charge should have known that we were not likely to give a transit pass for goods from the interior. The shipper has made no complaint to this office. If he do, we can, as I have told the Superintendent, issue a receipt for the full and half duty paid to us. The station must have made some mistake about the flag. Stevens went on board, but could find no national ensign of any kind. The only flag he saw

(2)

with anything foreign about it was one with the characters for the Standard Oil Company on it. However, the junkmaster says he did not fly this at Wusung. I have called the Chin Pao Fa a "junk", as she really is nothing else. She only differs from an ordinary junk in having a few boards on either side of the bow which, on a close view, make that particular part of her look slightly like the bow of a foreign ship.

which accused of extortion.

You will also notice a case among the Correspondence in which one of the Native Customs Lushih was charged with endeavouring to extort 10 cents for returning a junk's papers. The sum is very small, but of course the principle is immense. The Lushih denies the charge, and the accuser has brought no witness. So I have been unable to take any steps against the former. But I have made a change in the office practice which will probably prevent any abuse of the kind. The Assistant, Mr Huang Hou-ch'ing, now takes charge of the papers of all junks and delivers them himself on clearance.

Native Customs Tariff, rules, &p.

The translation of the Native Customs Tariff is finished and Mr Huang is now codifying the rules. Also Stevens is progressing with the map. He goes about the creeks whenever the weather is fine enough and is gradually getting the outlines of them and fixing accurately the positions of our out-stations.

Weather.

There has been a good deal of rain here of late. The number of rainy days in May was 20 and there were very few

13

days during the month on which the sky was clear. Yesterday the thermometer was in the eighties and people were in whites. But in the afternoon it started raining, with the result that the temperature has gone down some degrees and thick clothes have been resumed.

One of Sir Richard Dane's men, Mr Brauns, from Hangchow is down here just now. I have put him up. He is trying to find out why the southern half of Chekiang only yields about half the revenue on salt that is derived from the northern half. He thinks smuggling has most to do with it.

Salt Inspector

S/O

INSPECTORATE GENERAL OF CUSTOMS,

PEKING, 16th June, 1914.

Dear Mr. Acheson,

I have duly received your S/O No.3 of 3rd June.

New Likin Tax on Timber. I hope the compromise which may be arrived at will not take the form of reduction of the Native Customs duties. You had better watch this.

Yours truly,

Acheson, Esquire,
WENCHOW.

S/O

INSPECTORATE GENERAL OF CUSTOMS,

PEKING, 23rd June, 1914

Dear Mr. Acheson,

I have duly received your S/O No.4 of 10th June.

Taxation of Junk at Wusung by Taxing Station.

I confess I do not understand this question. In what capacity did we clear the junk - Foreign or Native Customs - and if the former, why do we have anything to do with junks.

Yours truly,

Acheson, Esquire,
WENCHOW.

O NO.5.

Custom House,

Wenchow, 24th June, 1914.

DEAR MR AGLEN,

tive
stoms and
kin.

I have duly received your S/O letter of 16th instant. No action that the Likin people can take will affect the Native Customs directly; no matter what they do we will carry on our work as usual. But the existence of three taxing establishments functioning side by side and taxing the same goods at the same time is objectionable and an anomaly only to be met with in China or some backward country like it. During the first days of this month, when the timber merchant were refraining from business on account of the new imposition, some junks that had entered to load timber left the port empty, but the trade is going on now much as before, our collection to date is as good, perhaps, as it would have been under normal conditions, and I hardly think we

16

have suffered much as yet. The tax is not taken off, but it has been temporarily suspended pending the result of a petition to

(2)

Hangchow, bonds being given by the shippers for the amounts leviable. But, although the action of the Likin Office may not have harmed us on the present occasion, it might very well have done so, and, so long as the present state of things continues, we shall remain exposed to perturbations by the proximity of other offices doing the same work. The Native Customs labours at a disadvantage vis-a-vis the two other establishments, in that they enjoy tariff autonomy and can manipulate their charges at will and in any manner that is likely to fill their coffers. But such manipulations may at the same time cause reduction in the volume of the trade and consequent falling off in the Native Customs receipts. I suppose, however, any protest on our part would be resented as unwarrantable interference.

Native Customs tariff, regulations, map.

I have got the draft of the Native Customs regulations ready; the tariff has been finished some time. There now remains the map of the river and canals showing the stations and trade channels. Stevens is working at this whenever he has the opportunity. But the weather is so unfavourable that surveying is most of the time impossible. We are not attempting anything like a regular survey. My only idea is to give the true positions of the stations and the approximate outlines of the canals. However even this requires observations of distant objects, which can only be made in clear weather. In May there were 20 rainy days and this month there have already been 16 days on most of which it has been too wet to do any out-of-door work.

(3)

The temperature is rising and the nights are getting hot.   Temperature

I remain
Yours faithfully,

signature

The former Taotaiship is going   Intendancy
to be revived under a new name and the holder of the office will be styled the Tao Yin (   ). The first Tao Yin is to be a man called Sun Chih-wei (   ), a native of Chekiang, I believe. The Superintendent of Customs thought he would be appointed, but has been disappointed.

S/O No. 6

Custom House,
Wenchow, 4th July, 1914.

Lorcha Chin
Pao Fa.

DEAR MR AGLEN,

I have duly received your letter of 23rd June concerning the lorcha Chin Pao Fa. We registered this vessel as a lorcha in November of last year, charging her Hk.Tls 100 and issuing to her a certificate of registry received from the Superintendent. The authority for our only charging Tls 100 instead of Tls 300 is contained in Inspectorate despatch to this office No.99/7663 of October 1903. The Chin Pao Fa is certainly very little like a foreign vessel, but there are other lorchas trading here that are nearly as Chinese as she is, being simply junks with a few superficial alterations. Properly speaking, a lorcha means a foreign hull with a Chinese rig, but this has not been strictly adhered to by the Customs. The rules are not explicit on the subject. Going by Circulars Nos 22 of 1873, paragraph 5, and 24 of of 1874, paragraph 2, junks can be registered at our offices as well as vessels entirely of foreign type.

(2)

~~that had very little of the foreign style about them.~~ As the Chin Pao Fa is registered in our office, of course she enters and clears at the Foreign Custom House and the Native Customs ~~do not~~ have nothing to do with her.

ore Likin. The new likin which came into force on the 1st of last month does not appear to have hurt our Native Customs revenue, our collection for the month being Tls 3,400, or over Tls.300 more than the collection for June 1913. But the revised likin tariff for the province ~~has come~~ came into force on the 1st of this month and it is almost certain to work no harm ~~to our mischief~~. There has always been likin charged on timber passing ChIng T'ien (   ), a place about 40 miles up river, on its way down stream to Wenchow. Formerly the levy on logs ~~here~~ at Ch'ing T'ien was 8 cash a piece. But under the revised tariff it will be no less than 96 cash a piece, or 12 times what it was before. This cannot fail to affect the trade, and, as a matter of fact since the 1st of the month no timber has come to this port ~~down river~~. Later on I will let you know more on the subject. Perhaps things will not turn out so badly. Strikes are sure to take place and probably reduction in charges will follow ~~be made~~.

eather. We had a couple of hard blows during the month which cooled the air without doing any great damage. In fact we have had hardly any hot weather as yet.

I remain Yours faithfully,

James Acheson

S/O   Inspectorate General of Customs,   19

PEKING, 7th July, 1914.

Dear Sir,

I am directed by the Inspector General to acknowledge receipt on the 6th July, of your S/O No. 5 dated 24th June.

Yours truly,

[signature]
Private Secretary.

J. Acheson, Esquire,

WENCHOW.

S/O

Inspectorate General of Customs,

PEKING, 14th July, 1914.

Dear Sir,

I am directed by the Inspector General to acknowledge receipt on the 11th July of your S/O No. 6 dated 4th July.

Yours truly,

[signature]

For Private Secretary.

J. Acheson, Esquire,

WENCHOW.

O NO. 7

Custom House,

Wenchow, 21st July, 1914.

DEAR MR AGLEN,

tive Customs.   I have been giving every attention to your despatch No.532/51,902 regarding the preparation of a map of this destrict, the formulating of rules for the Native Customs, alphabetical arrangement of the tariff, reduction of expenses, etc. I am also busily engaged in doing all that is required by Circular No.2206. I have got together a mass of information and have done a lot of arranging of material and in a short time will, I hope, be able to do all the reforming work that is possible. But at present the preparation for the introduction of the new tariff must take precedence of other things. I saw the Superintendent yesterday. He has received similar instructions to mine and he told me that he received them a fortnight ago and that they are to the effect that the new tariff must be introduced in a month, i.e., in a fortnight from now. I had written to him previously, in reply to a despatch of his on the subject, saying that the introduction of the new levies should commence at all our stations at the same time, and I repeated this to him at our interview. Our present tariff list comprises nearly four hundred articles. There is no one year in which all are imported and exported, but those that pass the Customs amount to a good many, and the making of a list

(2)

of them ~~with~~ ~~for any one year~~ giving all the particulars required to get a bird's eye view of the difference that the contemplated alteration of the duties ~~would~~ in make--quanties and values for a year, amount of duty collected, present and proposed rates of duty, amount of duty that would have been collected had new rates been in force--~~needs~~ requires a good deal of time and I am still in the middle of doing it. The Superintendent gave me a list which he had had compiled, but it does not agree with mine and I have given it to Mr Huang to see how the discrepancies arise. In so far as I can see the new rates will increase our Native Customs revenue considerably. I asked ~~him~~ The Superintendent if he thought there would be much opposition to the change, and he said that merchants were sure to oppose any raising of the tariff, but that it could be made all right. I have told the Writer to find out what public opinion was on the subject and he says the recent increase in the likin has created some feeling against the government ~~and~~ which will make difficulties for us that would not otherwise have ~~arisen existed.~~ ~~My idea in making a list of the duties as above is to be able to see exactly what we are going to do as well as to give yourself the information in the fourth paragraph of Circular No. 2206.~~ In so far as I know there is one ~~or two~~ articles at least on which the Foreign Customs tariff would bear ~~too~~ very heavily. There is a very coarse kind of paper exported from here in considerable quantities. It is worth only Tls 2 or less a picul and to charge such inferior stuff 2 mace a picul duty would be to impose a duty of 10% ~~and also~~ which would amount to

— 26 —

(3)

5 times what it has been paying hitherto under the old tariff. It would seem that in such a case an exception ought to be made. As regards reduction of staff and lessening of expenses, I question if this can be done to any advantage. But, in any case, it will be better ~~to postpone any action of this kind until we see~~ not to undertake anything of the kind just as we are about to introduce a higher tariff ~~of duties~~ which is sure, at the first go off, to result in increase of attempts to evade pyment of duty. I am rather inclined to make more use of the men we have than to reduce their number. I am beginning with the foreign Tidewaiter (Mr J.S. Lee). Hitherto this officer has been mainly occupied with examination of junk cargoes, a work which occasionally can be left to the Chinese Examiners, provided they know they are liable to be checked at any time. The work of the natives at the outstations needs more supervision. These employees are stationed at the places where the inland canals join the main river and their principal duty is to see that junks do not land or ship cargo at unauthorised ~~places~~. Cargo is sometimes landed and shipped at their stations and they collect duty on it; but whether they hand over all they collect or not I have no means of knowing. With certainty However, in order to have some sort of a check upon the tidings, I am making Lee study the stations and their surroundings and the canal traffic with a view to ~~establishment~~ ing ~~a patrol of~~ having him visit the stations frequently and patrol the canals and in this way make as sure as possible that no malpractices go on. I in-

(4)

tend issuing duty receipt forms to each station and making a rule that when any duty is paid an acknowledgement of it shall be given. In this way cargoes of boats met with on the canals can be checked. This is impossible now, as no duty receipts are given by the stations at all.

Shui-wu Ch'u and Superintendent on ~~l~~practices.

A few days ago I received a despatch from the Superintendent stating that ~~the Shui-wu Ch'u had instructed~~ he had received instructions from the Shui-wu Ch'u to the effect that false declarations to the Customs were of frequent occurrence and that he should consult with the Commissioner and make secret investigations in the matter. I suppose the recent Shanghai case has set the Ch'u on, but there may be some hidden object in its instructions ~~to the Superintendent~~. Perhaps this is to obtain more control over the Foreign Customs. I talked about the subject to the Superintendent yesterday. I told him that there was bound to be some smuggling, but that I believed the amount of this at Wenchow to be small. I said the despatch of the Ch'u was in general terms and that no action could be taken on it except to see that work was done as well as possible and that opportunities for smuggling were reduced to a minimum. To-day his Weiyuan, who attends every day at the Native Customs where he does absolutely nothing, though receiving from the Commissioner pay at the rate of Tls.50 a month, called to see me. He showed me ~~some~~ a despatch which the Superintendent had written him instructing him to examine into the way the Customs work was done and to find out regarding false

(5)

declarations. Another despatch instructed him to make out a schedule of the Native Customs property. He said he had told the Superintendent that, as he was paid by the Commissioner, he could not well carry on investigations about Customs work without my permission and he told me he had come to see me and ascertain my views on the matter. I informed him I did not want him bother himself about how we did our work in the Foreign Customs, but that, all the same, if he became aware of any abuses going on I considered it his duty to let me know and I added that I saw no objection to his informing the Superintendent as well. With regard to the Native Customs property, I told him if he liked to write out for the Superintendent what he knew about it, I could make no objection. I think the Superintendent is doing no more than carrying out the Ch'u's instructions, but he might have been more straght with me in the matter of setting the Weiyuan to report on what went on in the office. With regard to Customs property, when I went to the Native Customs a few days ago I met two strange Chinese, apparently officials, coming out of the office. I asked Mr Huang who they were and he said they were two deputies from Hangchow sent to find out about Customs building. I ought to have been notified that they were coming, but they did no more then look round the place. With regard to the Superintendent, he feels his position here in having a high sounding title

(6)

with hardly any functions and in having to draw his allowance from the Commissioner and he would gladly welcome any change that would restore his office to something like what it was in pre-Revolution days. This explains, no doubt, his action in examining independently into Customs matters. In former times a Taotai would always have ~~consulted~~ let the Commissioner know what he was doing in such cases.

ather.
Last week a typhoon passed inland between ~~here~~ Wenchow and Foochow. The wind blew here with great force. Part of my compound wall was destroyed, but we suffered no other damage. For a couple of days there was a great deal of rain, but we have now got dry weather again. The summer heat is on us ~~now~~ and I suppose the temperature will remain as it is until the end of August.

I remain
Yours faithfully,

James Acheson

O NO. 8

Custom House,
Wenchow, 12th August, 1914.

DEAR MR AGLEN,

Native Customs.

I have sent the Native Customs rules to the Superintendent for his consideration, and I have received them back from him with only a couple of trifling alterations. I will now proceed to publish them first in proclamation form and then in the form of folders, of which I will have several hundred printed and distributed among all concerned in the junk trade. But the junkmen are a very ignorant lot. Few of them can even read and very many of them will be able to still plead ignorance of the law which, in China, is allowed to constitute an excuse. However, we shall have done all possible. The map is now complete enough to show the stations within the 50 li and to give one a fair idea of how the land lies about here. The tariff was finished long ago and has only been waiting for the map.

The war.

We are far removed in Wenchow from the scenes of the tremendous events now taking place in Europe and the sound of the clash of arms does not reach us. But indirectly we are bound to suffer from the war, and I expect we shall soon feel its effects on our trade and in the raising of prices and the diminution in the purchasing power of the standard of value.

(2)

ather.   Since the date of my last letter we
have had it very hot, more so than I ever experienced it in
either Hainan or Pakhoi. Hot winds came from the west and
scorched and dried up everything and made people feel very
uncomfortable. For the last few days, however, the temperature has been more agreeable, especially at night, and I
hope we shall soon be into the autumn werther.

       I remain
       Yours faithfully,

Just as I am writing a squall of wind and rain has come on.

There may be a typhoon somewhere near us. Another good

blow would probably break up the summer. The country around

is badly in want of rain; the rice especially is suffering

and the price of it has gone up.

S/O

Inspectorate General of Customs,

PEKING, 25th August, 1914.

Dear Sir,

I am directed by the Inspector General to acknowledge receipt on the 18th August of your S/O dated 12th August.

Yours truly,

Richardson
Private Secretary.

J. Acheson, Esquire,

WENCHOW.

O NO. 9

Custom House,

Wenchow, 26th August, 1914.

DEAR MR AGLEN,

stal parcels.

I am sending you a despatch in reply to your No.547 which will, I think, tell you all about how we deal with Postal parcels here.

tive Customs.

One of the Native Customs Examiners died a few days ago. I am not replacing him. I am issuing his pay to ~~the end of the month~~ date of death, and ~~but~~ am paying no gratuity to his family. I have not yet decided if any of the sub-stations can be abolished. What they collect is very little, but their principal raison d'etre lies in what goods they are supposed to prevent being landed at the wrong places. The Examiners and Watchers at them are all unreliable if left to themselves, and it is only by ~~making~~ care that the Tidewaiter pays them frequent and unexpected visits that I can keep them in anything like the straight path. But the current in the river runs swiftly, and with ~~the~~ our sampans and ~~row~~ gigs we can do little but drift up and down. To get to the farthest station and back may take two days if the tides do not suit. I should like to have a motor launch, but the cost has prevented me from mentioning the subject so far.

gistrate.

Our Magistrate's term of office has come abruptly to an end. He has been very assiduous in levying

(2)

fines for breaches of the opium laws, but not just so conscientious in disposing of the money, a considerable portion of which seems to have found its way into his own pocket. The consequence is that he was unable to hand over the balance to the new Taoyin, who called on him to hand in his accounts as soon as he (the Taoyin) arrived. There is as yet no healthy public opinion in China and malversation in office does not ~~meet with the social disapproval which alone can~~ result in any social ban. Our Magistrate is going to Hangchow where, no doubt, he will be severely censured. ~~and~~ But his offence is venial and, after he has handed over a fair portion of his takings, he will receive absolution and, after a short retirement] will probably *get a billet somewhere else.* ~~be made a Magistrate of some other district~~.

oyin.   The new Taoyin is a Hunan man of the old style and would seem to be more of a reactionary than a progressive.

ather.   Weather still hot here, though somewhat cooler than it was at the end of July.

I remain
Yours faithfully,

James Acheson

S/O

Inspectorate General of Customs,

PEKING, 1st September, 1914.

Dear Sir,

I am directed by the Inspector General to acknowledge receipt on the 1st Sept. of your S/O No.9 dated 26th August.

Yours truly,

Richardson
Private Secretary.

J. Acheson, Esquire,

WENCHOW.

CUSTOM HOUSE,
Wenchow, 17 September, 1914.

DEAR MR AGLEN,

Native Customs.
I have been turning out the cargoes of junks lately, but have been surprised to find the manifests and cargoes fairly in agreement. We have found a quantity of goods brought on board by the sailors, mostly very cheap stuff, as it has been the custom for a long while past to allow the crews of junks to supplement their meagre pay (about $1.50 a month each man) by private trading, I have not imposed any heavy penalties in the cases of such seizures as we have made. But I have let the brokers know that anything shipped must be applied for and that the sailors must pay duty on their ventures as well as merchants. The junkmen are a very illiterate, rough, undiciplined lot and it is almost impossible to make them understand rules as we read them.

Case of British Consulate.
On the 20th of May last I sent the draft form of lease which I had drawn up for the leasing of the British Consulate here to the Consul in Ningpo, but I have not yet received it back. The Consul has written me privately that he thinks it must be in the Crown Advocate's office, but that is all he can tell me. We have paid no rent for the house yet. It is a fine house

(2)

but, being situated on Conquest Island, it is not quite suitable for a Customs residence. In stormy weather it is always difficult and sometimes dangerous to cross the river and at any time it is inconvenient. However, there is a scarcity of foreign residences in Wenchow and there is nothing better to be got just now.

Brigandage. The Chinyün district (   ), to the north-west of here, is troubled with brigandage. A force of 200 soldiers led against them by the local General has been defeated. But reinforcements have been applied for, and, no doubt, tranquillity will soon be restored in the disturbed district.

Trade and Revenue. Trade is very dull here just now. Prices in Shanghai are low or uncertain and there is very little exportation. Our collection last month was under Tls.2000 and, so far, it does not promise to be any more this month. The Native Customs revenue has fallen off also. But this is chiefly due to the slacking off in the export of timber which is to be looked for at this time of the year.

Weather. On Sunday and Monday, 6th and 7th, we had typhoon weather--high wind and heavy rain. In the two days the amount of rain which fell was over 9 inches. There was a strong freshet in the river on Monday and neither the Harbour Master nor the Examiner could get across. But I have not heard of much damage up the country. The weather here now is quite cool and enjoyable and autumn.

S/O

Inspectorate General of Customs.

PEKING, 29th September, 1914.

Dear Sir,

I am directed by the Inspector General to acknowledge receipt on the 27th Sept of your S/O No.10 dated 17th Sept.

Yours truly,

Private Secretary.

J. Acheson, Esquire,

WENCHOW.

S/O No. 11.

CUSTOM HOUSE,

Wenchow, 6th October, 1914.

DEAR MR AGLEN,

Native Customs.

I have had Lee, the Tidewaiter on Native Customs duty ~~stopping at the out Native Customs out station~~ making a prolonged stay at one of the Native Customs out-stations to try and ascertain how much is collected at it and in this way obtain some sort of check over the reports of the Chinese Examiner in charge ~~of it~~. A case occurred lately in which one of the Examiners was accused of not reporting all he received. I got hold of the ~~books~~ account books of the importing shops, but the difference between the ~~sums~~ total of the sums they had entered as paid to the Customs differed very little from what he Examiner had returned as ~~collected.~~ having been paid to him. ~~I was surprised at this agreement~~ I am hardly inclined, however, to regard this as conclusive evidence that he ~~is perfectly~~ reports every cent he collects, as this would be too much to expect from a man who is only paid ₵12 a month and whose work there is no means ~~at the head office~~ of checking with any degree of certainty. Lee has ~~been~~ spent several days at the out-station and has obtained some idea of the amount of business ~~done~~ there; but he says that for four or five days ~~there~~ at a time there may be nothing imported at all and then a day

(2)

will come when several junks will come to unload. I should say that fish is the only commodity allowed to be landed at these sub-stations. On account of the importing going on so irregularly, Lee has only been able to form a very rough estimate of what sum the station should yield. But it is possible the native Examiner may give him credit for the moral effect of his visit be good for the revenue.

Tidewaiter Lee.   I should like to bring Lee to your notice. He is a very efficient officer. He has a good appearance and a polite address. He takes interest in his work and is most willing to perform any duty required of him. He is studying Chinese. I have not examined him, but he looks forward to passing an examination next year. With regard to his private life from all I have heard, he is very steady and very well conducted. I do not wish for a better officer.

Revenue.   Our Maritime Customs collection continues low, being about the same as that for August, which was under Tls 2000. But the export of timber is commencing to go ahead again and the revenue of the Native Customs shows increase. I should say that both Foreign and Native duties show increase for the nine months just

(3)

over the ~~passed~~ indeed dutiable for the same period of last year.

Weather.   The weather continues ~~cool and~~ enjoyable ~~It is still warm in the daytime, but the sky is bright, and~~ days warm but ~~the atmosphere is dry and the~~ nights ~~are~~ quite cool.

I remain

Yours faithfully,

James Acheson

Bank of China.   A branch or sub-office or agency of the Bank of China has been opened here and the head of the concern has called on me and handed me a letter which purports to be from the provincial head office in Hangchow and has asked me to give him the Customs business. But the man is an old yamen hand with a shady reputation and, in addition, the letter he handed me, though it is written on paper which has printed on it the name of the Bank, yet the seal over the date at the end bears the characters 杭州分金庫印 The communication is not satisfactory and I have ~~given it back to the man~~ and told the man I must have a letter with the seal of the Bank before I could entertain any proposals from him.

CUSTOM HOUSE,

S/O NO. 12.

WENCHOW, 12th October, 1914.

DEAR MR AGLEN,

Self-protection and neutrality.

In my Non-Urgent Correspondence for September ~~October~~ you will see ~~a correspondence~~ some letters that have passed between myself and the Superintendent on the subject of revolvers carried by Germans passing through here for Shanghai. The case is one of first impression and none of the rules regarding arms or neutrality exactly apply to it. In fact it may be resolved into two cases, the carrying of arms into the port and the handing of them over to Stevens and the Captain of the Kwangchi. Divided thus the rules may be made to apply to a certain extent. ~~I regarded~~ The Germans were in ~~p&#~~ plain clothes and without military arms or accoutrements of any kind. The revolvers in question were very diminutive weapons, almost small enough to be carried in the waistcoat pocket. I regarded the men as perfectly within their rights in having in their possession such weapons for self-protection and it seemed to me that the Captain might properly have ignored them. That he did not was, of course, entirely his own affair. Stevens accepted one of the weapons simply in order that the possessor of it might be able to get away. ~~None of us~~ We all thought it better that they should not be detained in Wenchow. The action of Stevens in taking over the weapon comes under Circular No.1520, paragraph 3,

(2)

(b). He ~~did what he had a perfect right to do~~ acted perfectly in accordance with the rule there laid down, except ~~in~~ that he did not apply to import through the Consul prior to the introduction into the port of the arms. The Superintendent seems to take a more serious view of the matter than I have done and has ~~applied to~~ reported it to the Wai-chiao Pu. ~~With regard~~ I have told him that Stevens retains the revolver ~~weapon~~ and will hold it to his order. With regard to the one which was taken by the Captain of the Kwangchi, there would not seem to be any rule that exactly applies to this part of the case. If we regard it as having been taken from a passenger by the Captain of the ship, the latter would appear to be within his rights in having it added to the armament of ~~his ship,~~ the ship, and that I thought should be done at the port where ~~the vessel~~ she was registered. This is all I have to say regarding the matter. In so far as I know, the Superintendent has received no answer as yet from ~~the Board in~~ Peking. Perhaps the Board thinks that any violation of neutrality that may have taken place here is slight in comparison with what is going on at Tsingtao.

                            I remain
                        Yours faithfully,

INSPECTORATE GENERAL OF CUSTOMS,

PEKING, 20th October, 1914.

S/O

Dear Mr. Acheson,

I have duly received your S/O No.11 of 6th October.

<u>Native Customs : rumoured malpractices at an out-station.</u> Is this station properly under your control? A change of Staff seems indicated together with frequent inspection from Head Office.

Yours truly,

Acheson, Esquire,
W E N C H O W.

S/O

INSPECTORATE GENERAL OF CUSTOMS,

PEKING, October 20th, 1914.

Dear Mr. Acheson,

I have duly received your S/O No.12 of 12th October.

<u>Arms seized from German passengers.</u> If this case has been reported to the Wai Chiao Pu by the Superintendent you should report it officially. I do not quite understand it but it seems to me that Stevens should certainly have handed over the revolver to you to be sent to the Authorities.

Yours truly,

Acheson, Esquire,
WENCHOW.

S/O NO. 15

CUSTOM HOUSE,
Wenchow, 24th October, 1914.

DEAR MR AGLEN,

Native Customs tariff.

My despatches Nos 3036 and 3037, which go with this, will tell you about the new Native Customs tariff which the Superintendent has got the Board of Finance to approve for this port. As an attempt at a 2½% tariff I do not see any objection to it. It will increase our revenue, but not to the extent that a tenth of it will suffice to run the establishment, supposing the trade to remain as it is. With regard to this year's revenue, we have collected nearly Tls 23,000 to the end of September, and, with the new tariff introduced from the first of next month, we may have a record total at the end of December. Of course it must be remembered that a very great proportion of our imports do not pay duty here, which makes the revenue appear small in proportion to the value of the trade. A 2½% tariff is not high enough to make a Custom House pay properly, especially an establishment like the Native Customs which deals with a host of very small craft, the movements of which it needs an abnormally numerous staff to efficiently control.

Ans.

With regard to the revolver given by the German to Stevens and which I told you about in my last

(2)

letter, in so far as I know the Superintendent has received no reply ~~to~~ on the subject from the Wai-chiao Pu. Stevens has the weapon still.

A couple of days ago we had rain and a north wind and it got quite cold. But it has turned sunny again and feels warm.

I remain
Yours faithfully,

S/O NO. 14.

CUSTOM HOUSE,

Wenchow, 28th October, 1914.

Native Customs.

DEAR MR AGLEN,

I have duly received your letter of 20th ~~of~~ instant ~~in which~~ in reply to my letter regarding rumoured malpractice at one of our outstations. You ask me if the station is properly under my control. Yes, I have ~~full control over all the out-stations in so far as any interference on the part of the Superintendent is concerned~~ as full control over all the Native Customs stations as is it possible to have, considering their distance from Wenchow and the very inferior ~~style of~~ (which I have means) of communicating with them. When the case occurred to which I referred in my letter No.11 I changed the Watcher at the station. *It was he that accused the Examiner. But he had no proof.* As regards inspection from Head Office, I have Lee occupied most of the time in boarding junks unexpectedly, both in the harbour here and down river and he has ~~made~~ *effected* some seizures which will ~~have the effect of~~ making the junk people more careful in the matter of declarations to the Customs. I have a perfectly free hand as regards arrangement of the work and the handling of the staff and the Superintendent has never bothered me in ~~regard~~ respect of such matters. In connection with seizures he has only interfered once and ~~~~ that was when we seized some goods down the river which

(2)

were being taken out of the port without having been ~~rep-~~
applied for. They turned out to be the property of a man of
note here, a former Censor under the Manchu dynasty. ~~He~~ The
Superintendent
sent his Weiyuan round to me to ask ~~me about the seizure
and~~ if ~~it~~ the goods could not be released. I said it was
a clear case of attempting to evade export duty ~~and a fine
should be and my decision in such a~~ and that the owner
should be fined, but that, if the Superintendent thought ~~it~~
a case that
should be dealt with specially I was quite willing to hand
it over to himself to deal with as he thought right. The
Weiyuan said this was fair and went away. But the next day
he came back and told me that the Superintendent ~~was~~ would
rather not decide the case, but preferred that I should settle it. So I levied a fine of Tls 5, which was paid without
demur. That was nearly two months ago, and I have heard nothing
more concerning the matter. I should say that the goods
concerned were a quantity of vegetable tallow, the duty on
which was Tls 1.278.

Self-protec-　　　I have also received your letter concerning the
tion and neu-
trality.　　arms handed over by the Germans and will officialise ~~son~~
in respect of what occurred.

　　　　　　　　　　　　　　　　I remain
　　　　　　　　　　　　　　　Yours faithfully,

INSPECTORATE GENERAL OF CUSTOMS,

S/O

PEKING, 3rd November, 1914.

Dear Mr Acheson,

I have duly received your S/O No.13 of 24th October.

Revolver seized from German passenger and retained by Mr Stevens. It should be handed over to the Superintendent.

Yours truly,

Acheson, Esquire,
WENCHOW.

S/O

Inspectorate General of Customs,

PEKING, 10th November, 1914.

Dear Sir,

I am directed by the Inspector General to acknowledge receipt on the 3rd Nov. of your S/O No.14 dated 28th October.

Yours truly,

C. W. Richardson
Private Secretary.

J. Acheson, Esquire,

WENCHOW.

NO. 15.

CUSTOM HOUSE,
Wenchow, 18th November, 1914.

DEAR MR AGLEN,

Revolver case.   I send you with this my official report on the matter of the revolver given by the German to Stevens. It is the Chinese way, when a case occurs which is not expressly provided for in any particular, to bring it under some rule, the spirit of which can be made to apply to it and, had the case in question been referred to me at the time, I would most likely have brought it under the transhipment clause (Rule No.8) of the Arms Regulations of Circular No.1520 and have given permission to the Germans to retain the weapons and apply for the Superintendent's huchao at Shanghai. The third paragraph of Circular No. No.2266 applies better to the case than any preceding rule, but this Circular had not been received when the affair happened. But in any case I hardly think that any rule can override the right of a man to carry a weapon to protect himself when on a dangerous journey. The Germans came here in a junk and through waters infested by pirates, and I do not see how their possession of the revolvers on landing here could have been looked upon as an offence or how we would have been justified in seizing them. The revolvers were not military weapons in any sense, the one that Stevens took being so small that I can cover it completely

(2)

with my hand. As to our desire to get the men out of the port, they were men bent on a desperate errand--going to Tsingtao for no other object, if they followed the Emperor's orders, than to get killed, they were not likely to be particularly careful as regarded their behaviour, and there was no official of their nationality to exercise any control over them. If they had not gone by the Kwangchi, they would have had to wait here several days and it would have been a serious question who should put them up. We all had a good deal of sympathy for them and were willing to assist them as much as we properly could. But I think you will understand how unwilling we were for them to remain here longer than necessary. If Stevens had refused to accept the revolver in the way he did and had said that the case must be referred to the Chinese authorities, delay would have occurred and the steamer would likely have departed leaving them still here. And the community would have blamed him.

I have enclosed in my despatch two copies of the Chinese version, one for the Inspectorate and one for the Shui-wu Ch'u, should this be required. The correspondence appended to the former consists of only one letter, the first I wrote to the Superintendent on the subject. It was sent on the 18th of September. The next day his Weiyuan brought it back and pointed out that I had only stated that one man had carried the revolvers, whereas there were altogether eight men. I altered the one into

(3)

　　　　　　　on the 19th
two and returned it together with a second letter in which
I went more fully into the matter. In the first letter I
　　　　　　　　　　　　　　　　　via Amoy
said the men had come from Siam and had come overland to
Wenchow. This was correct enough. One or two of them had
come from Siam, going by what dropped from them, and I understood at the time that they had travelled from Amoy to
　　　　　　　　　　　way
Wenchow part of the overland. However, I left out these
details in my second letter. The first letter I did not
think it necessary to include in the Non-Urgent Correspondence for September. All the other letters, however, will
be found there, and so I have not ~~recopied~~ had them re-
copied in the Chinese ~~copy of the Chinese~~ version intended
for the Inspectorate, though all are appended ~~to~~ the copy
intended ~~to~~ for the Shui-wu Ch'u.

　　　　I trust my report of the case will enable you to
clearly understand it.

　　　　　　　　　　　　　　　　I remain
　　　　　　　　　　　　　　　　Yours faithfully,

　　　　　　　　　　　　　　　　[signature]

P.S. Letter No.81 from the Superintendent in the Non-Urgent
Correspondence for September refers to two other Germans
who did not come with the eight and who left by another
steamer, the Yung-ning.

S/O NO. 16

CUSTOM HOUSE,

Wenchow, 25th November, 1914.

DEAR MR AGLEN,

Revolver case.

I have duly received your letter of 3rd instant stating that the revolver given to Stevens should be handed to the Superintendent. I now write to say that ~~it has been handed over to him~~ I have done this. It was handed over before ~~the de~~ I sent off my despatch No.3044, but both the despatch and the Chinese version had already been drafted and I did not care to alter them.

Native Customs.

I am sending you with this my despatch No. 3045 giving you all the particulars you asked for regarding the Native Customs and also enclosing the map showing the various stations and other important places around here. With regard to the Rules, Rule No.1 states the junk anchorage limits in theory. But junks anchor outside them ~~to a great extent~~. Strict adherence to rules is not understood by the junkmen and I never try to bind them down to the letter of the law. Rule No.19 relates to Special Permits. We always charge the inland steamers that run between here and places on the coast, ~~but not the launches which ply on the~~ and which enter and clear on arrival and departure, but not the launches which run on the canals and only report when they pay tonnage dues. Also we do not charge the junks, though if they work on Sunday we fine them. I think we

(2)

(just as well might) let them work on payment of a small fee and I am in communication with the merchants on the subject.

Rice case.　　　　I have a rice case on hand at present. It is to a certain extent similar to the one I had in Pakhoi, with the difference that in the present case I have done nothing but refer the matter to the Superintendent who passed it on to the Taoyin, who has resented the interference. Briefly the case is as follows:--Rice comes here occasionally from Fukien in junks in small quantities and the importations have never been covered by huchao. In the beginning of this month a junk brought in 80 bags and we accepted the manifest as all right, though there was no document for it, as we had been done on former occasions. While it was still on the junk and before we had given it a permit to land, it was seized by the Taoyin's people. and confiscated. I got a petition about it which I sent to the Superintendent with a complaining letter about the cargo being taken out our hands in such a way. The Superintendent seemed to agree with me and, after he had gone to the Native Customs himself and made independent enquiries, he sent on my complaint to the Taoyin. The latter maintains that, as the rice had no huchao, it has been rightly confiscated and has told the Superintendent that he should look after matters better and I was being misled by people under me. I have replied to the Superintendent saying that I had looked very carefully into the case and he that we had passed the rice in the same way

(3)

as had in done in past years by former Taotais and Superintendents and that to take ~~the rice~~ away from our control in such a way was equal to saying that the Customs were conniving at smuggling. *I added that* ~~and that~~ if we were to change our practice, we must issue a proclamation, otherwise any confiscation by us of imported rice would be protested against as contrary to what we had done before. I have not yet received his reply. I will officialise on the matter in a few days.

Wither. Weather just now getting colder and people have started their fires.

I remain

Yours faithfully,

James Acheson

I should add that the Taoyin's people seized the rice on the charge of having been clandestinely shipped in Wenchow and it was only when they found that this charge could not be sustained that they brought the accusation of no huchao. When I wrote to the Superintendent I thought the junkman had been accused of trying to export the rice, which I knew he was not.

INSPECTORATE GENERAL OF CUSTOMS,

S/O

PEKING, 1st December, 1914.

Dear Mr Acheson,

I have duly received your S/O No.15 of 18th November.

<u>Revolver Case.</u> I think under the circumstances that the revolver might well have been retained. The point is however, that as it was handed over, it cannot be retained privately by a Customs employe.

Yours truly,

Acheson, Esquire,
 WENCHOW.

INSPECTORATE GENERAL OF CUSTOMS,

S/O

PEKING, 8th December, 1914

Dear Mr Acheson,

I have duly received your S/O No.16 of 28th November.

<u>Interference of Taoyin in a case of rice import.</u>   You will have to press this case: if there was any irregularity it was not the business of the Taoyin's people to interfere. Ask the Superintendent to report to the Ch'u if you are unable to obtain redress locally.

Yours truly,

Acheson, Esquire,
W E N C H O W.

No. 17

CUSTOM HOUSE,

Wenchow, 15th December, 1914.

DEAR MR AGLEN,

rice case.

I have duly received your letter of the 8th regarding the interference of the Taoyin in a case of rice import, in which you say I will have to press the case, and ask the Superintendent to report it to the Ch'u. But I fear the Superintendent is too much of a trimmer to be of any help. He will do nothing against the Taoyin. One reason is that the two are kindred spirits and spend most of their time in gambling together. He has spoken me very fair in all his despatches. But he and the Taoyin understand eachother and have acted in concert. The case has been settled as far as the Taoyin is concerned by the Magistrate wringing a confession out of the master of the junk that he shipped some of the rice down river and that he intended not to land here, but to carry it out of port again. This, of course, would be exporting rice, which is prohibited and the confession is held as justifying the Taoyin in having confiscated the cargo. But an important point in the case is left out of consideration, and that is that the junkmaster, on arrival in port, declared the rice to the Customs, which, of course, meant that it could not have been re-exported without our consent. As a matter of fact the Taoyin knows quite

(2)

well that he is in the wrong, but he has had to save his face and he has done so by means of a fiction. How can anyone do business with people who are so childish as to hide their heads in the sand and imagine nobody can see them! The case began in exactly the same way as the Pakhoi case. The Taotai's people went on board the junk to make a squeeze. They first demanded $50, but finally came down to $15. The junk people refusing even to pay this, they trumped up the charge of intending to export, which they had to prove, if not by fair means, then by foul. But, all the same, I think my protest in the matter will prevent the same thing taking place again. At the first, when the Taoyin was riding the high horse, his people even went on board steamers to search for rice and the police searched the luggage of passengers. But there is no interference by any of his subordinates now. I did not say anything about these other cases, considering that the important thing was to see the Taoyin back in the case of the junk first of all. This I have succeeded in doing to a certain extent. In spite of his strong pronouncement that any rice coming in without huchao must be confiscated, the Superintendent, in his last despatch to me states that we had better continue as before. He said The putting out of a proclamation and changing our practice would mean that rice from down river could not come here, as the small junks could not get huchao for the little lots they carry. As luck would have it, another

(3)

junk came in ~~three~~ days ago from Fukien with 100 piculs of rice and no huchao. As I wanted to be perfectly sure, I sent the Writer to see the Superintendent and ask if it could be released. He said yes, and it has been taken ashore without, in so far as I know, being interfered with by anyone. The Superintendent said the putting out of a proclamation and changing our practice would mean that the rice from down river could not come here, as the small junks would not be able to get huchao for the puny ~~small~~ lots they carry. ~~But~~ you will not ~~fully~~ understand the case fully, however, till you get my despatch. I have written the English version of it, but the translation of it into Chinese and the copying of it with all the correspondence will take some days. I shall ~~sent~~ let you have it as soon as possible.

Office safe.   I have given our old office safe to the Native Customs. ~~I got no offer for it that would have been worth taking~~ I offered to sell it for $100, but couldn't get anything like that for it, so, rather than practically give it away, I sent it down to the other establishment. It is still some use — better than none at all — and will come in handy in case we happen to seize anything valuable and of small bulk like opium that we want to keep for a few days.

Typewriter.   Our Hammond typewriter I also sent to the Native Customs on the receipt of the Underwood from Shanghai.

Fins.   Circular No. 2281. I have arranged

(4)

with the Superintendent to adopt the Kiungchow procedure with regard to coffins, i.e., in the case of any coffin imported, to make the importer get a guarantee for it and then write to the Superintendent giving all particulars as to where it has come from and is going to, etc., so that he may inform the officials nearest the place of intended burial. This system was started by me in Hoihow and worked very well. *Coffins imported only need the guarantee.*

Further.

Very bright, dry and pleasant weather just now. The sun during the day is quite warm, though the hoar frost is on the ground in the mornings.

I remain

Yours faithfully,

Inspectorate General of Customs,

PEKING, 29th December, 1914.

Dear Sir,

I am directed by the Inspector General to acknowledge receipt on the 28th Dec. your S/O No. 17 dated 19th Dec.

Yours truly,

Richardson
Private Secretary.

Acheson, Esquire,

WENCHOW.

1915 年

O NO. 18.

CUSTOM HOUSE,
Wenchow, 4th January, 1915.

DEAR MR AGLEN,

ce case.

I send you with this my despatch ~~No.~~ reporting the rice case, about which I have written you semi-officially. The attitude of the Superintendent throughout it has been unsatisfactory. His despatches to me have seemed to indicate that he was supporting me, but, in reality, I believe, it has been the other way. He and the Taoyin are bosom friends and, as I have already said, spend most of their time in gambling together. They do not want to fall out with eachother. And another thing is the Superintendent considers his position here as unsatisfactory. I have never in the least attempted to ignore him, and any changes I have made in the work of either the Foreign or Native Customs, if they affected the public in any way, I have consulted him about. At the same time, the collection is entirely in my hands and I maintain control of the staff, and it is easy to understand how this goes against his grain. The Writer has told me that the Taoyin's despatch ~~to him~~ was put together by the both of them and that they spent a day and a night ~~to~~ in concocting it. And the last despatch of the Superintendent ~~ent the~~ in which he encloses me copy of the bogus confession

(2)

of the junkmaster, contains a very lame ~~excuse~~ ^(second thought) for the action of the Taoyin. I have not returned any answer to this, as the confession is such a patent fraud that I feel certain the Superintendent himself does not believe it any more than I do. *The whole thing is simply laughable.* And I thought, too, that any attempt on my part to deprive the Taoyin of the little satisfaction which he ~~seemed to~~ derived from the statement forced from the junk-master would only irritate him the more without doing any real good. He knows quite well that the Customs did what was right and, since the time the rice was seized on board the junk, his people have not interfered with our work. I am still on very good terms with the Superintendent. With regard to the Taoyin, in my despatch (which I drafted in December) I say he does not appear to regard me with unfriendly feeling. But I probably did not judge right. On New Year's day the Superintendent called upon me and on the 2nd I had a visit from the T'ungling; but neither the Taoyin nor the Magistrate has come near me. This seems to mean that the former is offended. I regret this, but I do not see how I could have passed over the seizure of the rice right from under our control. It was such an impudent proceeding on the part of the Taoyin's people. Had there been no Superintendent here and I had been writing direct to the Taoyin, I would have addressed him in a somewhat apologetic manner--sorry to have to complain about his people, etc. But as I was writing to the Superintendent,

(3)

whose interests in the matter were identical (or should have been) with my own, I considered it right to put the case straight to him and tell him what I thought about it. As you can see from my despatch, the Superintendent went himself to the Native Custom House before he passed on my complaint and enquired independently into the case and expressed his belief that the rice had been imported from Fukien. If he helped the Taoyin to write the reply, I really am at a loss to conceive what his idea was, except that he wished to see the Commissioner, whom he regards with jealousy, get a set-back. But the despatch of the Taoyin betrays so much ignorance and is so self-contradictory, that it can hardly be taken seriously. The Taoyin is the principal official here and evidently regards any criticising of his acts as savouring of lese majestie. All the same, the end of the whole case is that we are going on as before and passing rice cargoes from Fukien without any huchao and that in spite of his emphatic declaration that all rice imported without huchao must be confiscated. I should say that since the arrival of the Chêng Ch'üan Li several more junks have arrived with rice from Fukien. You will note at the end of my despatch that the Superintendent says I should draft a proclamation. As a matter of fact, neither he nor I could do any such thing. If a trade which for generations has been free between here and Fukien ports is to be subjected to restrictions, I shoudl should say that no less authorities than the Governor of the two

— 71 —

(4)

provinces could prescribe these. The best way is to do as we are doing--continue as before.

With regard to the accusation in the paper against the Weigher, Yen Po-chuang, I am pretty well convinced that both the Superintendent and the Taoyin knew all about it from the first. The newspaper concerned, the Hsing Pao, is partly owned by people in both their yamens. And you will note that the Magistrate shirks giving his decision in favour of either party. What he says about Yen writing to the paper himself and ~~in this way~~ correcting the accusation is ridiculous. A nice handle it would have given the editor! The Taoyin was riding a very high horse at the time and backing up the Chi-ch'a Chu and the accusation was, no doubt, designed to curry favour with him by trying to put the Customs more and more in the wrong. A couple of days after the appearance of the first paragraph, there appeared another paragraph saying the police had made a seizure of opium on the S.S. Kwangchi ~~and lauding the Taoyin for his well-rewarding watchfulness.~~ I believe, ~~the~~ however, the seizure was made on the street and not on the steamer. In talking with the Writer, the Superintendent said that, if the case went to Peking, he would say that there were faults on both sides --that the Taoyin's people should not have gone on board the junk to make a squeeze, while the Customs employees should not have colluded with the rice merchants. I say in my ~~last as~~ semi-official letter that the Taoyin's people went on board the junk to make a squeeze, and demanded first $50 and came down to $15. My authority for this is the Superintendent himself: he told it to the Writer. I presume, therefore, that there can be no doubt about it. With regard to the Superintendent's attitude in the case, he told the Writer that he had simply acted the part of a telephone--been nothing but a medium of communication between myself and the Taoyin. I am inclined to doubt the strict truth of this, however. That he did not want to put the Taoyin in the wrong is shown, among other evidence, by his not giving him the proper answer when the latter twitted him with having failed to investigate. Why didn't he say to the Taoyin--"it's you that have failed?"

But, to return to Yen Lo-chuang, the charge against him was evidently trumped. I do not in the least hold that Yen is more honest than the other Chinese on the staff. I mean to say that he had nothing whatever to do with the passing of the rice and that, after it had been confiscated, it was absurd to imagine that the rice merchants would go to him to get it back. Therefore I have done nothing against him. Wong Haiu Geng, the Assistant in the Native Customs, has complained to me that the Superintendent has also been talking about him as having done squeezing. He seems to dislike Wong. Exactly why, Wong professes not to know. He says that, when Bowring took over the Native Customs, he put him in charge of the establishment and he (Wong) was the means of turning

(6)

out some useless members of the staff whom the Superintendent had put in, and that this may have created an antagonism against him on the part of the latter. Notwithstanding the eagerness of the Chinese Government to replace the foreign staff of the Customs with their own people, the port officials, if my experience here goes for anything, certainly do not trust the latter anything like as much as they do the former. No Superintendent would think for a moment of suspecting an European or an American Assistant. I have told Wong that, so far as I myself was concerned, I would not take any action against him on the head of a mere assertion, unsupported by proof. The pay he gets is such that he ought to be able to live well and save money without the necessity of increasing it by any underhand means. He certainly is a very capable Assistant and very willing to do any work I ask him to do, and he knows the routine of the Native Customs thoroughly. However, what he has told me about the Superintendent has made me consider the expediency of bringing him up to the Foreign Customs and replacing him, for a while at least, by Aida. I hesitate to do this principally because it would increase the expenditure of the Native Customs by Tls.100 a month. Still I think we should have a man on the staff who could replace Wong, in case you transferred him.

Tariff.　　　　　With my despatch No.3051 I sent you our tariff tables. They give all the particulars called for by the

Circular, though you will likely only be interested in the figures of the two final columns, which give particulars regarding our new tariff. ~~The tables were finished before I knew anything about the Superintendent's new tariff.~~ With this tariff the present year ought to be a long way ahead of all preceding years in the way of revenue. But the one-tenth will still not suffice for payment of expenses The junk trade requires a scattered staff to deal with it and, consequently, ~~more men~~ a great many men in proportion to the volume of the trade. It is certainly not on account of the pay we give the staff--if we leave out the Assistant and the Tidewaiter--that our expenses exceed the limit. The Watchers get about half of what the Foreign Customs Boatmen get and the Examiners *none of* ~~about~~ *get* ~~the same as not as~~ much as our *head* Tingchai. And yet they are doing responsible work. At the out-stations the Examiners not only collect duties, but they even levy fines. The only one of the entire Native Customs Outdoor staff that I can depend upon is Tidewaiter Lee, and it is only by keeping him going around and inspecting and checking all the time that I can hope to keep within bounds the supplementing of their meagre pay by the rest. Among the Confidential Reports for last year is Stevens' Report on Lee, in which he ~~ways~~ recommends that ~~him to your~~ notice. be taken of the zeal with which he has been attending to his work. I would beg to second what Stevens says. Lee is an exceptionally good

Customs Officer, in addition to being a steady, well conducted man, generally speaking. He is working at Chinese, too. I consider that it would only be for the benefit of the Customs work if he were given some recognition.

Foreign Customs.

While speaking of the Native Customs staff, I may as well say that the staff of the Foreign Customs here is too small for the work. Lee does a little in the way of entering and clearing steamers; but there is no one except the Boatmen to attend to their working and the landing and shipping of cargo goes on any way at all. This is not as it should be and later on I will address you officially on the subject.

Weather.

The weather continues cold, but is quite agreeable. I think Wenchow has the best climate on the China coast.

I remain
Yours faithfully,

(9)

P. S. With regard to the accusation against Weigher Yen, an incident occurred on the day the rice was seized which may have been the case of this. About 5 o'clock in the afternoon, on that day after the office staff had left, four or five men from the Chi-ch'a Chü came to the Native Customs. Two of them entered the office and sat down at Mr Wong's desk in quite a free and easy manner and asked the Tingchai to show them the junk's papers. Yen happened to be on the premises and the Tingchai called him in to talk to them. Yen told them that the papers were locked up and that they could not see them. He further said to them that they had no right to come into the office and sit down at the Assistant's desk and he requested them to leave the place. They went away sullenly and evidently not best pleased with Yen's reception of them, and it is quite possible that the paragraph in the paper may have been the outcome of their ill will. In my despatch, referring to the paragraph of the 26th of November, I say that it was partly printed in large type and partly in small type. I enclose you a copy of the paper containing the paragraph, so that you may see for yourself. The whole thing bears the impress of malevolence, in spite of the writer's protestations as to the heavenly mission of journalism which appear in the paragraph of the 6th of December. As a matter of fact the paper is a low class, personal sort of print and every now and then it contains remarks which show that the editor enjoys poking fun at people. It would be a mistake to pay too much attention to the remarks of such a paper.

No. 19

CUSTOM HOUSE,
Wenchow, 5th January, 1915.

DEAR MR AGLEN,

In the first paragraph of ~~his memo~~ Mr Assistant Wong's memo to me, which forms Enclosure No.2 in my despatch No.3053, reporting the rice case, he says that the Superintendent enquired if there was proof that the junk entered on the 3rd. I believe he had some idea of trying to make it appear that Wong had really received the manifest after the rice had been seized and had put a false date on it. Because, a few days after, he sent for one of the Watchers, a man called Ma, who used to be his servant in Peking and who had accompanied him here. ~~He cross questioned Ma as to exactly what time the manifest had been handed in.~~ It happened that Ma was one of the three members of the staff who had gone with the manifest on board the junk to check the cargo. The Superintendent cross-questioned him very minutely as to exactly what time the manifest had been handed in to the Customs, but, of course the answers were bound to correspond with what I had reported. I have reason to believe that the Superintendent was disappointed in not having been able to catch Wong in ~~malpractice~~ doing what was wrong.

INSPECTORATE GENERAL OF CUSTOMS,

PEKING, 19th January, 1915.

S/O

Dear Mr Acheson,

I have duly received your S/O No. 18 of 4th January.

Rice Case. Having made your protest and drawn attention to the matter it will probably be best to let it drop.

Yours truly,

Acheson, Esquire,
    WENCHOW.

Inspectorate General of Customs,

PEKING, 19th January 1915.

Dear Sir,

I am directed by the Inspector General to acknowledge receipt on the 15th Jan. of your S/O No.19 dated 9th January.

Yours truly,

A. Richardson
Private Secretary.

J. Acheson, Esquire,

WENCHOW.

INSPECTORATE GENERAL OF CUSTOMS,

PEKING, 23 Jan 1915

Dear Mr Acheson,

In a recent s/o I suggested dropping your Rice Case, but I have since read your desp. No 3053 and am instructing you officially not to do so.

Yours sincerely,

F. A. Aglen

No. 20.

CUSTOM HOUSE,

Wenchow, 3rd February, 1915.

DEAR MR AGLEN,

case.

I have duly received your despatch No.574 instructing me to again request the Superintendent to obtain release of the rice or report the case to the Shui-wu Ch'u. I have done so. He will find it very hard to have to complain to head quarters about the Taoyin, but I suppose he will find it best to ~~do so~~ *until something*. I hear the Taoyin is leaving for another post. There have been a good many complaints about him and the people generally will not regret his departure. Also, the Hsing Pao, the newspaper that denounced Weigher Yen has been suppressed for writing similar remarks about the Magistrate's ~~people~~ *deputy*. Some people are sure to hang themselves if they only get enough rope.

Change of name lorcha.

My despatch No.3060 recommends that the lorcha Chin Tê Li be charged for permission to change her name. Chinese practice is very slack in the matter of vessels changing their names and, as I remark in my despatch, we used to have a lot of trouble in Pakhoi on account of it.

Bank of China.

I am ready any time to commence with the Bank of China. The proposed agreement may appear strange to you on account of stating no remuneration. But

(2)

it merely continues, with slight modification, the present practice, which has worked all right. When a Bank keeps the Customs money, the public regard it as being backed by the Government, and this brings it a lot of business. Hence the Banker is willing to lose by his connection with us now and then ~~buy the business.~~ Just now ~~At the present~~ he has to remit to Shanghai about $155 for every S'hai Tls111.40, so collecting at the rate of $152 means a loss to him of about $3 on every Hk.Tls 100 he collects. However, a couple of years ago the rate was the other way and he made money out of us all the time. In the agreement I have stipulated for receipts and payments to be at the same rate--$152. Such and arrangement simplifies work. ~~The country round here just now is fairly quiet.~~

Mr Rose, the British Acting Consul, was here from Ningpo in the middle of January. He came down to settle some outstanding cases. One was that of the erection of a wharf ~~by~~ which Ilbert & Co. of Shanghai wish to construct for steamers which they contemplate running here. I have no particulars regarding what ~~steamers~~ kind of steamers are intended, whether "Inland" or ordinary coasting. The place selected--they have already acquired the site--is outside the anchorage limits, as these are now defined, and I have told the Consul that if we have to send officers to the wharf to ~~examine cargo~~ supervise ~~working of~~ cargo, by coasting vessels we shall have to charge extra fees. But I said that in the case of " Inland" steamers reporting to the Native Customs, no charge would be made. This would seem to be in accordance with No.3 of the Rules on page 108 of Volume VII of

S/O NO.19.   CUSTOM HOUSE,

                                    Wenchow, 9th January1

(3)

the Circulars, which says that steamers registered for inland traffic may ply freely in the waters of the port. Later on, if any question should arise regarding the matter, I will write officially.

ntry quiet.
ather.

The country around here is fairly quiet just now. In the middle of the month we had a cold snap and the thermometer went down to 27. But the weather has become mild again and I suppose we have passed the coldest time ~~we are going to have during~~ the present season.

I remain
Yours faithfully,

INSPECTORATE GENERAL OF CUSTOMS,

S/O

PEKING, 17th February 1915.

Dear Mr Acheson,

I have duly received your S/O No. 20 of 3rd February.

<u>Revenue Collection by Bank of China.</u>

The agreement you have made seems satisfactory but it may require revision later. What dollars are current at your port besides Mexicans?

Yours truly,

Acheson, Esquire,
W E N C H O W.

NO. 21

CUSTOM HOUSE,
WENCHOW, 26 February, 1915.

Rice case.

DEAR MR AGLEN,

I am sending you with this my despatch concerning my request, ~~according to your instructions,~~ to the Superintendent to ~~ask the Taoyin to hand~~ get back the rice ex Chiang Ts'ai Li from the Taoyin, or report the case to Peking. The Taoyin says he has no rice to hand back, as it has been confiscated and sold, so the case is being referred to the Ch'u, going by what the Superintendent says in his despatch. With regard to the Taoyin, he is leaving in a few days and will hardly be ~~here~~ much affected by any decision the Peking authorities may come to on the subject. He is a man of ~~an arbitre has~~ an arbitrary, impracticable temper and cannot even get along with his own countrymen ~~people~~. He has been flouting ~~treating~~ the Hsün-an-shih ~~with contempt~~ and the latter, I hear, has objected to him, so he is being removed to Huai-yang (　　) in Kiangsu. There he will be near his patron, Chang Hsün, whose influence over him will perhaps ~~be beneficial~~ have the effect of making him keep his temper within proper bounds.

Native Customs staff.
Security Bonds.

I ~~am sending~~ have sent you a telegram asking if Circulars Nos 2,172 and 2,259 refer to Native Customs Lushih. The Circulars ~~do are not~~ have no Native Customs numbers and, in carrying out the instructions of the first,

(2)

the first, Mr Bowring only applied them to the Foreign Customs and did not require any bonds from the members of the Native Customs staff. A few days ago one of the Native Customs Lushih died. The Superintendent seems not to have received any instructions regarding bond securities and may possibly refuse to give me the written statement required by the second Circular. Therefore I want to be sure that the instructions apply to the Native Customs before demanding it from him. His Weiyuan came to the office and I let him make ~~a copy~~ copies of the two Circulars, but I question if the Superintendent will consider himself bound by them.

Assistants Aida and Wong.

I said in my S/O No.18 that I thought of sending Aida to the Native Customs and bringing Assistant Wong to the Foreign Customs. I think it will be a good move in more ways than one and I am making the change from the 1st of March.

Dollars current.

I have received your letter of 17th, asking what dollars are current here. About 70% are Mexican, and 15% Japanese yen issued before the adoption of the gold standard in Japan; about 5% are Hupeh and Kiangnan dollars, about 3% and about 2% of Kwangtung and of Peiyang dollars. Hupeh, Kwangtung and Kiangnan dollars are each worth about 99 cents Mexican and Japanese and Peiyang dollars about 98 cents Mexican.

Weather.

South winds are beginning to prevail and the temperature is becoming warmer.

I remain Yours faithfully,

The Superintendent ~~wants~~ has introduced a new form of duty receipt in four parts, outside the 50 li and has asked me to use it at our stations, instead of the hung-tan and also ~~use it~~ in the case of all payments of duty ~~in all the offices inside the 50 li~~. I have replied that it might be very convenient in some ways, but the use of it would about treble the work and I thought our present documents all right.

INSPECTORATE GENERAL OF CUSTOMS.

S/O

PEKING, 9th March, 1915.

Dear Mr Acheson,

I have duly received your S/O No. 21 of 26th February.

<u>Dollars current at Wenchow.</u> What happens when Japanese, Hupeh, Kwangtung and Kiangnan dollars are tendered in payment of duty - at what rates are they received ?

Yours truly,

Acheson, Esquire,
WENCHOW.

No. 22

Haikuan and Kuping taels.

CUSTOM HOUSE,
WENCHOW, 11th March, 1915.

DEAR MR AGLEN,

I send you with this my reply to your despatch No.578, asking about the rate we use in converting between Haikuan and Kuping taels. On receiving it I sent for the Native Customs Weiyuan and gave him the copy of the Ch'u's letter and asked him to find out what return was meant. He took the letter away to show to the Superintendent and shortly after brought it back with the enclosed small piece of paper which he said the Superintendent had written with his own hand. From the paper it can be seen that the Monthly Report on Collection and Remittance is alluded to. The sum of Tls 3,172.016 written on the paper is the Native Customs collection in Haikuan taels for January. Since the receipt of Circular No.1898, we have ceased entering Kuping tael figures in our returns, and no conversions appear in any of the statements we send to the Superintendent. But he reconverts the figures we give him into Kuping taels in the reports he makes to Pekking and, of course, disagreement is the result. I hope my despatch and this will make the matter clear to you.

DRUNKENNESS.

I have duly received Circular No.2332. I have posted it in the Order Book, but I am glad to say the cap does not fit any member of the staff at this port. In his

(2)

Confidential Report for last year Stevens said that Verner had the name of being a drinker. But, since I have been here I have not noticed any signs of ~~whisky~~ liquor about him. From my own knowledge of him I should certify him as a steady man.

ather.   The winter seems pretty nearly over. The temperature is becoming milder all the time and the days are lengthening out and fires are almost unnecessary.

I remain

Yours faithfully,

James Acheson

i-ch'a Chu.   The Chi-ch'a Chu has not outlived the departure of the Taoyin who established it. He set it up to give employment to some of his hangers on, but the only pay they got was what they got out of confiscations and fines. The result was unsatisfactory and the establishment ran foul of others besides the Customs. No one except the Taoyin had any use for it and one of the local prints writes its epitaph in anything but complimentary terms.

Inspectorate General of Customs,

PEKING, 23rd March 1915.

Dear Sir,

I am directed by the Inspector General to acknowledge receipt on the 20th March your S/O No. 22 dated 11th March.

Yours truly,

Richardson
Private Secretary.

Acheson, Esquire,

WENCHOW.

NO. 23.

CUSTOM HOUSE,

WENCHOW, 23 MARCH, 1915.

DEAR MR AGLEN,

Native Customs.   I am sending you a despatch with this asking for increase of pay for the staff of the Native Customs. Since the establishment came under us in 1913, so many checks have been introduced that the Examiners and Watchers cannot supplement their pay to anything like the extent that was possible to them formerly, and their bare salaries are not sufficient for them to live on in a way befitting the work they do. So they have been getting discontented, and hence the petitions I have received from them. If I check them any more closely than I am doing now, possibly some of them will resign or give trouble. I do not pretend that the increased pay which I have proposed will entirely counteract their propensities to malpractice. But it will give them less excuse to ~~desire~~ want to make money irregularly and ~~make them and~~ cases of squeezing, when they do occur, will meet with less sympathy. With the increased revenue, our expenditure will be getting down to within measurable distance of the one-tenth of the collection. But it is rather much to expect a Custom House like this, which has to look after an extent of river equal to that controlled by the Shanghai Office to run itself on the one-tenth of a 2% tariff. Formerly the Native Customs staff bore

(2)

about the worst name in the place for squeezing. But I think they have a better reputation now and better pay will make it easier for them to sustain their improved reputation. Since the 1st of this month I have had Aida in the Native Customs instead of Wong Hiau Geng and it is a change for the better, as the former, being a foreigner and dressing in foreign clothes, has more authority than a native. Wong is quite capable, but he is too much of the same style as the rest of the staff to carry a great deal of weight with them. With regard to the security bonds, this will be all right, as the Superintendent has asked me to go ahead and get a guarantee for each member of the staff.

lar and
l rates.

I have duly received your S/O letter of the 9th instant, asking about dollars current at Wenchow. In reply, I beg to state that Japanese (silver) dollars and Peiyang dollars are at present accepted at the rate of Hk.Tls 100 equal to $153.535 and that Hupeh, Kiangnan and Kwangtung dollars are received at the rate of Hk.Tls 100 equal to $152.763.

I remain
Yours faithfully,

NO. 24.

CUSTOM HOUSE,

WENCHOW, 26 March, 1915.

DEAR MR AGLEN,

I have sent you an application from Aida asking for a transfer to Dairen. Should you grant his request, the man you send to replace him ~~should~~ ought to be one who knows enough Chinese to do the Native Customs work. I think A Japanese is very suitable for this work. Because a Japanese has always a perfect working knowledge of Written Chinese; also, being a foreigner, he is invested with a prestige which enhances his authority, and, again, not being a Chinese subject, he need be in no fear of the Superintendip by Stevensent.

I am sending you a report by Stevens on a trip he made by "Inland" steamer from Ningpo to Wenchow. which gives some valuable information. You will see that the Chinese are establishing lights and buoys on their own account. I do not give the Chinese characters for Wu Ji Island, as I am not sure of them. It is ~~very likely~~ possibly the same as Wu Ji Rock (鷄娘礁), which appears on page 68 of the second issue of "Names of Places on the Coast", but the characters do not represent the name, as written alphabetically, which is apparently Chinese.

I have arranged to hand over the collection to the Bank of China on the 1st of May. The Agent

(2)

was absent in Hangchow for some time, and this has delayed matters. The present Banker has asked a full month according to the calendar to have everything ready to hand over.

ive Customs. One of the Native Customs Examiners, Wu T'ing-kan (胡廷幹) has died. For the present I am not intending to replace him, as I think we have got enough men.

ther. Weather foggy, raw and chilly and we are not into the summer just yet.

I remain

Yours faithfully,

[signature]

(The man who has died was at P'u-chou-k'ou, and I am transferring the Examiner at Ning-ts'un to P'u-chou-k'ou and sending a man to Ning-ts'un from the Head Office, where we can do with a man less. As time goes on Lee is getting a greater grasp of the work, and I am getting to know more and more about it myself. The supervision is increasing in efficiency and the native staff are doing more than formerly.

Inspectorate General of Customs,

PEKING, 30th March 1915.

Dear Sir,

I am directed by the Inspector General to acknowledge receipt on the 28th March of your S/O No. 23 dated 23rd March.

Yours truly,

Richardson
Private Secretary.

Acheson, Esquire,

WENCHOW.

INSPECTORATE GENERAL OF CUSTOMS,

S/O

PEKING, 6th April, 1915

Dear Mr Acheson,

I have duly received your S/O No. 24 of 26th March.

<u>Request for transfer to Dairen from Mr Aida.</u>

There is no vacancy at Dairen and if Mr Aida is transferred it will probably be to some other port.

<u>Lights and Buoys established by Chinese.</u> This is a new development and requires watching. Send copy of report to Coast Inspector.

Yours truly,

Acheson, Esquire,
W E N C H O W.

NO. 25. CUSTOM HOUSE,
WENCHOW 17th APRIL, 1915.

DEAR MR AGLEN,

Haikuan and Kuping taels.
    I duly received your despatch No.582 about Haikuan and Kuping taels. I will send you my reply in a day or two. The Superintendent says he explained clearly to the Ch'u that the Customs converted at the rate of 164 and that the statement that we convert at 163 must be an error on their part.

Tidewaiter Lee.
    Tidewaiter Lee is very grateful for his promotion, which I can only say he has well deserved. He has done excellent service and the increased efficiency of the Native Customs staff and the improvement in the method of doing the work are very largely due to his willing~~ness to work~~ and ~~his~~ intelligent performance of his duties.

Death of Examiner. Native Customs.
    Another of the Native Customs Examiners died a couple of days ago. I am not replacing him for the present. ~~Since The present~~ Three of the Examiners have died since I came here and I have not replaced any of them. Their pay amounted altogether to $40 a month, or $480 a year. I think, however, the staff is about as low now as we can let it go and I shall have to ~~replace the next man who withdraws~~ fill the next vacancy that occurs.

Dismissal of Native Customs Lushih.
    In my S/O No.21 I said that one of the Lushih in the Native Customs had died. The Superintendent

(2)

sent me a man, called Ch'êng (　) to replace him to whom the staff in the office very much objected, as they said he had a bad reputation and the Superintendent sent him to us simply in order to be rid of him. I told them the Superintendent was responsible and, as soon as the man appeared, I duty installed him. However, a very short time after he commenced work I began to hear stories about his charging for clearances papers. I should say that the duty receipts given to junks on clearing (hungtan) are not made out until after the cargo has been checked on board with the applications. This checking generally takes place after 4 o'clock and the hungtan is often not ready till half past 5. It has therefore been the practice for the Lushih to remain and issue it and at the same time hand back the junk's papers. This work was the duty of the new Lushih, Ch'êng. A few days ago I received a petition from half a dozen of the Native Customs brokers stating that Ch'êng had forced them to pay him 20 cents for every junk he cleared for them. The whole six brokers came to the office and, in the presence of Ch'êng, stated that they had paid him the money. Ch'êng denied having received any money from them. But I told him there were too many against him and I there and then dismissed him. I have to wrote to the Superintendent and asked him for another man. He replied to my letter stating he was sending man, but he made no remarks regarding the dismissal. I am now endeavouring to alter the rule so that the clearance papers shall be issued by the Assistant. The brokers have been told that on

(3)

vens.

ather.

days when they want to clear their junks they must hurry up with their applications, so that the checking may be done earlier. The native staff cannot be trusted farther than one can see them.

I have given Stevens leave to go to Shanghai ~~for three or four days~~. His daughter is going to be married and there is no one to perform the ceremony in Wenchow. So the event is to come off in Shanghai. He will be absent only for ~~four or five days~~ about a week.

Weather rainy most of the time. It is getting warm. It was 85 on Sunday, but it has cooled off a little since.

I remain

Yours faithfully,

[signature]

I have received your letter of the 6th and will send a copy of his report on his trip to the Coast Inspector, whom he will be able to see when he gets to Shanghai and the two can talk the matter over.

INSPECTORATE GENERAL OF CUSTOMS,

S/O

PEKING, 27th April, 1915.

Dear Mr Acheson,

I have duly received your S/O No. 25 of 17th April.

<u>Dismissal of Native Customs Lushih recently nominated by Superintendent.</u> It is not necessary for you to accept anyone nominated by the Superintendent. If he sends you a man whom you have reason to suspect you can certainly refuse to appoint him and ask the Superintendent to nominate another. The Superintendent does not appoint.

Yours truly,

J. Acheson, Esquire,
   WENCHOW.

No. 26

CUSTOM HOUSE,

Wenchow, 6th May, 1915.

DEAR MR AGLEN,

ive Customs.   I am sending you with this a despatch regarding a new form of duty paid certificate which the Superintendent wishes me to introduce inside the 50 li. He says it has been used ~~with good effect~~ outside the radius with good effect. I have held out against introducing ~~the form~~, because it would increase the work and would be no improvement. If it were brought into use here, I do not say we would require more staff all at once. But any addition to the work makes reduction of staff more difficult, and it is reduction we should strive after. As a matter of fact the Superintendent has no one he can trust, and the only plan he can think of for keeping his people straight is by juggling with documents and making one man check another, the two being at a distance that makes collusion unlikely. But, with a reliable white man to supervise the work, such cumbrous methods are unnecessary. I have considered Lee entirely trustworthy, and I hope Stocks will be the same. The application is the main document, around which abuses can most centre. In making out the other papers of junks, there is little room for illicit gains. I hope I shall not be instructed to introduce the quadruplicate

(2)

certificates. We make out too many documents as it is. The cargo certificate is not wanted when a junk has a hungtan.

Lushih

I have duly received your letter of 27th of April. Notwithstanding what I had been told about the Lushih, I could hardly have refused to appoint him, as I had no proof against him. I put the objection of the staff to him down to personal ill-feeling. He was, no doubt, a sea lawyer and a mischief maker, and I think the office is well rid of him on general considerations.

Duties.

The Native Customs duties for April only amounted to Tls.2,891, as against Tls 2,657 for the same month of last year. With the new tariff and equal trade, the collection should have been half as much more. One reason for the short receipts was falling off in the export of timber on account of the political situation being unsatisfactory.

I am very sorry that Lee is transferred. He is an excellent man for the Native Customs work. He is a Chinese student and is making good progress in the language. His manner with the Chinese, too, is polite and agreeable, and I should say he is liked by all the natives with whom he comes in contact. He deserves to get on in the Service. I was very glad to receive your telegram saying I could keep him till Stocks came. The Native Customs work here is carried on at a great many different points and Lee is so well acquainted with the peculiarities of each place that he is the proper man to initiate his successor.

The weather is getting warmer. There has been a good deal of rain of late.

      I remain
      Yours faithfully,

Inspectorate General of Customs,

PEKING, 18th May, 1915.

Dear Sir,

I am directed by the Inspector General to acknowledge receipt on the 14th May your S/O No. 26 dated 6th May.

Yours truly,

Acheson,
Private Secretary.

J. Acheson, Esquire,

WENCHOW.

CUSTOM HOUSE,

WENCHOW 24th May, 1915.

DEAR MR AGLEN,

I handed over the Customs business to the Bank of China on the first of the present month and am reporting this officially to you by this present mail and sending you copy of the Agreement amended as instructed. I received the Inspectorate despatch instructing me to make the transfer on the 25th of February. But, as mentioned in my S/O No.24, the absence of the Agent delayed matters. Also the month's notice from the 1st of the month which the Kung I Bank asked for added further to the delay. Again, I have delayed reporting the transfer because the Kung I Bank asked me to allow it to remit the revenue balances to Shanghai instead of handing them over to the Bank of China. The Manager explained that the Bank, for some months past, had lost a good deal of money on the Customs remittances on account of the high value of the tael. I knew that the money was safe, as the Kung I Bank and, besides, I held a security for it from a very large timber concern. So I consented. He wished to defer the remittance to the 21st of the present month, but I told him he must give me his draft on Shanghai the middle of the month. I posted his cheques on the 15th and have not received the acknowledge-

(2)

ment of the receipt of the money from the Hongkong and Shanghai Bank. As a matter of fact Kung had the money all right on the 1st of the month, but exchange was getting more favourable and he wanted to wait. The delay has not affected our Accounts (as we usually remit about the middle of this month). The Bank of China is doing our business quite satisfactorily.

I remain

Yours faithfully,

[signature]

ive Customs .   The timber business here is still very slack and our Native Customs collection for this month is much less than we expected. I shall likely have to apply for a second Supplemantary Grant foɾ eh the quarter, as we shall hardly have enough to pay the June expenses.

Inspectorate General of Customs,

PEKING, 8th June, 1915

Dear Sir,

I am directed by the Inspector General to acknowledge receipt on the 4th June your S/O No. 27 dated 27th May.

Yours truly,

Acheson,
Private Secretary.

Acheson, Esquire,

WENCHOW.

No. 28

CUSTOM HOUSE,
Wenchow, 12 June, 1915.

dismissed
shih and
arantee.

DEAR MR ABLEN,

I am sending with this my reply to your query about the Lushih whom I dismissed. Requiring from the Superintendent an avowal that the bond was actually in his keeping might have been resented by him as an unnecessarily close observance of form. But there was no occasion to make use of any guarantee ~~they the~~ when the Lushih ceased to belong to the staff. The petition against him gave a list of eight junks for whose clearances he had charged 20 cents each--total $1.60. The amount was very small and the petitioners did not ask for refund of it. If I had paid them back the money, it was possible that a number of other claimants would have come forward, some putting in false claims that might have made the case look like one of conspiracy against the man, with the result that the Superintendent might have asked me to retain him. But he had a bad name and was objected to as a colleague by the rest of the staff. I was glad, therefore, to have the opportunity of getting rid of him. It is so unusual for Chinese to come forward and give evidence that I did not want to do anything that might have ended in their testimony being called in question. I paid the Lushih his salary in full to date of dismissal.

ive Customs
lection.

The Native Customs collection for May

(2)

is disappointing, having only been Tls 4,400 odd, as against Tls 4,200 odd for the same month of last year. Had the trade been as good this year, ~~we should have collected~~ our collection ought to have been nearer Tls 6,000. But I think we shall nearly make up for ~~the f~~ it this month. Up to the 8th we have received Tls 1,400 and, at this rate the month's receipts should be over Tls 5,000, as against Tls 3400 odd for the June of 1914. The trouble with Japan upset business a lot. ~~It made~~ The unsettled condition of things made the timber merchants unwilling to give credit to firms at other ports, and so sales fell off. However, the timber is stacked in the timber yards and we are bound to get the duty on it sooner or later. I do not expect the collection for the whole year will be much under expectations. We shall not want an additional grant for account N.

gtan cargo.

I am going into the question raised in your despatch No.599 concerning the passing free here of ~~goods imports~~ under hungtan from ports in the Chekiang province. It is only to be expected that, if the tariff at Ningpo, for example is lower than here ~~and they still seem still to be working on the old tariff there, with and addition of 6 mace per tael, which, however, does not bring it up to the Wenchow fi rates~~ imports for here will be passed through that port. However, since we introduced the new tariff ~~here~~, our imports have remained about the same as they were before and our import duties are about what they should be. Later on, when I have found out more on the

(3)

subject, I will write officially. The Native Customs stations in the province south of here and for some distance north of us are all under the Wenchow Superintendent, who has informed me that the tariff which we use is also in use in all the offices under him.

e case.

I have duly received your despatch No.600, regarding the rice seized from under our control by the Taoyin. I talked to the Superintendent about the case a few days ago. I presume he has also heard from the Shui-wu Ch'u about it. He said he had been handicapped in the matter by others telling him he should support the Taoyin rather than the Commissioner, but he maintained throughout that I was his colleague andthat he was bound to side with me. Now that a ruling exists, such a case will not, he says, occur again. He said the Taoyin had blundered in backing up the Chi-ch'a Chü. I ~~said that~~ 'the Taoyin had a bad temper and ~~the Superintendent~~ said that was a fact.

ive Customs -stations.

I regret that, ~~I made an incorrect statement~~ in my despatch No.3087 about the quadruplicate duty receipts, I made an incorrect statement in saying that the Examiners rendered their accounts once a month. The Examiners at the river front stations in Wenchow, at the time I wrote the despatch, only handed over their receipts once a month; but those at the more distant stations paid what they collected once in ten days. Since the beginning of this month, all the stations pay in their receipts to the Bank

It continues to rain a lot. We have had one or two hot days, but no prolonged spell of heat as yet.

I remain

Yours faithfully,

[signature]

A few days ago the Superintendent came to see me and asked me if I could procure subscriptions amoung the staff to the domestic loan of the present year. I have got him about $2,500 and he has thanked me very profusely. The people do seem to have come forward very readily with their contributions. Distrust of their officials still exists and is not without foundation.

INSPECTORATE GENERAL OF CUSTOMS

S/O

PEKING, 29th June, 1915.

Dear Mr. Acheson,

I have duly received your S/O No. 28 of 12th June.

<u>Domestic Loan: subscriptions obtained from Staff at Superintendent's request.</u> Superintendents have been pressing for subscriptions to the loan from Staff elsewhere and I have been asked for my views. I have replied that we have nothing to do with the private investments of the Staff and that, beyond giving publicity to prospectus and regulations, nothing is to be done by Commissioner to influence anyone.

Yours truly,

Acheson, Esquire,
  WENCHOW.

CUSTOM HOUSE,
WENCHOW, 5th July, 1915.

NO. 29

nks and
cuments.

DEAR MR AGLEN,

You will see in my Non-Urgent Correspondence for June copies of despatches that have passed between the Superintendent and myself regarding junks and documents. In the middle of May I addressed him saying that junks from other provinces never handed us their documents and we should have these, so as to have a better check on imports. I sent him the draft of a proclamation which I thought might be issued. It stated that, after two months, the Native Customs would begin to demand from junks, whether from ports in the Chekiang province or from ports in other provinces, such documents as had been issued to them by the Custom Houses at the places where they had shipped their cargoes. The Superintendent approved of the proclamation and it was issued in our joint names. In the beginning of June the Fukien merchants petitioned the Superintendent and myself on the subject. They stated that junks were not like steamers reporting to the Foreign Customs, which only visited a limited number of ports. Junks traded up and down the coast and called in at any places where it might be possible to sell or buy cargo advantageously. Sometimes a junk with cargo covered by Customs documents would discharge part of it at a way port and come to

Wenchow with the rest. Of course, in such a case the cargo would not agree with the documents. There is, no doubt, a good deal in what the petitioners say. But I believe the real reason why they do not want to produce their documents

(2)

that a lot of the cargo brought in junks here from ~~other~~
ports in other provinces is shipped at places where there
are no Custom Houses and so has paid no export duty. They
view the proclamation as the first step towards putting an
end to this and consequently object to it. But their very
objecting shows that there is a lot of non-duty-paying trade
carried on along the coast to the detriment of the Native
Customs revenue. The Superintendents wrote to me asking me to suggest some
way of ~~working~~ carrying out the proclamation so as not to
interfere too much with the business of the merchants. I
replied (described) the procedure that I thought should be followed.
I said there was no reason at all why the merchants should
object to produce the documents they had received to cover
cargo and that we ~~would~~ need not raise any question except there
were evidence of ~~smuggling~~ clandestine shipment-- ~~some goods~~
~~entered in the documents and others~~ partly ~~in excess of it~~.
With regard to goods declared as from a place without a Custom House, I said the best thing to do would be to take note of
such casks ~~these places~~ and communicate with the Superintendents of the
Custom Houses nearest ~~to each~~ the places. Of course it would not
be worth while doing this except the non-duty-paying ~~trade~~ cargo
amounted to something considerable. No doubt importers will
give fictitious names; but I think we can gradually arrive
at a knowledge of the various places in the Fukien province
where goods of various kinds come from. Fukien is the province ~~where nearly all the~~ --not counting Chekiang--where
nearly all the junks come from that bring cargo. ~~A good man~~

— 119 —

(3)

As to giving a document to cover cargo re-exported from here that was uncovered by any document issued by the port of original import, I do not see how we could do this. The abuses that exist are about as old as the Native Customs (establishment) itself and it will take some time to eradicate them, though they may be got rid of in time by proceeding slowly and step by step.

Registration Chinese vessels.

The Ministry of Communications seems to have been a little premature in issuing the regulations given in Circular No.2212. There are four launches running on the canals here. They had Inland Certificates issued by this office and, at the time of receipt of the Circular, were duly warned that their Certificates could not be renewed unless they produced Registration Certificates from the Ministry. That was a year ago, but they have produced as yet no Certificates from the Ministry. Consequently, their Inland Certificates have been called in, as they have expired, and I have informed the Superintendent that the launches are now running without any authorisation from this office.

Staff.

I am very well satisfied with Lee's successor, Stocks. He seems to take interest in his work and to check the native staff effectively. With one good Outdoor Staff man who is active and keeps on the go all the time and works intelligently, I do not think abuses can exist to any great extent. I hardly ever receive a petition against any of the Examiners or Watchers, which looks as if

(4)

they were running straight.

ppy heads.   I have received despatch No.604 instructing me to claim the reward laid down in Circular No.2334. *(for the seizure of poppy heads)* But the Examiner estimated that the amount of poppy seeds contained in the heads or capsules did not amount to more than about 2 taels in weight. At the rate of $4 a picul, the reward issuable would have only been half a cent. So I have made no application to the Superintendent and there will be no reward in the case.

tive Customs llection.   The Native Customs collection is recovering. I expect the duties for ~~this~~ June will be about ~~Tls~~ Tls 4,500. We haven't got in the Station accounts yet. Junks are clearing with timber all the time and the present month *should* ~~will~~ also show a good collection.

ather.   Though well into July, we ~~havnt~~ *have* had very little hot weather as yet. There has been a good deal of rain which has kept it cool.

I remain
Yours faithfully,

S/O

INSPECTORATE GENERAL OF CUSTOMS

PEKING, 29th July, 1915.

Dear Mr. Acheson,

I have duly received your S/O No. 29 of 5th July.

<u>Proclamation issued jointly by Superintendent and Commissioner in rê junks arriving with cargo not covered by documents in proof of payment of Export Duty.</u> Junks should of course produce such documents as they carry in their own interest, but there is no law preventing them from trading at places where there are no Native Customs Houses. What we have to do is to insist on a proper and true declaration of what is on board and to charge duty on it

Acheson, Esquire,
   WENCHOW.

it according to our Tariff and regulations. I do not think it would be wise to press this matter too far and it would certainly have been better if you had consulted me before you took any steps and involved the Superintendent in a proclamation.

Yours truly

NO. 30

CUSTOM HOUSE,
Wenchow, 25th July, 1915.

DEAR MR AGLEN,

I have been laid up for about a fortnight with inflammation in the ear, fever and bronchitis and have been able to do very little. However, I am glad to say that I am getting all right again and am at the office every day.

The fish shops have petitioned against the Examiners for not reporting what they collect and not giving duty receipts and also for charging higher rates than proper. I believe the truth is that the Examiners have been keeping too much of the squeezing to themselves. ~~The~~ How to deal with the ~~levy~~ fish importation is the most difficult problem of the Native Customs here. Because the fish, especially the fresh fish, is rushed into the port in the early hours of the morning in numbers of small junks. It is landed at various jetties and taken straight to the shops. With the best will possible I do not think the Examiners could obtain proper tally of it, ~~Corrupt, as they necessarily are from their training and associations, it is the easiest thing for them~~ and the checking of their work by anyone else cannot be effected by any means I can think of. Under the circumstances therefore and considering how corrupt they are from up-bringing and association, it is only to be expected that they should take advantage of the facilities so ready to their hand for enriching themselves at the expense of the revenue. Hitherto we have been rather slack in only requiring from them general statements each day of the total quantity of fish passed and the duty leviable upon it. Now I am requiring them to give a daily detailed statement of the import by each shop and the amount of duty payable by it and when a shop pays any duty it must be entered in the day's statement. The Lushih will keep a ledger with a space for each shop where the imports of the shop will be entered as well as the duties paid by it. Most of the fish is taken delivery of by the large shops, but some of it is retailed from the junks. Duty is paid on this by the junks and here is where malpractice is so easy, as we can exercise no effective supervision over these petty transactions. But the large shops know about them and have some idea of what they amount to and I am going to try and procure from them statements that will serve as some kind of a check on the doings of out staff. The foregoing will constitute a show of doing the work in a more thorough manner. But I have little hope that it will entirely stop abuses. The likelihood will be that the Examiners will be driven to collude with the shops and the pickings will be shared. In your despatch No.532 of April last year you suggest an arrangement by wich the shops would pay a lump sum

(3)

and we would withdraw the staff at the Fish Station. I have sounded them on the subject and they say that, on account of the new tariff which is to come at Ningpo on the 1st of August, they are uncertain how the fish import here will be affected and the most they could offer to pay would be Tls 200 a month. Considering that up to the end of June we have received over Tls 1,600, the offer is quite too small. I can do better by improving the mode of checking. The great difficulty in the way is that we have no means of finding out, even approximately, the actual quantity of fish that comes in. The Tidewaiter is frequently on duty along the river front in the early hours of the morning, but he can only form a rough idea of what happens to be imported on the particular days when he is on fish duty. The import is not constant, but varies with the months. However, I will add that, though the revenue suffers a lot from malpractice, viewing the matter from a practical standpoint, there is not so much to complain of. Here is the duty received from the Fish Station for each year from 1912:--

    1912. Tls 194.
    1913. ,, 1,108.
    1914. ,, 1,229.
    1915, to end of June. Tls 1,646.

Our collection for this year ought to be about Tls 3,000. You will see that our receipts have been increasing by leaps and bounds. This partly due to the new tariff, but

I have tried to get at the importation by enquiring from the shops. A short time ago the head of the principal shop told me he would estimate the value of the fish imported during a year at $150,000. Duty at 2½% on this would be nearly $9,000, say about Tks 6,000. I fear we shall never attain to these figures in collecting. ~~But with improved methods we may approach it within measurable distance.~~

(4)

the increase commenced before this came in, so it must be partly attributed to improved management. ~~But~~ there is still room for more improvement and I shall adopt the best measures I can think of.

Bamboos.   Last December the bamboo exporters petitioned the Superintendent against the same two Examiners that run the Fish Station. They said that more money was paid as duty than was reported by them and complained that they could not obtain receipts for duty. They gave a statement of what they had exported for the ten months January ~~to the end of~~ October and, as well as could be gathered from it, their export amounted to about 130,000 bamboos, if duty on which, at one cash apiece--old tariff rate--would have amounted to about $130. According to the returns of the Examiners only about 115,000 bamboos were exported, the duty on which was about $115. The difference between the exporters and the Examiners was only $15. Spread over a period of ten months, this meant--supposing it to have been pocketed by the two Examiners--only 75 cents a month each, quite an insignificant sum. ~~But~~ And the statement of the bamboo exporters was made out in a very unintelligible manner and ~~I had~~ there was no proof that it was perfectly correct. So I told the Superintendent that it was impossible to ~~fix blame~~ locate the error. I said we had begun a new system with the new tariff and that the Examiners had strict instructions to collect according to it, and that there would be less cause

(5)

for complaint in the future. I thought the matter was ended, but a few days ago I received a petition saying that the Exporters had referred the case to the Ts'ai-chêng Pu. They complain that the new tariff rate of 8 mace a hundred represents about 5% on the value and they ask in their petition if the Peking authorities know about it, or if This is simply a local imposition. I have informed them that the tariff had the sanction of the Board and was notified to the public by proclamation posted broadcast. I told them also that it had been printed and copies given to the merchants and that anyone could get a copy on applying to the Native Customs. The fact is the new tariff was adopted at too short notice— four days only. It is really only a local tariff. In so far as I know Ningpo is still working on the old tariff of two hundred years ago, though I believe new rates are to be introduced there from the 1st of August. But changes should be made simultaneously, at least in so far as they affect the same province. I have told the bamboo men that all complaints must be made at once and that if an Examiner acts improperly or refuses to issue a receipt for duty paid, the matter should be without delay referred to the Head Office, where it will be set right, but that it is impossible to enquire into cases that have taken place months before.

s' documents.   I have duly received your letter of 26th regarding the proclamation in the matter of junks' documents. I first thought of them at the time of the rice case. If the junk had had a document showing where the rice had been shipped

(6)

it would have made the case much more easily dealt with. Subsequently I began to hear that cargo was being landed down river without being reported to the Customs and it seemed to me that, if we could get the export documents, we would be in possession of one means of checking this irregularity. About 70 per cent of the junks that come here load their cargoes at places where there are Custom Houses, which issue them clearance documents, and we may as well have these. I am not forcing the junks in the matter, but I expect in time to bring them into line.

Kaneko has arrived and Aida has left for Shanghai. I am very sorry he has gone. a very capable and willing worker. I like what I have seen of Mr Kaneko. His English very good, which is an important point I am placing him in the Native Customs. I cannot send Wong back there, as the Superintendent is too much down upon him.

There are typhoons about and we are having hot, west winds which are very unpleasant.

I remain
Yours faithfully,

S/O

Inspectorate General of Customs,

PEKING, **14th August** 191**5**.

Dear Sir,

I am directed by the Inspector General to acknowledge receipt on the **9th inst** your **S/O No.30** dated **29th July**.

Yours **truly,**

C. Acheson,
Private Secretary.

. Acheson, Esquire,

W E N C H O W.

NO. 31.

CUSTOM HOUSE,
WENCHOW, 19th August, 1915.

DEAR MR AGLEN,

kerosene drums.   I have answered your Circular about kerosene drums. The plan of identifying them by the numbers could not be made to work here, I fear. Even if the numbers could be read, mistakes in transcribing them could hardly fail to occur--a 2 might be written for a 3 or a 9 for a 7, and a mistake of the kind once made would lead to confusion later on. The way all other cargo is identified is by the marks on it, and I think this is the only practical way of identifying kerosene drums. The Customs would have to find some means of stamping the metal, but this would likely be possible.

Writer.   I have written to ask an increase of pay for Writer Ts'ao. He has had a good deal of work of one kind or another since I have been here and has always done it willingly. Of late, for example, I have given him a lot to do in examining the books of the fish shops and finding out where these agreed with or differed from those of the Examiners. This has occupied him days at a time, the said books being not easy to understand. He has been quite a number of years without any rise, and I think it only fair to him to bring his name before you.

(2)

oting
staff.

My despatch No.3104 gives the history of piloting by members of the staff here in so far as I have been able to ascertain it. It is a custom almost coeval with the opening of the port and would be difficult to abolish, though there may be objections to it. All the money the Lin brothers make by their piloting amounts to little and it would hardly be fair, considering the hardship, to make them do it for nothing.

ive Customs
/uan.

I have written asking for an increase of pay for the Native Customs Weiyuan. He does no work for me and, as far as the running of the establishment is concerned, it would be just as well without him as with him. But he is recognised as a member of the staff and paid from Account N, and feeling slighted in being made an exception of pay. I will say for him that he is a very agreeable man and never attempts to interfere with the work and never gives any trouble. I do not think $60 a month for a Weiyuan is too much.

ve Customs
iners.

I have been trying to find out the extent of the abuses that have been going on at the Fish Station, but without very much result so far. The Examiners' books and those of the fish shops do not agree, but in some cases the former contain more duty than the latter. I have no doubt there has been squeezing. But there is very little

(2)

written evidence of it. Under the new system which I have introduced, the Examiners keep ledgers in which they enter clearly--not in grass character--the quantity of fish that each shop imports day by day with the duty on it. Every ten days the total is made up and the Head Office calls upon the shops to pay. The discontent of the fishmongers was caused really by the raising of the tariff. Certain fishery products pay now ad valorem ~~which formerly~~ *paid specific duty*. These products differ very much in value, while resembling eachother so closely that it is very difficult to distinguish between them in the early hours of the morning when they are landed. So *had to* We have lumped *them* these together to a great extent I have told the shops that we are quite *willing* to charge *strictly* ~~true ad valorem duties on them~~ *according to values* on condition that they will abstain from rushing them on shore *in cargos* ~~with such haste that our Examiners cannot possibly distinguish between them. The shops see the force of are willing to strike a bargain. I have told them that our E the boats must wait until our Examiners have gone on board each junk and properly inspected its cargo before any of it can be landed.~~ The shops are willing to ~~strike a~~ bargain and I have now made a new departure and introduced the rule that no junk can discharge till the Examiner has inspected her cargo. I expect things will be better ~~now~~, though we shall be still dependent on the Examiners' reports.

The Civil Governor of the province,

(4)

Mr Ch'ü Ying-kuang (屈映光) arrived in Wenchow on the in the cruiser Ch'ao Wu (超武) on a tour of inspection, 2nd. On the 3rd he went up river as far as Ch'ing-t'ien (青田); returned from there early in the morning of the 5th; left same day for Shanghai en route for Hangchow. At the time he arrived I was still suffering from the effects of the inflammation in my ear and was deaf on the one side. So I sent Mr Kaneko on board the cruiser on its arrival to present my compliments. On the departure of the Governor I also sent Mr Kaneko to see him off.

ive Customs
k: memo and

I have finished the draft of a memorandum which gives a complete description of how the Native Customs work is done at present. But, as the practice still admits of improvement in a good many respects, ~~there is no~~ and as I ~~am~~ change it from time to time, there is no use my sending you a copy of ~~it as yet.~~ the memorandum as yet. ~~I am also~~ Stevens, also, is working on a revision of the map which I sent you in my despatch No.3045 of last November. I want to have this as complete as possible and it will be some time before it is finished.

:her.

The night winds are getting a little cooler and the summer is approaching its end.

I remain
Yours faithfully,

James Acheson

I see from one of the local papers that Our late Taoyin, Mr Tso Ti-chow ( ) with whom I had the trouble over the rice, has been denounced to Peking for improper treatment of the people when he was here. I daresay his confiscation of the rice will form an count in the indictment against him. The paper says that the Governor has been instructed to report on the case.

INSPECTORATE GENERAL OF CUSTOMS,

PEKING, 31st August, 1915.

Dear Mr Acheson,

I am directed by the Inspector General to acknowledge receipt of your S/O No. 31 of 19th August, and to reply as follows :-

<u>Piloting by Customs Staff</u>. What approximately is the piloting worth to them a year? They cannot, of course, be expected to pilot for nothing, but the question is whether they can act as pilots and still retain Customs employment.

<u>Pay of Native Customs Weiyüan</u>. If he does no work and is also useless the

Inspector

Acheson, Esquire,
    WENCHOW.

Inspector General cannot understand why you recommend increase in pay. The pay he receives should be adequate in these circumstances.

<u>Native Customs Examiners and abuses at the Fish Station.</u> Your foreign tidewaiter should occasionally check the doings of these examiners.

Yours truly,

L. Acheson,
Private Secretary.

CUSTOM HOUSE,

WENCHOW, 10th September 1915.

DEAR MR AGLEN,

oting staff.

I have duly received your letter of 31st August. I will make up an account of the earnings of the Lin brothers as pilots for the past two or three years and send it to you.

ive Customs miners.

The Tidewaiter keeps a fairly close supervision over the doings of the Fish Station Examiners. But of course he cannot be looking after them the whole time. ~~The problem of how to keep the Native Customs Examiners~~ and Watchers straight is exactly the same as confronts Tramway Companies at home as regards their car conductors. A vast amount of ability has been brought to bear on this problem both in England and America, but without ~~completely satisfactory results~~. The new system which I have started of keeping the Station books will afford a check which has hitherto not existed. Until I began the new entries in system the books were written in grass character in a very slovenly manner and it was extremely difficult to ~~check~~ find out from them what had been imported and what duty had been paid. The Examiners now keep a Liu-shui pu (   ) The entries in this book have to be written clearly and neatly and according to system. It is entered up daily, the entries being distributed under the names of the various

(2)

ious shops or individuals who have imported fish during the day. Every morning the journal is sent to the Head Office where the Lushih copies the entries into abstract books, which are looked over by the Assistant. My first idea was to have all the books kept at the Station. But it afterwards seemed to me rather better to have the abstracting done in the Head Office, as the knowledge that their entries would be rearranged and copied in another office would tend to make the Examiners more careful. At the same time our check over them is a good deal short of perfect. The problem of how to keep the Native Customs Outdoor Staff straight is the same as confronts Tramway Companies at home as regards their car conductors. A vast amount of ability has been brought to bear on this problem both in England and America, but without very satisfactory results, and I suppose a solution can hardly be expected in China.

petre.

In my Non-urgent Correspondence for August you will notice some letters that passed between the Superintendent and myself regarding an importation of saltpetre. I released it before I had your authority partly because 'Tp' the request of the Superintendent, who stated that it was urgently needed and that authority from Peking was sure to arrive and partly because the Tidesurveyor informed me that if we kept it much longer the quantity would be very much diminished, as it was melting away. It had been stored in the China Merchants godown for 10 days. Your telegram arrived the day after I released it.

ther and crops.
So far we have been free from typhoons or inundations this year. There was a fair amount of rain in July and a long way more in August than last year in the same month. The rice crop bids fair and the orange trees are laden with fruit, the country is quiet and there is little to interfere with business. So if we get through this month without mishap, the trade of the second half of the year should be good. Since the 3rd the weather has been quite cool at night, though still hot in the daytime. The autumn tints are on the trees and the first north gale will likely strip a good many of their leaves off. We have now left the summer behind and in a month or so will be getting a taste of the winter.

I remain

Yours faithfully,

Inspectorate General of Customs,

PEKING, 20th September, 1915.

Dear Sir,

I am directed by the Inspector General to acknowledge receipt on the 18th Sept. your S/O No. 32 dated 10th Sept.

Yours truly,

L. Acheson,
Private Secretary.

Acheson, Esquire,

WENCHOW.

No. 33

CUSTOM HOUSE,

WENCHOW 24th September, 1915.

DEAR MR AGLEN,

piloting by staff.
            I have duly received your despatch No.620 regarding piloting by members of the staff and will carry out its instructions. In your letter of the 31st of August you ask about how much the piloting is worth a year. We have not been keeping very clear accounts of the fees paid. Stevens, however, has gone over such records as have been made and has made the total earnings of the men for the last 22 months to have been $610 which, divided between the two, would give each about $14 a month. From ~~this time~~ now on each time one of our men pilots a vessel, the fee will appear in Account D, so you will be able to keep track of what they ~~their earnings~~.

re Customs.
            You will notice from the the Requisition for the Supplementary Grant for Account N for the December quarter that out Native Customs expenditure is increasing. This is partly due to the general increase in the pay of the staff in April last. But it is more largely due to the fact that the Assistant is now Mr Kaneko who has Tls 250 a month, while up to the end of last February ~~it~~ was Mr Wong Haiu Geng, who had only Tls 100 a month. I have already said that I changed the latter to the Maritime Customs, as the Superintendent objected to him. The ~~latter~~ Superintendent

(2)

was very friendly with Aida, who understood and appreciated his poetry and he told Aida that if he did nothing but sit in his chair in the Native Customs Office, he would be more use there than Wong. He ~~said that Wong~~ remarked that the brokers who did business there were nearly all Foochow men and that Wong favoured them unduly. The Superintendent also told me at an interview that Wong was not to be trusted. I replied that ~~Wong~~ would likely be replaced by another Chinese Assistant one day. He said another Chinese Assistand would be just as bad ~~as Wong~~. With regard to my own opinion in the matter, I think the Superintendent's dislike to Wong is unreasoning. The ~~latter~~ Native Customs is, no doubt, better run by a foreigner than a ~~native~~ Chinese; there is more discipline among the staff and the public have more confidence in the establishment. But, as far as conduct and ability are concerned, I have no fault to find with Wong at all. He knows his work and is very willing to do it and his manners are agreeable. And he is very capable as a translator of English into Chinese. Any translation he makes is so good as regards the Chinese composition that the Writer need hardly alter a character in it. And he works very rapidly too. I have made enquiries about his doings outside the office and have been told nothing bad about him. Still the fact remains that the Superintendent will have none of him, and I think it best to keep the two as fart apart as possible. But I should be sorry if Wong

(2)

were transferred, as another Chinese Assistant would not likely be as good.

We are having our first taste of winter. A north wind has been blowing for the last two days and the thermometer is in the sixties. We have had some rain, too, which the country needed.

I remain
yours faithfully,

Inspectorate General of Customs,

PEKING, 5th October, 1915.

Dear Sir,

I am directed by the Inspector General to acknowledge receipt on the 4th Oct. our S/O No. 33 dated 28th Sept.

Yours truly,

V. Sandercock
Assistant Private Secretary.

Acheson, Esquire,

WENCHOW.

No. 34.

CUSTOM HOUSE,

WENCHOW 12ᵗʰ October, 1915.

DEAR MR AGLEN,

NATIVE CUSTOMS:

My Non-urgent Correspondence for September concerns the Native Customs entirely and is rather voluminous. It contains some long communications to and from the Superintendent regarding documents and charges against the staff. There still a great many improvements to be made in the work before the routine can be considered satisfactory. With regard to the first subject, "Cargo and Documents", the conveyance certificate which has been introduced will be better than the invoices stamped by the Customs. The traffic on the canals is difficult to watch and entails considerable expense looking after it. Subject No.2 concerns two more cases of interference with our work. In the first case, the seizure was made on board the steamer and was, perhaps, stronger than the second, in which the rice was taken from the godown and before it had been shipped. But I think we must consider all goods that have been declared to us and are covered by our documents as inviolable, no matter whether they are on board ship, or in a godown, or even on the street. The replies to my letters in the matter are not completely satisfactory. The rice was not returned to the Customs, as I requested,

(2)

But it was released, which is the main point. The Superintendent is very unwilling--most likely he is unable--to take the part of the Commissioner against the territorial officials, and I suppose I must rest content with something less than receipts. With regard to duty receipts, matters are greatly hindered by the continued insistence by the Superintendent on the superiority of the quadruplicate certificates. I described these to you in my despatch No.3087. I still think the use of them would take a lot of time without any adequate result. But the Superintendent will not give up the idea. He has introduced the documents outside the 50 li and tends to resist my not having introduced them inside the radius. The Lushih in the Head Office are still not worked to the full extent of their capacity. But I want to keep any spare time they have for attention to work which I may make myself. The keeping of the books of the Fish Station which I added to the duties of the junior man occupies a considerable portion of his spare time, and neither Lushih has much leisure left. There are still more reforms to be made which will likely take up all that remains to them. At present the duty receipts used by the stations in form and some are sealed by the Superintendent while some only bear the seal of the Weiyuan. My despatch No.249 was written to have this want of uniformity remedied. The Chuangyuanchiao and Ningtsun stations, being distant, are

(3)

allowed to pass local exports for coast ports and to issue hungtan for these. The nearer stations do not issue hungtan. But they must have some kind of receipt to use when they pass exports for places in the neighbourhood, so that it can be known if cargo going down river has paid duty or not. The whole trouble has been about the form of this receipt. All the cargo that passes the nearer stations is for places in the neighbourhood and so is a good deal of what passes Chuangyuanchiao and Ningtsun. Such cargo does not want hungtan and it seemed to me that, where it was concerned, all the stations, near and far, had better use the same form. So I asked the Superintendent to let me have seven books, one for each station that might want it. You will see from his reply that he is undecided what to do. He says it was never intended that duties should be paid to the stations, but he knows quite well that the people that import fish at Puchou, for example, which is two miles down river, would not be willing to come all the way to Wenchow to pay duty. go in boats down the river and the men, for example, would resent it if they were required to apply. So there is no way but to issue some kind of local receipt. With regard to the quadruplicate certificates at the Head Office, whatever might be possible, I feel certain, if the stations had to make out these documents, there would be a lot of confusion. And it would be absurd to make out four documents for a few candareens of duty.

— 149 —

(4)

The Superintendent says he has referred the matter to Peking, and I am curious to know what answer he will get.

practice. Under the heading "Malpractice" is ~~an ordinary case~~ given some correspondence regarding a case in which ~~I~~ an Examiner resigned whom I was going to discharge for neglect of duty and ~~I~~ was discharged a Watcher for being generally unsatisfactory.

rges against miners. Under the heading given in the margin are ~~two communications~~ a despatch and a letter to the Superintendent concerning old cases (which I thought was finished but which has been) brought up again. In my S/O No.20 I told you about the fish and bamboo men. The Superintendent ~~is satisfied with~~ has nothing to say against what I ~~told~~ wrote to him ~~about~~ regarding the former, but the difference between the exportation of bamboos as reported by the exporting shops and (as shown by our books) ~~by the Examiners~~ still sticks in his mind and he is ~~not all~~ at all ~~satisfied~~ content that I did not dismiss ~~them~~ the two Examiners concerned. He came and called upon me and showed me a despatch from the Ts'ai-cheng Pu, ~~which had~~ to which the bamboo men had carried their complaint. The despatch made a good deal of the use ~~issue~~ by the Examiners of different ~~kinds of duty receipts~~ forms in issuing duty receipts. Copies of these were sent to the Board which sent them to the Superintendent with instructions to explain why the forms varied. The Superintendent ~~all~~ produced an original receipt which had ~~been issued~~ received from the bamboo men in Wenchow and showed it to me as proof positive that the Examiners had ~~issued~~

(5)

He declared that he could not be responsible if men in whose appointments he had had no say whatever were allowed to carry on in such a manner. On the receipt he gave me there were two impressions of ~~small~~ a small seal. I could not read the characters, so I asked him to let me retain the document. ~~He consented to leave them with me.~~ When I returned to the office I showed the receipt to Assistant Wong and he at once said that the seals were those of the Haifang, another local taxing establishment, and that the document had not been issued by our Examiners at all. ~~Was it not strange that the Superintendent did not discover this fact himself?~~ I gave back the receipt to the Weiyuan and asked him to point out to the Superintendent that it had not been issued by us. The form, however, was one which was in use by ours as well as by the Haifang station before the Examiners went there and they continued to use it until the new form was issued to them. It was certainly very strange that the Superintendent did not know this and stranger still that he did not notice or, if he did, did not think that I would find out whose the two seals were on the particular form he produced as his proof. I have heard nothing more from him concerning ~~the subject~~ this particular branch of the subject. With regard to the collection of duty, he made a great point of the fact that they Examining charged 350 cash as the equivalent of 2 mace, the duty on 100 bamboos, and he called in one of his accountants who stated that 2 mace should only be 302 cash. That seemed to be to be very low, but I could not refute

(6)

the statement
not refute ~~it~~ at the time, so I said I would make enquiries. You will see by my letter that I went pretty fully into the matter, enquired from the cash shops and inspected the cash received by the stations, and that I told the Superintenent that 350 cash for 2 mace was not an overcharge. Besides I pointed out to him that, as the Examiners have to do the work of the Bank, they cannot be blamed if they do happen to charge a little extra ~~more at one time~~ to make up prospective loss. It is important to consider this in dealing with the Native Customs staff. The currency is perfectly chaotic and so long as it remains in its present state, so long will it be impossible to properly check receipts ~~easy for the staff to dodge enquiry~~. ~~In my letter No.30 I said that the discrepancy of 115,000 bamboos in the bamboos meant only $15 of duty for ten months, or 75 cents a month for each Each Examiner. If they claimed that this was due to their losses by exchange, I do not see how we could disprove the statement.~~

~~One reason, the principal perhaps, why~~ the Superintendent wanted the Examiners discharged ~~was~~, I think, that they had not been nominated by himself. They were appointed by Bowring before there were any rules on the subject. The Superintendent talked a good deal during our interview about the men having really been appointed by Assistant Wong. He said the Commissioner could not, of course, be expected to know anything about the characters ~~of Chinese in Wenchow, except through other Chinese. Xu~~

(7)

~~is a man of a jealous disposition, I think, and he evident~~ly wants the Native Customs staff to consist only of his own nominees. In time this will be so, but I ~~cannot be expe~~ do not consider it right to discharge men for the purpose of bringing it about. Another reason why he wanted me to get rid of the Examiners was probably that the bamboo men had ~~petitioned him~~ stated in their petition to him that he was the Superintendent and could do what he wished and they prayed him to deliver them from extortion. However, as there was not a single ~~charge in the petition~~ one of the charges they brought that, when enquired into, showed any wrong doing on the part of the two men, I could not take any action against them.

With regard to the relations between the Superintendent and myself, we have only differed regarding two matters, quadruplicate duty receipts and the question of dismissing ~~dismissal of~~ the Examiners. We are on quite friendly terms and are like~~ly to remain so.~~

TIME CUSTOMS:
ing Cu Nguong.

I shall be very sorry to lose Mr Ling Cu Nguong. He is a first class man--reliable in his work, steady in his conduct and agreeable in his manners. I have had him as Secretary and Accountant for a year and I do not want a better man. I have taught him typewriting. He proceeded according to the method I explained to him and his proficiency as a typist leaves little to be desired. For the last year he has typed all the despatches for Peking

(8)

and I venture to think you have found them as well done as any others. I hope his successor will be something like him.

Stevens has been laid up for the last 4 weeks, principally with fever, which has weakened him a good deal. He did a lot of surveying on the canals during the hot months for the new edition of the Native Customs map, and he was constantly in the sun. Also, on one occasion, by the awkwardness of the boatman, he was thrown into the creek and got one or two mouthfuls of dity water. He says he never suffered from fever before, and I am therefore inclined to attribute his present indisposition to his recent out of doors work. But he is getting all right again and does not appear as if he would be the worse for the illness.

Since the date of my last letter the ~~weather~~ has got warm again. We have had some rain and the atmosphere has been damp. The weather is more that of ~~one~~ spring than autumn.

I remain
Yours faithfully,

INSPECTORATE GENERAL OF CUSTOMS

S/O

PEKING, 26th October, 1915.

Dear Mr Acheson,

I have duly received your S/O No. 34 of 12th October.

<u>Goods seized while under Customs control: should any but correct settlement of cases be accepted in view of Superintendent's attitude ?</u>   Not at all. You were supported in the previous case by the Shui - wu Ch'u.

<u>Quadruplicate Duty Receipts.</u>   The question of quadruplicate receipts has come up elsewhere. If you report officially you will get instructions.

<u>Charges against Native Customs Examiners:</u>
Superintendent's

─── Acheson, Esquire,
　　　WENCHOW.

Superintendent's queries re duty receipts issued.

I do not like the idea of the "Examiners" collecting duty, and I wish some other system could be arranged. "Examiners" ought to examine and if necessary issue a duty memo. but duty should be collected independently of them.

Yours truly,

NO. 35.

CUSTOM HOUSE,
Wenchow, 6th November, 1915.

R MR AGLEN

IVE CUSTOMS.
lection of
by
niners.

I have duly received your letter of 26th October.

With regard to collection of duty by Examiners, the system is, no doubt unsatisfactory, though, so long as we have out stations, it cannot be avoided. However, the station which ~~collects~~ contributes by a long way the most duty is the Fish Station at Wenchow, and ~~I have~~ the Head Office has now taken over the collection ~~of the duty on fish~~ any work that used to be done by it, and with good results. In your despatch No.532 of April last year you remarked that the method of collecting duty on fish was ~~most~~ uneconomical and that it might be advisable to compound for a lump sum with the dealers and withdraw our staff. ~~But this is hardly necessary now. During the 9 months ended 30th September last~~ At that time the collection was a little over Tls 1,000 a year, while the expenditure (at the Station) was Tls 357, or over 33%. But During the 9 months ended 30th September last, the ~~collection~~ sum collected amounted to Tls 3,306, while the expenses were only Tls 342, or little over the one-tenth ~~of the collection. There are ob The farming out of revenue is generally productive of abuses and~~ All the stations used to be farmed out ~~abuses resulted that are still in existence,~~ but the result was a number of abuses that we have not entirely got rid of even yet.

(2)

The fish dealers, for example, are very dilatory in paying their duties. They are supposed to pay once in ten days, and at the end of each ten days the Head Office now issues each shop a memo for the amount due on the fish imported during the period. When I commenced the present system, in ~~~, some of the shops would not pay for about 3 weeks. They have no guarantees, so I could not foreclose. However, I have now made a beginning in the way of refusing a shop that is behind with its duties permission to land its cargo without first paying. I think I can bring them into line by doing this. But they have been allowed to go on in a slack manner for generations, perhaps, and the speeding them up will take a certain amount of time.

With regard to the status of the Examiners, it is not the same as that of Examiners in the Maritime Customs. The Chinese name for them is Szu Shih (　　) and they are all men of some education. They rank higher in the estimation of the rest of the staff than the Lushih, in fact. They are not at all of the same class as the Watchers, and will not do any rough work such as hauling about of packages. But they are quite good as Examiners and their bonds of $50 each are sufficient to cover any amount of duty they are likely to have in their hands, now that the Wenchow fish dealers pay direct to the Head Office.

(3)

Sulphur seized.

On the 19th of September a junk arrived from Formosa having on board 50 piculs of sulphur. It was entered in the manifest and application was made to land it. The applicant was told that he must obtain authority to import from Peking, and the sulphur was landed by ourselves and placed in the Native Customs seizure room. After ten days, not having received the necessary authority from the Shui-wu Ch'u through yourself, I wrote to the Superintendent and asked him to apply and to apply by telegraph to Peking for instructions, as the Customs had no proper place to keep such dangerous cargo. A couple of weeks after, he wrote me saying the Ch'u instructed that the Sulphur was to be handed over to the local Armoury. I accordingly communicated with the Armoury, gave them the value of the Sulphur and asked them to send for it and issue to the Customs two-tenths of the sum named. I thought it right that the Armoury should send for it and bear the expense of conveying it, as they were getting eight-tenths of the value. At the time, I viewed the matter as an ordinary case of seizure and did not include the letter regarding it in my Non-Urgent Correspondence for September. Therefore I am not including the other letters in my Return for October. But I now think the letters should have been included and so I mention the case here. As the seizure was made by order of the office, there is no reward and the two-tenths remain in Account N.

(4)

druplicate y Receipts.

In my despatch No.3087 of May last I said about all I had to say regarding the Quadruplicate Duty Receipts which the Superintendent has been wanting me to introduce. I saw him a couple of days ago and he said he had asked instructions from Peking concerning generally and had received a despatch from the Ts'ai-chêng Pu on the subject, but that he would wait until he heard from the Shui-wu Ch'u as well before communicating with me in writing. As soon as he does this I will write you a despatch regarding the matter.

ice rference.

My Non-Urgent Correspondence for October only comprises two communications. With regard to the one concerning Police interference, the Taoyin is largely right in holding that the Police can seize goods from incoming passengers landing at a wharf guarded by a Customs staff. But as, in the case in question, no seizure actually took place and, as the constable got two months inprisonment, I did not feel called upon to argue the case further.

enue.

The Native Customs collection for the first twelve months of the new tariff --November 1914 to October 1915--is Tls 4?,000 nearly. I estimated that the annuall collection would be about Tls 45,000 and, if it had not been for the political disturbance in the Spring, when the timber export is at its best, the amount would have been little short of this figure.

ITIME CUSTOMS.
Ling and Mr

Mr K'o Yu-p'ing reported here on the 29th of October. He was relieved from Duty in Foochow on the 12th of October and left there on the 19th. arrived in Shanghai on the 22nd. No steamer left for here till the one of the 27th in which he took passage. Perhaps he might have left Foochow a little earlier, but it is hardly worth while the Commissioner for information on the subject. I like what I have seen of him. He intelligent and willing and his manners are agreeable. I kept Mr Ling till he arrived, as I ventured to think that he was of more account in this office than in Shanghai. I trust Mr Unwin has not been inconvenienced.

rns.

Our Returns tables-- Annual, PartII--do not properly represent the trade of the port, and I have been revising them. I have tables made out showing all the articles five years, and I have selected from them those Tls 4,000 and over and made new lists which I have arranged in accordance with the "List of Headings" recently received with Printed Note No.441. The revised lists differ very greatly from those at present printed and I am sending them to Mr Taylor to see what he will have to say regarding the trouble involved in making such extensive changes in the already set up type. The new arrangement of headings is exactly that of Part I and Part III

(6)

~~piling of the Returns tables.~~ and it is also my idea to ~~enter the~~ observe the same sequence in entering the ~~articles~~ in the Returns books and to enter with each heading its number in Part III. This plan cannot fail to be of advantage, in compiling the Returns tables, comparing them together, etc.

Last week we had north winds and temperature down in the fifties; but ~~for~~ the last three days the wind has been in the south, the thermometer has risen again and it has rained a good deal.

I remain

Yours faithfully,

Inspectorate General of Customs,

PEKING, 23rd November, 1915.

Dear Sir,

I am directed by the Inspector General to acknowledge receipt on the 16th Nov. our S/O No. 35 dated 6th Nov.

Yours truly,

Acheson,

Private Secretary.

Acheson, Esquire,

WENCHOW.

No. 36

CUSTOM HOUSE,
Wenchow, 26th November, 1915.

DEAR MR AGLEN,

Things are very quiet here just now. The crops for the year have been good, rice is cheap, the people seem contented, and I hear of no trouble anywhere around.

Natural gas.

You may have noticed in the papers an account of natural gas at Wenchow. Nothing has come of it as yet, and I have asked the Head of the Methodist College here, a man who has a knowledge of geology, if anything was being done to exploit the place and if he thought there would be any money in doing this. Here is what he wrote to me:--

"I have heard that all the vents have been filled up, as the farmers do not wish to have a continual succession of people tramping over the fields. There is nothing being done as far as I know, and I have made enquiries in trying determine the cause."

"I believe that there is rock about 10 feet below the surface of the field and if the gas comes from below this and not simply from decaying matter above the rock, then the cause may be either a gas well or there may be coal. In either case of course there would be money in it. Boring or even digging down below the rock surface would probably get at the source of the gas.

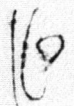

"I do not think the supply is exhausted."

NATIVE C
Fish

Our Native Customs revenue from fish is very poor this month. At first I thought importation from Ningpo might have something to do with the falling off, as they seem to be still working on the old tariff there, which is lower than ours. But this is not so. The fish is not being imported. The weather of late has not, it appears, been favourable for fishing and very few are being caught. At present fish are very dear here. I question if our ~~fish~~ collection will amount to much over Tls 100 for the present month. Last November, the first month of the new tariff, it was over Tls 200.

Quadrupl
duty rec

In my last letter I stated that I was expecting to hear from the Superintendent what the Shui-wu Ch'u wanted done in the way of duty receipts. But I have not yet heard from him on the subject. However, the receipts that we are using are all right, and I certainly do not want any change that will mean more work.

Weather

The beginning of this week was wet and gloomy, but at present the weather is dry and bright. Wind from the north-west.

I remain Yours faithfully,

Inspectorate General of Customs,

PEKING, 14th December, 1915.

Dear Sir,

I am directed by the Inspector General to acknowledge receipt on the 4th Dec. of your S/O No. 36 dated 26th Nov.

Yours truly,

L. Acheson,
Private Secretary.

—— cheson, Esquire,

WENCHOW.

37.

CUSTOM HOUSE,
Wenchow, 22 December 1915.

DEAR MR AGLEN,

Police and contraband.

I am sending you a despatch with this reporting some correspondence I have had with the Superintendent concerning the searching of passengers' luggage by the Police. I happen to have a copy of the English Customs Consolidation Act of 1876, and it is distinctly laid down in this that the Police have the right to seize prohibited goods if they find them; but that any seizures they make must be handed over to the nearest Custom House. Of course English law does not necessarily hold good in China, but the principle shown forth in the Act is one which may be applied anywhere. The Taoyin feels in duty bound to do all he possibly can to prevent arms getting into the hands of the lawless people in his circuit and wants to thoroughly satisfy himself that people coming to Wenchow do not unauthorisedly bring arms with them. I think the proviso that all seizures must be handed over to the Customs should maintain our jurisdiction free from invasion.

Superintendent and revolutionaries

On the 17th the Superintendent sent his Weiyuan to me with a telegram from the Shui-wu Ch'u stating that Sun Yat-sen had large funds at his command and was corrupting Chinese students in Japan. The telegram that

(2)

a careful look just was to be kept for students returning from Japan and that any found carrying contraband or bearing letters of instruction from Revolutionaries were to be arrested and handed over to the territorial authorities. The Weiyuan said the Superintendent would like to send his own ~~men Wei~~ deputies on board steamers to examine documents carried by passengers, as revolutionary papers would likely be ~~in ap-~~ ~~p/~~ to the ordinary reader quite harmless, ~~but would~~ convey secret meanings which only advanced literary students would be able to detect. I agreed to Weiyuan boarding steamers and searching luggage for documents and ~~gave the~~ sent the Superintendent four written authorities to hand to those he might depute for the purpose, so that they could make themselves known to our people.

NATIVE CUSTOMS.
Fish.

In my last letter I stated that our Native Customs collection on fish had fallen off, and I did not expect it to be much over Tls 100 for the month. As a matter of fact it was under Tls 60. The import had ~~fallen off~~ diminished so much that the head of the principal shop came to see me and, if things didn't improve, he would have to ~~stop~~ close business. He said the reason of the falling off was that the fish was all going to Ningpo, where the tariff was lower than here. I asked him how it was that they didn't go ~~to Ningpo~~ then as soon as we started the new tariff. He said the two Examiners who were then in charge of the Fish Station were not strict, but that, since they were transferred

(3)

in August, the two men who succeeded them last applied the rules rigidly and examined minutely, so that all lots paid the full amount of duty, ~~that~~ and that, on account of this, the fish boats went ~~elsewhere~~ to Ningpo, where the Customs exacted less. He drew a comparison between the two or three hundred taels we collected in former years and the thousands we get now and said that such and increase must affect the trade. All this afforded food for reflection. But I could hardly believe that the decrease in the import was entirely due to the Customs. I enquired at the Native Customs ~~if~~ how the quantity of fish which came from Ningpo ~~was~~ this quarter compared with the same quarter of last year and found that this year it is less. I have written to Wilzer on the subject, but have not yet received his reply. I am glad to say, however, that things have now changed for the better. It was on the 14th that the head of the fish shop came to see me. But the day or two after, importation began to revive and is now about normal. Yesterday I sent for him and asked how was business with him. He said it was all right and admitted that the reason for the falling off was largely the weather. ~~Though~~ This is ~~what I~~ the reason I gave in my last letter. The new Examiners at the Fish Station are, no doubt, more strict than their predecessors, but I cannot blame them for this. I have seen the new Ningpo tariff and compared it with our own. The rates in the two agree fairly well, and do not differ enough

(4)

enough in any instance to make it worth while importing via Ningpo. So I think it better to maintain the practice as it is in the hope that the importers will get used to it in time, which is likely, now that the rates at Ningpo have been increased also.

MARITIME CUSTOMS.
Increased pay asked for some Chinese employees.

I am sending you a list of a few members of the Chinese staff whom I consider deserving of a little more pay and hope you will see your way to allowing it. A little addition every now and then to a man's pay keeps him in heart and makes him work all the more diligently.

Weather.

The weather has been uniformly dry ~~and dry~~ since the date of my last letter. The north winds have blown steadily and we have had ~~the~~ thermometer down in the thirties.

I remain

Yours faithfully,

1916年

NO. 38.
CUSTOM HOUSE,
Wuchow, 10th January 1916.

167

DEAR MR AGLEN,

NATIVE CUSTOMS:
Reporting of
duties by Sta-
tions.

In my Non-urgent Correspondence for December you will see a letter which I wrote to the Superintendent regarding reporting of duties by the Stations. Under the old system the duty on all goods passed during a month were ~~placed~~ entered in the duty account for that month, though the practice of allowing the fish shops to pay once in ten days resulted in there being always some amounts outstanding at the end of each month. If the shops were long about paying these, the Examiners generally advanced the money themselves. As the amounts involved were very small, I did not think it worth while interfering with the practice ~~until~~ the Banker objected to date his certificate on the last day of a month when the balance it stated was that of some days later. As you will see from my letter, the first change I made was to carry the accounts for the third ten days of a month over into the next month. But the Stations render separate accounts to the Superintendent and ~~for this~~ the people in his yamen complained that the Stations accounts did not agree with ours. So I made the second change, which ought to be final. At present, though goods passing a Station are entered in the Station books as

(2)

formerly, under the date they were passed, they are not reported to the Head Office or the Superintendent until duty has actually been paid on them. The system of giving credit for duties without security is certainly not in accordance with general Customs practice, but the amounts owing are always small, and the system has been going on for a very long time and is well understood. The Banker now states in his monthly balance certificate exactly what balance he has in hand on the last day of the month. This, of course must differ from our duty account, which must include what has been collected during the last days of the month, by the out-Stations but cannot be handed over by them until the beginning of the next month. (the disagreement) I am adjusting in the balance schedule under the heading "Difference" and hope the Audit Secretary will pass it. I see no other way of arranging the matter. You will see that the difference in the Bank's account is small, only amounting to Tls 14 odd. But our revenue return now represents facts, which it did not formerly. The Superintendent would not give any reply in writing to my letter. He simply sent his Weiyuan to tell me that I could arrange the matter as I liked. He has always shown a reluctance, which I cannot quite understand, towards making any changes in accounts or duty receipts. However, when things are straight, no one can object to them.

The Native Customs collection for 1915 is disappointing, having only amounted to Tls 35800 instead

(3)

of the Tls 45,000, which I said I expected it would reach. However, if the trade had been ~~equal to~~ as good as that of 1914, the receipts would certainly have been much greater and probably have reached or even passed expectations. But the conditions that have prevailed for the last year and a half have ~~upset~~ interfered with commerce everywhere. ~~I hear~~ Chinkiang, for example, is one of our best customers in the way of buying timber, but I hear there are piles of Wenchow timber stacked there for which there is no sale. Business is ~~nowhere~~ not booming in China ~~and~~ the demand for house accommodation is slack, and ~~woodwork~~ building material is not in great request.

However, ~~But~~ I am glad to say the collection on fish has even exceeded my expectations. Here are the ~~figures~~ amounts collected, or rather reported as collected, during each year from 1912 to 1915. They are partly a repetition of what I gave in my letter No.30.

    1912. Tls. 194.
    1913. ,, 1,108.
    1914. ,, 1,229.
    1915.   3,190

I feel sure the revenue from the down river Stations might also be increased, ~~but~~ if I could check the staff as I can do at Wenchow. But the single Tidewaiter ~~which~~ I have for Native Customs work can only spare a day now and then for ~~out-Station~~ inspection ~~so~~ of the out-Stations, so these are left to a great extent to their own devices.

(4)

DOMESTIC LOAN.	In June last various members of the staff here, including myself, subscribed to the Domestic Loan of the year. The second ~~instalment~~ six months' interest is due, but none of us have received our coupons and are unable to claim it. The others who have subscribed have asked me several times when they are going to get their scrip. I hope it will soon be issued.

Weather.	From about the beginning of the month until a couple of days ago, the weather was quite mild, but it has turned cold again and we have had a fair amount of rain.

I remain
Yours faithfully,

INSPECTORATE GENERAL OF CUSTOMS,

S/O

PEKING, 11th January, 1916.

Dear Mr Acheson,

I have duly received your S/O No. 37 of 22nd December.

<u>Contraband : query rê right of Police to search for.</u>   So long as the searching for arms is done on shore I do not see that it concerns us !

Yours truly,

Acheson, Esquire,
   WENCHOW.

INSPECTORATE GENERAL OF CUSTOMS,

S/O

PEKING, 25th January, 1916.

Dear Mr Acheson,

I have duly received your S/O No. 38 of 10th January.

<u>Domestic Loan, 1915 : subscribers on the Staff have not yet received scrip, etc.</u>. You and the others should apply for the scrip to the Agency who took your subscription. Did you subscribe through a Bank ?

Yours truly,

—heson, Esquire,
WENCHOW.

No. 39.

CUSTOM HOUSE,
Wenchow, 5th February 1916.

DEAR MR AGLEN,

stic Loan.   I have duly received your letter of
25th January regarding staff subscriptions to the Domestic
Loan. The various members of the staff who subscribed handed their subscriptions to me and I sent them on, together
with my own contribution, to the Superintendent, who lodged
the money in the Bank of China, as I have been informed by
the Bank. A few days ago I wrote to the Superintendent and
he has replied that he has told the Bank to hurry up with
the scrip. He has sent me the Bank's letter in reply to his
and it is to the effect that the Bank has telegraphed to
Peking and expects that an answer will not be delayed. From this
I conclude that things are all right, and I am not apprehen-
sive regarding my own money, though the others who took
shares would like to be reassured.
The next half year's interest will be due on the 12th of
April, and I trust we may all have our coupons by then.

(2)

~~it only right to oblige him in return~~.

Business quiet.

Things are very quiet here just now. Business will, no doubt, wake up again after the New Year holidays and I suppose the ~~coming~~ year will be at least as good as the last in the way of trade. But, until the war is over in Europe and people get some idea of what the future is going to be in China, there is hardly likely to be much of a boom in anything that savours of progress in this part of the world.

Weather.

I think our winter is about over. On the 24th of January the thermometer went down to 27 and we had snow; but the cold did not last long and for the last week it has been quite mild. The spring is on us and the trees will soon be in full leaf again. This winter has not had nearly so many days of low temperature as last winter, and I can speak of the past summer in a similar way. The weather was not nearly so hot as it was the year before.

I remain

Yours faithfully,

[signature]

Inspectorate General of Customs,

PEKING, 22nd February, 1916

Dear Sir,

I am directed by the Inspector General to acknowledge receipt on the 14th Feb. your S/O No. 39 dated 8th Feb.

Yours truly,

Acheson,
Private Secretary.

cheson, Esquire,

WENCHOW.

NO. 40.   CUSTOM HOUSE,

                    Wenchow, 22nd February 1916.

DEAR MR AGLEN,

                In my S/O No.31 of the 19th of last
August I stated that I had finished the draft of a memorandum on the working of the Native Customs here and that Stevens was engaged on a revision of his map of the canals. At the time the practice of the establishment was still in a transition stage. Now, however, it has reached, in so far as the Head Office is concerned, something like final shape, and I have thought it time to bring the memo up to date and send you a copy. Stevens, also, has completed the map, and I think it right that the Inspectorate should have a copy of it too. I am accordingly sending you with this a despatch enclosing the memorandum and the map, and I hope you will find them useful when questions regarding Native Customs work here come up. I need not say much about the memo. It contains a description of the work as it is done at present. But, of course it will get out of date and will need occasional revision. The map is really the more important of the two. As I say in my despatch, it is a reduction from a larger map--the original. It is quite accurate enough for such purposes as you are likely to

(2)

ly to need it. That is to say, it shows the network of the canals and the positions of the various Customs Stations. But our facilities for the reducing of maps here are very limited, and the copy now sent does not exhibit things so clearly as the original does. ~~But hr~~ Stevens is now perfecting this latter. He is drawing a new copy which I intend to send to Shanghai to be reproduced there both in large and small size. We want about half a dozen copies of the former. The latter, reduced by scientific process, will give the smallest lines and tracings with a accuracy that could not be attained by hand. We will need about fifty copies of the smaller size, so as to always have a copy ready to hand anytime it becomes necessary to explain Native Customs matters to the Inspectorate. I think Stevens deserves a lot of credit for the work he has done in this direction. The map will be of lasting use to the office and will fill a want that has been long felt.

ITIME CUSTOMS.   The new rules for yüntan--Circular 2442- are not working very smoothly. Cotton yarn is imported from Ningpo under Special Exemption Certificate and Yüntan. When the destination on the latter is entered as Wenchow, we cancel it and it is of no use to cover the cargo farther. The merchants complain, however, that goods are imported at Wenchow to be divided up and distributed among various districts and they cannot possibly give the various destinations beforehand and at time of export ~~from~~ Ningpo.

(3)

The previous practice of reissuing fresh yuntan here on receipt of Special Exemption Certificates worked very well. But, from all accounts, it did not suit the T'ungchüan, whose receipts were kept down by our issue of free transit passes. ~~I have been told that~~ I presume therefore that the more strictly we enforce the new regulations, the better the Provincial Government will be pleased.

ificates Board of Communications. Considerably over a year and a half has gone by since we received Circular No. 22/2. But I have not yet seen a single registration certificate issued by the Board of Communications. The result has been a good deal of invenience. Steamers are running on the canals without any Inland Waters papers, and when a steamer from seaward happens to enter and apply for an Inland Certificate, she has to petition the Superintendent, which means delay and trouble that did not formerly take place.

stic Loan. I am glad to say that we have at last received the scrip for our shares in the Domestic Loan, and will be able to claim our interest when the time comes.

er. Since the date of my last letter there has been a cold snap with a slight fall of snow. But the cold did not last long, and the weather is mild again.

I remain

Yours faithfully,

No. 41

CUSTOM HOUSE,
Wenchow, 26th February 1916.

DEAR MR AGLEN,

MARITIME CUSTOMS.
property; lists,
plans and photographs.

I am sending with this my reply to Circular No.2432, calling for lists, plans and photographs of the Customs property here. What I send are the lists, etc., of the ~~concerning~~ Maritime Customs property. In a short time I will also let you have those concerning the Native Customs. My reply is considerably overdue. The reason is that the only man I have who can draw plans is Stevens. When I got the Circular he was still engaged in surveying for the map of the canals and he was taking such an interest in this work and doing it so well that I did not like to interrupt him. So as favourable days came, he continued to go down river making his observations. The making of the plans of the property was therefore not proceeded with at once, and this has caused the delay in sending them. I trust no inconvenience has resulted. I should say that the most of the plans ~~sent were~~ have been drawn from measurements ~~made~~, as there were no office copies ~~to~~ from which to reproduce them.

Registry of
Finance, statistics for.

With regard to Circular No.2471, I asked the Superintendent regarding forms, and he sent me them already filled in by his own people. So I am not do-

— 185 —

(2)

ing anything more in the matter. In looking over his returns, however, I noticed that he had ~~entered~~ re-written the character
兴 in the 常 ordinary colums. This means that the Account D receipts have been omitted. But, as the receipts in this Account only amount here to about Tls 1,000, the omission will not
appreciably affect any return covering the receipts of the whole country. And as he has already sent off the returns, he cannot well amend them. So I am saying nothing to him about it.
The north wind is blowing again and we
are having another spell of cold.

I remain

Yours faithfully,

No. 42.

CUSTOM HOUSE,
Wenchow, 6th March 1916.

VE CUSTOMS.
ce and
seizure.

DEAR MR AGLEN,

In my Non-urgent Correspondence for January you will have seen mention of another case in which the police acted wrongly in regard to certain rice that had come under our jurisdiction. As the Ningtsun Watcher could not by himself have removed the rice to the Customs Station, it was natural that he should ask the police to assist him and quite wrong of them to insist on taking possession of it. You will see the end of the case in the Correspondence for February. The Superintendent did not reply to my letter until the 8th of February, though in the meantime I had heard from his Weiyuan that the rice would probably be given back to us. In his reply the Superintendent said that the Magistrate was enquiring into the case. But, as the rice had first been seized by our Watcher, it seemed to me that it was a case that should be investigated by the Customs, and not by the Magistrate. So I wrote again to the Superintendent pointing this out to him. He did not give me a written answer, but on the 25th he sent his Weiyuan to inform me that, if the Ningtsun Customs sent to the Police Station for the rice, it would be handed over. I thought that, under the circumstances, the police should send it back

(2)

themselves, and I told the Weiyuan so, but he seemed to think the point unimportant, and I did not insist. So our Examiner sent for and received it back. The quantity he received having was considerably short of what was seized. Our people did not waigh it at time of seizure--they had no chance to do this. But the quantity the police reported to the Taoyin was Piculs 21.15, and what they handed over to us was only Piculs 16.13. Asked to explain the difference, they said that their steelyard differed from that of the Customs to the extent of Piculs 2.40 and that the remainder of the difference was due, no doubt, to a mistake in weighing and to the depredations of mice. They offered to make it up to its extent Piculs 2. As there was no way of disproving their statement, I thought best to let the quantity short delivered stand for their share of the prize money. On a former occasion, when the police made a seizure by themselves and handed it over to us, I gave them half the proceeds as their reward, the Native Customs Weiyuan having informed me that this was the custom here. On the present occasion, if the police had carried the rice straight to the Customs, as requested, I would likely have issued them a quarter of the proceeds, and this was represented approximately by the short handed over. With regard to the reward issued to the Watcher, I made this two-tenths of the amount we actually received. This was about 25% less than the original quantity and the

(3)

rice was, in addition, damaged by having been kept so long and ~~only sold for~~ did not sell for as much as it would originally have fetched, so the reward ~~given~~ did not come to much more than the one-tenth of the value of the whole lot seized. Such a mode of settling a case may be open to objection, but when the police mix themselves up in any matter it is, ~~as a rule,~~ impossible to deal with it in accordance with strict rules. They are ~~only~~ simply coolies and can only be expected to act as such. Their story about the difference of scale, mistake in weighing and the mice was an invention. The shortage was due to their own pilfering. They did not think they would have to deliver up the rice to us.

The companies that run the steamers between here and Ningpo under Inland Certificates via non-treaty places en route are commencing to build wharves for their vessels with godowns attached. This will facilitate both passenger and goods traffic and I am offering no objection ~~to it~~. But I have informed one company that contemplates putting up a jetty at the down river extremity of the junk anchorage that we ~~cannot~~ shall always spare officers to examine in their godown, as it will be rather far from the Native Custom House. Hitherto the steamers have moored in the stream and we have been unable to keep the sampans from boarding them when coming in. With wharves to go alongside there will be no use for sampans, and the Customs will have less trouble. Of course I always get Stevens to report on

(4)

how the projected structure will affect navigation before giving permission to go on with the work.

As I read the Inland Waters instructions, steamers under Inland Certificates carrying native goods - not counting factory products - from one treaty port to another should pay Maritime Customs export and coast trade duty and not Native Customs duty, except they come from or go to inland places. However, the native goods carried by steamers plying between here and Ningpo under Inland Certificates only pay one Native Customs export duty at Ningpo and nothing at this end. This is because their cargoes are always declared at Ningpo as for T'aichow (   ), a place about half way between Ningpo and here. They hand us the Ningpo documents and we accept these as exempting the goods from import duty, considering them hungtan cargo from another Chekiang port. This procedure is, of course, very favourable to the steamers, as the one Native Customs duty is only about a third of what the export and coast trade duty would be, and the practice has gone on for so long that there would no doubt be opposition to alteration of it. But it is not fair to the China Merchants Company. As to alteration, it would likely make no real difference. Because, if we were to charge full and half duty on any Ningpo cargo that came on here from T'aichow, I fear the merchants would simply change their documents at that place and things would be just the same as before. The trading of vessels

rs of
...and
...mers.

under two different sets of regulations tends to **confusion**.

Another point in connection with Inland steamers on which there is some difficulty is that of their papers. When I issue an Inland Waters Certificate to any vessel I always retain her ~~other papers~~ national register ~~or any other certificates she may have. Some ports do not~~ This is according to the instructions, as I read them, and it seems to me requisite for the protection of the **revenue**. Because, if we return the register, there is nothing to prevent her loading cargo at non-treaty places, without paying duty at all, at cheap duty rates, or perhaps and carrying it to a foreign country -- Formosa, Hongkong, etc. Shipmasters object that they must have their papers or risk being treated as pirates. But I ~~regard~~ think that is their look out.

her.

For the last two days we have been having a rain of dust, brought down, no doubt, by the recent north gale; to-day we are having ordinary rain instead.

I remain

Yours faithfully,

[signature]

P.S. After having finished the foregoing letter, I received a letter from the Superintendent stating that he had received a letter from the Taoyin stating that the seizure of the rice was a Customs seizure and should be dealt with by the Customs and that instructions had been given to the police to hand it over to us.

INSPECTORATE GENERAL OF CUSTOMS,

S/O

PEKING, 7th March, 1916.

Dear Mr Acheson,

I have duly received your S/O No. 40 of 22nd February.

<u>Yüntan for Factory Products : new rules not working smoothly.</u> The rules are being re-considered. It is intended that the factory products should have the fullest protection from Yüntan inland.

<u>Steamers not provided with Certificates from Board of Communications, and I. W. S. N. Certificates.</u> Steam launches should not be allowed to run inland without Inland Certificates

———— cheson, Esquire,
   WENCHOW.

Certificates. You should take the question up with the Superintendent and get him to address the Board.

Yours truly,

182

Inspectorate General of Customs,

PEKING, 14th March, 1916.

Dear Sir,

I am directed by the Inspector General to acknowledge receipt on the 6th March of S/O No. 41 dated 26th Feb.

Yours truly,

L. Acheson,
Private Secretary.

——cheson, Esquire,

WENCHOW.

INSPECTORATE GENERAL OF CUSTOMS,

S/O

PEKING, 21st March, 1916.

Dear Mr Acheson,

I have duly received your S/O No. 42 of 6th March.

<u>Inland Waters Steamers ; query re duty treatment of cargo.</u> This is a matter which I think you might thrash out with your Ningpo colleague. It is, I believe, a matter of convenience that Inland waters steamers are handled by the Native Customs. Strictly speaking they should enter and clear at the Maritime Customs, and when carrying cargo between treaty ports pay Maritime Customs duties

——cheson, Esquire,
 WENCHOW.

duties. Under the rules steamers are allowed to trade between treaty ports viâ inland places, but they are engaged in inland trade and, if they desire to take advantage of the privilege which puts them on the same footing as junks, they should not ship cargo from treaty port to treaty port direct unless it is destined for an inland place beyond second treaty port, or if they do so they should pay the ordinary export and Coast Trade duties. Thus cargo shipped from Ningpo to Taichow is entitled to Native Customs duty treatment, but strictly speaking it should be landed at Taichow. If re-shipped it should be covered by a document showing that it originated at Taichow and not at Ningpo. The whole question of the duty treatment of Inland waters steamer cargo is very unsatisfactory and nowhere clearly laid down. But the principle of the Circular rulings seems fairly plain. If I were

were the Ningpo Commissioner I would refuse to clear cargo for Wenchow except on payment of Maritime Customs duties giving the usual documents, and if cargo should be shipped to an inland place I would take steps to see that it was bona fide destined for that place.

Yours truly,

NO. 43

CUSTOM HOUSE,

Wenchow, 8th April 1916.

DEAR MR AGLEN,

try quiet.   Business here is going on pretty much as usual. The country around is perfectly quiet and the political troubles of the time have not affected the population of these parts as yet.

There has been a great export of alum during the last quarter. The destination has been Russia, I am told ~~so far as my information goes~~. I have not been able to ascertain exactly what it is wanted for there; but I presume it is for tanning purposes. There must be a tremendously increased demand for leather now ~~in Russia~~ for military accoutrements of various kinds.

Inland Waters Steamers, duties   I have duly received your letter of 21st of March regarding payment of duties by Inland Waters Steamers on cargoes carried between here and Ningpo and will try to get things properly into line.

Lo-ti shui.   I got a petition a few days ago from a number of Chinese merchants complaining that foreign goods under transit pass had been subjected to lo-ti shui. I replied to them that, in the tariff issued by the T'ung-chuan, it was stated that the Ts'ai-cheng Pu had ruled that such duty was leviable and that I could do nothing to help them. When Lord Elgin negotiated his treaty in 1858, he did not intend that any levy beyond the half tariff duty was to be imposed. But the Chinese do not appear to have read the treaty this way, and the British Government gave up the whole thing in 1868. So I suppose transit pass goods have to pay in the interior whatever charges the officials like to lay upon them.

The sun is getting hot in the daytime Weather and I fancy the ~~winter~~ cold weather is about over.

I remain

Yours faithfully,

[signature]

There is also an outward transit case on at the present time. A Japanese firm took out triplicate memoranda in October to purchase tobacco in the interior. They made the purchase all right, but, before they could remove the goods from where they were stored, the officials demanded the Tobacco Monopoly tax. The firm has referred the matter to the Consul General and has asked for an extension of the six months allowed in which to exchange memoranda for passes.

NO. 44.

CUSTOM HOUSE,

Wenchow, 17th April 1916.

DEAR MR AGLEN,

ssion
f
ince.
    A proclamation was posted in the evening of the 14th announcing the independence of the Province of Chekiang. Everything is perfectly quiet here and there is even a paucity of rumours and no trouble seems anticipated. I am going on as usual with the Bank of China, only I am keeping the balances as low as possible. The Superintendent and Salt Department have still got their money in it. But, to make sure, I tried to send you a telegram on the 15th asking if the Bank were safe. However, the Telegraph office refused to accept messages for places outside the Province and I posted it to the Shanghai Commissioner and asked him to wire it from there.

nd steamers.   The steamers running on the inland waters have now got their certificates all right from the Board, and have issued them the usual Customs papers. Immediately before writing to the Superintendent on the 16th of March, I enquired from the steamer people if they had received their Peking papers, and they said not. I fancy the Superintendent had received them only a day or two before I wrote him, and issued them after he got my letter.

    You will see also from my Non-urgent Correspondence for March that, on the request of the Superintendent, I released a consignment of saltpetre for the Armoury. In reply to my letter No.338, the Superintendent stated that he had telegraphed ~~to hurry up~~ the Chiang-chün. But I hear this official has now disappeared, and in this case I presume we shall have to do without it.

This morning I received a ~~letter~~ despatch from the Superintendent conveying a request from the Taoyin to disallow the export of treasure, on account of the shortness of dollars in the place. The despatch enclosed a proclamation which he asked me to post outside the office. I have done this, though I question if it is good political economy. I suppose the Taoyin has the right to lay an embargo on any article if he thinks the export of it is likely to lead to trouble.

Weather getting warmer all the time.

I remain

Yours faithfully,

Inspectorate General of Customs,

PEKING, 18th April, 1916.

Dear Sir,

I am directed by the Inspector General to acknowledge receipt on the 15th April of S/O No. 43 dated 8th April.

Yours truly,

L. Acheson,
Private Secretary.

——— Acheson, Esquire,

WENCHOW.

NO. 45.   CUSTOM HOUSE,
                  Wenchow, 24th April 1916.

DEAR MR AGLEN,

Influenza.   There has been a mild form of influenza
prevalent here and from the 10th to the 15th I was ~~partly~~ to a
certain extent
laid up with it. I went to the office every day, but stayed
only an hour or two. ~~The result on the work was that~~ The
                              unwell for a few days and was
Office Writer was also ~~laid up and~~ absent from the office
on the 10th, having caught the same complaint. The result
on the work was that some of the returns were delayed. ~~I
am all right now.~~ The Native Customs Accounts were ready
before the 10th, but I kept them a day or two before going
through them. The Collection and Expenditure was detained
on account of the Bank in Shanghai being late in acknowledg-
                                            from
ing a letter asking it to make a transfer ~~for~~ our tael to
our dollar account. We couldn't close our books till we
knew how many dollars the taels realised. I am all right
~~unications~~ again.

UNICATIONS: Our communications are disorganised.
Telegraph.
The Telegraph Office will not accept messages for places
outside the Province. ~~Yes~~ On the 22nd I wanted to send
a telegram to the Hongkong and Shanghai Bank asking if two
remittances sent some days ~~ago~~ had been received. But the
Telegraph Office would not forward it. So I sent the Writer

(2)

with it to the Superintendent and told him to say that the telegram must be sent. The Writer came back and informed me that the Superintendent had sent it with a letter to the Military Commandant and he guaranteed that it would go all right.

t Office.   There is something wrong with the Post Office. For some months past letters have been going astray and we now register any cover of the least importance. The Missionaries have complained to me on the subject and I have informed the Postmaster. He says the censorship that is exercised by the authorities has likely something to do with it. Deputies from the Taoyin's yamen come to the office and look over the letters and may mislay them. And I believe in Shanghai the same thing takes place.

her.   If the weather keeps on getting warmer, we shall have to start the punkahs in a day or two.

I remain

Yours faithfully,

INSPECTORATE GENERAL OF CUSTOMS,

S/O

PEKING, 25th April, 1916.

Dear Mr Acheson,

I have duly received your S/O No. 44 of 17th April.

<u>Prohibition by the Taoyin of the export of Treasure.</u> So long as foreigners are not affected I do not suppose any question will arise.

Yours truly,

Acheson, Esquire,
　　WENCHOW.

Inspectorate General of Customs,

PEKING, 2nd May, 1916.

Dear Sir,

I am directed by the Inspector General to acknowledge receipt on the 1st May your S/O No. 45 dated 24th April.

Yours truly,

L. Acheson,
Private Secretary.

—— Acheson, Esquire,

WENCHOW.

NO. 46.   CUSTOM HOUSE,
                    Wenchow, 10th May 1916.

DEAR MR AGLEN,

of river
canals.   Stevens has finished the third edition
of his map of the Wenchow River and Canals and has sent it
to Shanghai to find out cost of lithographing. I shall be
very glad when we have got a supply of copies in the office.
It ~~is~~ with it a very useful work.

her
ao-ch'ing.   In my Non-urgent Correspondence for
April you will see a case ~~of assaulting a woman~~ in which
one of the Native Customs Watchers, Ma Pao-ch'ing has been accused of assaulting a woman. When questioned about the
matter, ~~the Watcher~~ denied the charge and ~~offer~~ said the
case was got up against him by smugglers whom he had been threatening
to denounce. I should explain that ~~Ma~~ he is a favourite
of the Superintendent ~~of~~ whose carter he was formerly in
Peking. As the case consisted of charges and counter
charges, I did not think I could come to any decision on it
that would be satisfactory to both the Superintendent and
the woman. So I told her to go to the Magistrate. She
duly petitioned the Magistrate. But, as he did not seem
willing to move in the matter, I wrote to the Superintendent
my letter No.342, saying that the case concerned the good
name of the Customs and asking him to request the Magis-

(2)

trate to carefully investigate it. I received no reply and the Writer told me he had heard that the Superintendent had written nothing to the Magistrate. On the 22nd the woman came to my house and handed me a second petition. She said she could get no satisfaction from the Magistrate and seemed in great distress and asked me to help her to get her wrong righted. The same day I sent the Writer to the Superintendent to say that I was awaiting the decision of the Magistrate before taking any action regarding Watcher Ma. When the Writer came back he told me the Superintendent appeared at a loss how to proceed. He said the penalty for libidinous assault was ten years imprisonment and he did not think the Watcher was guilty of the offence. He expressed a wish that I would wait a few days before pressing the case any further. The next day I received a petition from Ma tendering his resignation. No doubt the Superintendent told him to do so. People generally believe that he did attempt to assault the woman in the way she stated. Her case was weak, however, as she is neither the wife nor the concubine of Tuan, but only his mistress, and (before the assault occurred he had ceased living with her) and has refrained from assisting her in any way connected with the case. He has kept out of it entirely. The Superintendent has sent me another man in place of Ma, and I presume the matter does not concern the Customs further. I think myself the woman has not received the satisfaction to which she was entitled. But

(3)

my experience of wanton confiscations of rice goes very far to show that Chinese officials consider their own face as of more importance than justice and that claimants for this with nothing else ~~on their~~ but right on their side obtain it or not according as it suits the judges.

The latest news from Hangchow is that Governor, Ch'ü Ying-kuang (   ) has been displaced by the senior General, Lü Kung-wang (   ) ~~and that the Province is~~ The Province is now under military control, and I believe both the Taoyin and the Superintendent are going to resign. If the latter depart, I shall not issue the monthly allowance until I receive instructions regarding it from yourself.

I remain

Yours faithfully,

The export of treasure has ceased apparently since the date of the Taoyin's prohibition; none has been declared to us since then. But I fancy it is going away all the same. Dollars are easily concealed in luggage and they must be exported (shipped), as the exports of merchandise are not sufficient to pay for the imports.

INSPECTORATE GENERAL OF CUSTOMS,

PEKING, 23rd May, 1916.

Dear Mr Acheson,

I have duly received your S/O No. 46 of 10th May.

Staff : charge of alleged assault against Watcher Ma Pao - ch'ing. The case is one for the Magistrate not for the Customs to investigate and decide. Does the Superintendent nominate Watchers or did you ask him for a man specially in this case ?

Yours truly,

―― Acheson, Esquire,
WENCHOW.

NO. 47.

CUSTOM HOUSE,
Wenchow, 31st May 1916.

DEAR MR AGLEN,

I have duly received your letter of 23rd. In reply, I beg to state that, whenever there has occurred a vacancy on the Native Customs staff for Lushih, Examiner, or Watcher, I have always asked the Superintendent to nominate a man to fill it. But I have not always accepted the man he has sent. As soon as Ma Pao-ch'ing resigned I applied to the Superintendent for a man to replace him; he sent me a duly qualified man and I have accepted him and placed him on the pay sheets. But, on a former occasion, when I had applied for a man for the same post, he sent me one who could neither read nor write Chinese. I told him such a man would not do and he sent me another who possessed the required qualifications. There has never been any friction between us on this point, and the Superintendent has never tried to control the staff in the carrying out of their duties.

I fear the provisions of Circular No. 2518 will have to remain in abeyance for some time, or so long as the Province remains independent. There is a small gunboat or launch here which belongs to the Water Police, but she has not yet hoisted the new flag and I have done

(2)

I have consulted with the Superintendent regarding her, but he thinks we can do nothing. So I have ~~nothing~~ not done anything in the way of bringing her under Customs control.

Office of Taoyin.

The post of Taoyin is abolished from today, and from to-morrow the Magistrate will be the principal territorial official in Wenchow. I hardly think the change will make much difference, as the two men who have occupied the position of Taoyin have been noted for taking things easy and letting the Chih-shih do the work for them.

Stocks and Chinese study.

Stocks knows a fair amount of Chinese, considering his advantages. He has studied a lot since he came here and will improve more and more, now that I have had your instructions copied out for him. ~~Also, he now knows exactly what is expected of him, which he did not before.~~ Hitherto he has been working a good deal in the dark, but he now knows exactly what is required of him. Also, I have given him several of my own books that I used to study from, including Williams' Dictionary, and he has now an equipment for work that he did not posses before. He is apparently very anxious to progress in Chinese, and I think a bonus would stimulate him to greater and greater efforts.

Weather.

Weather becoming summer-like and a few of us are already in whites.

I remain Yours faithfully,

Inspectorate General of Customs,

PEKING, 20th June, 1916.

Dear Sir,

I am directed by the Inspector al to acknowledge receipt on the 15th June at S/O No. 47 dated 31st May.

Yours truly,

Acheson,
Private Secretary.

cheson, Esquire,

WENCHOW.

S/ NO. 48

CUSTOM HOUSE,
Wenchow, 20th June 1916.

DEAR MR AGLEN,

Mourning observances.

I have duly received Circular No.2534, regarding mourning observances for the late President. But I have read it in connection with your telegrams of 7th and 9th, saying I was to follow the local authorities in the matter. I have been in consultation with the Superintendent and he has said that he would not dare to take any official or public notice of the event so long as Chekiang remains hostile to Peking. Therefore I have not half masted the Customs flag, used black-edged paper or a black seal. I notice, however, that Ningpo is using black and blue on documents ~~partially~~. A good many days before I received Circular No.2534, the Superintendent received the Chinese of it from the Shui-wu Ch'u, but he has never communicated it to me, contrary to his practice, which is to send on to me copies of any Peking instructions that are likely to concern the Customs. He received ~~instructions~~ directly from Hangchow to full-mast his flag in honour of Li Yuan-hung and I followed him in ~~thi~~ this. But since the 14th ~~of this month~~ I haven't hoisted our flag at all.

Hue stamps.

Shortly after the Province had declared its independence, ~~the~~ and when the Superintendent was in-

(2)

tending to resign, he asked me if I would take charge of his stock of revenue stamps, amounting in value to some $5,000 and contained in four boxes. I told him if the number were less, so that ~~I could~~ the spare room in the safe would be enough to accommodate them, I would take them, but that I had no secure place to keep articles amounting to so much valui and in bulk. ~~But I think he is retaining his post~~ I have heard no further from him on the subject. I believe he is retaining his post. The fall of the Yüan family is a sore disappointment to him, as he was a personal friend of the eldest son and expected great things when the father was proclaimed Emperor. ~~I should be sorry if Mao left Wenchow, as I have got on very well with him and a change of Superintendent might easily mean notso pleasant a man.~~

[B]ish [Cons]ulate.

Mr J. Bradley of the British Board of Works was here a few days ago. He told me the Government would be willing to sell the Consulate and he mentioned $25,000 as the price. He said he would write officially when the matter was settled. The amount is stiff, but the house is very solidly built and is well suited for the Harbour Master. I think we should secure it if we get the opportunity.

[Commi]ssioner's House.

The lease of the Commissioner's house will expire on the 31st of December of this year. On the 17th of May I wrote to Mrs Soothill, the landlord, who lives in England, asking if she was willing to renew the lease

(3)

for another six years on the same terms. At the same time I asked if she would be willing to sell the house and at what price. Her answer should arrive towards the end of July. The house is not nearly so well built or so picturesquely situated as the Consulate. But it much more easily to get to and from it. Personally I prefer it. The chief objection to it is that it has no tennis ~~ground~~ lawn, and to make one would necessitate an extension over ground now occupied by a public road and houses that it would take a good deal of money to purchase. Of late I have been looking after a ~~piece of ground~~ lot that would do for a Commissioner's house and give all the garden and lawn space wanted. But the owners ask $2,000 for it, ~~which is out of the question. The size of~~ it is only two-thirds of an acre ~~about~~, and the Missionaries got a piece of ~~ground~~ lot not far from it measuring an acre ~~for $800.~~

Temperature fairly ~~The weather is still~~ cool ~~for the time of year.~~

I remain
Yours faithfully,

INSPECTORATE GENERAL OF CUSTOMS,

S/O

PEKING, 4th July, 1916.

Dear Mr Acheson,

I have duly received your S/O No. 48 of 20th June.

Mourning for late President : local procedure followed in accordance with telegraphic instructions. Quite right!

Yours truly,

Acheson, Esquire,
  WENCHOW.

NO. 49.

CUSTOM HOUSE,
Wenchow, 7th July 1916.

*the
mourning
and
office seal.*

DEAR MR AGLEN,

I did not send off any of the returns due to be posted at the end of the quarter until the 4th instant. The period of mourning for the late President did not expire ~~to~~ until the 2nd, and I waited for the expiry, so that there should be no question regarding the colour used for the official seal. We have been using red all the time ~~for~~ in the General Office.

*Inland
steamers.*

You will see from my Non-urgent Correspondence that I have been in communication with the Superintendent regarding the inter-treaty-port duties of inland steamers. After receiving his reply I posted a notice in the Native Customs General Office that ~~full and~~ goods for Ningpo must pass the Maritime Customs *here* ~~and pay duty there~~ and also that goods from ~~there~~ *Ningpo* direct, if they havn't ~~done this~~ *passed the maritime customs there*, must make up the difference at this end. They *steamers* are now shipping at Ningpo under transit pass, but this would seem to be all right if we go by Circular No.1367. ~~With regard to the entering and clearing~~ So long as steamers are working under ~~different~~ *a plurality of* regulations, paying duties according to two tariffs and reporting to two Customs Houses, so long will it be possible for them to evade the law, and to keep them ostensibly within this and prevent their openly

(2)

evading it, is about the most we can do. With regard to the entering and clearing of the steamers, your despatch No.651/60,664, ~~your~~ does not approve of guarantees. But I have not liked to stop a ~~practice~~ privilege they had enjoyed for so long, ~~as~~ --discharging cargo before entry at Customs--and I have ~~now~~ made the agent of each steamer deposit a sum of Tls 20, which is ample to cover the import duties of any trip, and ~~they are now made to pay~~ all export duties before ~~receiving~~ clearance.

You will notice also in my Non-urgent Correspondence a couple of letters that have passed between myself and the Superintendent on the subject of the Native Customs duty on tea. In the old tariff two kinds were specified, Fine and Coarse, but in the new tariff only Fine Tea appears. This is a serious omission, because the kind that passes the Native Customs is almost invariably Coarse Tea, so when it came to the question of omitting one or the other, it was the Fine Tea that should have been left out. When the tea season commenced last year, the lushih seems to have considered that the single designation meant all kinds of tea, and when the Coarse Tea was declared, he charged it at the ~~single rate~~ new tariff rate of T1.0.625, which meant an ad valorem duty of, at least, 6¼%, as the falue of it, at the most Tls 10. The merchants made no complaint to me at the time, so the charge made by the lushih was passed unnoticed. Had the matter been referred to me

(3)

I should have ruled without hesitation, and without any reference to the Superintendent, that, as Coarse Tea is not mentioned in the tariff, the proper duty to charge on it would be 2½% ad valorem. The Superintendent replies to me as if he thought the question was one of alteration of the tariff. You will see that he has referred the matter to Hangchow, so I suppose there is nothing to be done locally till we hear from there, and, in the meantime, we must continue to charge as we have been doing, which will not increase our revenue, as Coarse Tea will probably cease to be exported from Wenchow, I have no doubt, and will probably be shipped at Pingyang, instead, where the Customs are farmed out by the Superintendent to a man who pays him so much a month. The farmer is supposed to charge according to the tariff, but so long as he pays his monthly amount, I fancy the Superintendent does not much concern himself whether he sticks to the tariff or not.

Farming of revenue.

A couple of cases have occurred here which have put me much against the farming of taxing establishments. In May last year, at the time when the quadruplicate duty receipts were being introduced, a raft was passed here for Taichow and paid duty to our Head Office. On arrival at destination, our hungtan was ignored and duty was levied again on the raft. I received

(4)

a petition from the exporter, which I sent to the Superintendent, who replied that he would write to the Ningpo Superintendent. After some months, having received no further reply and on being again petitioned, I wrote to him once more. He said he had duly written, but had not received any answer. The exporter continued to petition and I finally sent the Writer to ask the Superintendent if anything could be done. The Superintendent said he feared not, as the farmer of the station ~~that ignored our hungtan was no longer to control the station the same man~~ and the man at present in charge could not be held responsible. The other case occurred at Kanmen ( ) a station a little way north from the mouth of the Wenchow River and controlled by the Wenchow Superintendent. The station passed 3 piculs of artificial indigo at an exceedingly low value. But when I came to enquire about it, I found that the farmer of the station had been changed and there was no use investigating any further.

As the ~~man~~ cannot get justice locally, of course he ought to petition Peking, but I cannot tell him this, as it would be setting him on to make trouble for the Superintendent.

ter.

Very hot here just now.

I remain

Yours faithfully,

The Native Customs collection for this year is again disappointing. ~~We shall probably not have as~~ Up to the present we have not received as much as last year, and I question if our revenue for the twelve months will be much over Tls 35,000. ~~And~~ But I see no hope for improvement till things are in better shape both in China and in Europe.

S/O

Inspectorate General of Customs,

PEKING, 18th July, 1916.

Dear Sir,

I am directed by the Inspector General to acknowledge receipt on the 12th July of your S/O No. 49 dated 7th July.

Yours truly,

Acheson,
Private Secretary.

J. Acheson, Esquire,

WENCHOW.

NO. 50.

CUSTOM HOUSE,
Wenchow, 7th August 1916.

DEAR MR AGLEN,

N. CUSTOMS:
Practice.

My last S/O letter was written to you on the 9th of July, and ~~this letter~~ should properly have ~~been~~ written to you again before now. But about three weeks ago I was informed of malpractice on the part of the Native Customs staff, and since then I have been engaged in making enquiries on the subject and have delayed writing until I ~~should have~~ decided something. From time to time I had heard that the Chinese portion of the staff made money from the merchants and once or twice that Tidewaiter Stocks was not straight. There was never any direct evidence against him, but of late people here, including the Superintendent, have talked so much about him that I have had to tell him that I may ~~would have to~~ report what was said to Peking and he might possibly be discharged. I told him he could avoid this by resigning. He indignantly denied the charges and I told him I did not hold them as proven, but he has handed me his resignation and my despatch reporting it officially goes with this. In a day or two I will write you fuller particulars. In my telegram I say that his successor should be ~~known~~ more senior and known as reliable. The Outdoor foreign officer who oversees the junk work here has quite a considerable

(2)

erable trust. He has to keep watch over the doings of a staff which is thoroughly corrupt, every man of which will do anything for a bribe and will try his best to corrupt the morals of anyone ~~foreigner~~ set over him. I am told that Lee was offered bribes time and again but he always refused them and his reputation here is exceedingly good. The Superintendent praised him to me more than once and said he was a first class man and perfectly ~~absolutely~~ reliable. I do not mean to say that ~~absolute~~ any man can be guaranteed as absolutely ~~strai~~ straight. But a man who has been in the Service for say ten ~~a number of years has a Service character~~ and has been in positions where he has been free from direct oversight has come to be known as reliable or not, while a man of only two or three years standing has not yet a Service character. It has been the rule here to leave the Maritime Customs officer detached for Native Customs work entirely to himself, but I shall recommend my successor to instruct the Tidesurveyor to turn out an odd junk to see that the cargo agrees with the permits. However, in order to exercise a perfect control we would need better means of getting about than we have. Junks can easily take in ~~more~~ cargo down river. The only way ~~thing~~ to check this would be to have a fast launch that could catch them just as they were getting out to sea. ~~before they had left the mouth of the river.~~

'c lar 2533.

I duly received Circular No.2533 regarding the Native Customs staff and had the draft of my reply to it almost completed when the above case came on. I have

(3)

kept it back ~~till I had come arrived at some~~ pending decision ~~in the matter~~, but I shall now send it off in a day or two. I trust no inconvenience has resulted from the delay.

Circular 2527.   I have also received Circular No.2527. The Superintendent himself has supplied the statistics called for in it, so I need not do anything in the matter.

I remain

Yours faithfully,

CUSTOM HOUSE,
Wenchow, 12th August 1916.

DEAR MR BOWRA,

I enclose herewith amended copies of my despatches Nos 3146 and 3154. In the first are omitted the details required by Circular No.87 and the second omits the date and place of Stocks's birth. I trust the omissions have not cause you inconvenience.

Kind regards.

Yours very truly,

No. 51.

CUSTOM HOUSE,
Wenchow, 14th August 1916.

**NATIVE CUSTOMS.
Same practice.
Stocks and native staff.**

DEAR MR AGLEN,

In my last letter I said later on I would write you more particulars regarding Stocks. The first time I heard anything against him was a month or so after he arrived here, when Aida told me one day that the Office Writer had told him that Stocks had taken a bribe to allow cargo to go free on board a junk. He had no proof, so I did nothing but tell him--and Kaneko, after --to keep a close watch on Stocks. About a month later the Superintendent, when paying me a visit, talked a good deal about Lee and praised him for being perfectly upright and proof against any bribery. I mentioned Stockes's name, but the Superintendent then became silent, and I felt sure that the rumour that Aida told me about had reached him also. I heard nothing more in the matter until towards the end of last month, when Kaneko came to me bringing some Chinese documents which he said he had received from the former Watcher, Ma Pao-ch'ing, who had been allowed to resign in connection with a charge of libidinous assault (see my S/O No.46). One of the documents was an account of money received from Chinese shops having dealings with the Native Customs.

(2)

the Native Customs. It contained the names of twenty shops. Below ~~each name was~~ the names were written ~~various~~ sums of money varying in amount from $84 to ~~a quarter of a dollar~~ ~~to~~. 29 cents. The total was a little over $300. It bore no date. Below the above amounts ~~again~~ there were entered as received ~~[ ]~~ various other sums which ~~agreed~~ in most of the cases amounted to about the same as the sums first mentioned ~~apparently claimed~~. Further, in one corner of the document there were some entries evidently recording the distribution of the money received among members of the staff. ~~One entry was to the effect~~ According to one entry the sum of $43 had been given to a man named Yen ( ); another man designated as Ch'an ( ) had received $18, while $3 appeared as paid to someone named Hui ( ). Ma Pao-ch'ing stated that the account was for last October and ( ) ~~paper~~ had been made out by one of the Watchers, Yang Ming by name, from whom he had got it on the pretence of wanting to check it. The document ~~itself~~, however, even if I had picked it up in the street, bore ~~certain~~ evidence in itself of being an account (of money that had really been collected and of having been) made out by a member of the staff. ~~of money that had really been received~~. The names of the shops and the first entries under them were all of the same shade of black ~~colour~~ and had apparently been written at the same time, ~~while the sums received had~~ and with a pencil with plenty of ink in it, while the receipts were recorded in very faint characters, such as would be written by someone using his tongue going from shop to shop with a pencil in his pocket and ~~no~~ for his inkstone

(3)

inkstone ~~to rub it on. And who would levy contributions on shops and divide them among them Customs staff except a member of the staff? There was another document, which Ma said~~ was also written by Yang and it seemed to be in ~~the~~ same handwriting as the ~~other~~ first. ~~This was a list of members of the staff with sums of money paid to them. Stocks headed it with $54.58. Then followed the names Ch'en (   ), Feng (   ) and Yen (   ), the two first being~~

With regard to the names of those entered as having received money, Yen is evidently intended for Yen Po-chuang (   ), the Weigher detached from the Maritime Customs, Ch'ên is the surname of the Examiner known as Ch'ên Wei (   ) and also of the Watcher Ch'ên Fu (   ). I ~~do not know~~ cannot guess whom the third character, Hui, refers to. It seems to me quite certain that the statement was made out by a member of the staff, as who would levy contributions on shops and divide them among Customs employés except someone in the Customs? There was another document, which Ma said was also written by Yang, and it certainly seemed to be in the same handwriting as the first. It was a list ~~giving the surnames of~~ members of the Native Customs staff ~~with sums of money paid to them~~. Stocks's name headed ~~with $~~ $54.58. Then followed the names Ch'ên (   ), Fêng (   ) and Yen (   ) with $36.50 entered below each name. Ch'ên and Fêng are the surnames of Examiners ~~Ch'ên Wei and (   )~~ Fêng Chên-hsi (   ) and Yen evidently stands for Yen Po-chuang.

(4)

This document does not bear the same stamp of genuineness as the first, but, taken with it, must be allowed a certain amount of weight. The other documents did not throw any additional light on the case.

Being anxious to obtain as much evidence as possible before taking any action, I called on the Superintendent and asked him if he could procure me the books of half a dozen Chinese firms that I gave him the names of, as I would like to see if they contained entries of payments to members of the staff. He knew all about Ma Pao-ching's charges, but said that to seize the books of the firms would make the matter public and perhaps lead to our having to prosecute the accused and in this way create for us a lot of trouble without doing any permanent good. He suggested that I should call upon those implicated to resign. He spoke about Stocks and told me that he knew that he took bribes. And he recalled our interview of a year ago and said that his silence when I mentioned Stocks's name was meant to imply that he was the reverse of Lee. But with regard to the books of the firms, I was so very curious to know if they contained anything incriminating that I went with the Maritime to three the Inland steamer agencies and asked to see their accounts. Two showed me their books and one allowed me of the two

(5)

to take its books to the Custom House, where I examined them carefully and was rewarded by finding some useful information in them. I found a monthly payment to the Native Customs of from $15 to $20 which was called Chien-fei ( ), also a sum of $4 entered each month as a payment to the Watchers--there are four of them at the Head Office, so this means $1 each. There was one entry of $10 paid to Yen Po-chuang at New Year. I found nothing else of importance to the case in hand. The chien fei is evidently a charge of so much per package of goods which pass the Customs and it is evidently paid to the staff. There are altogether about thirty firms engaged in passing sundry goods through the Native Customs, and I presume each pays so much a month as chien-fei which in the aggregate is quite likely to amount to as much as the total of the first document which I have described--over $300.

As soon as I had collected the above evidence, I sent for Stocks and told him all I had heard about him. I showed him the list with his name and the $54.58 entered against it. He said the paper might have been made out by anyone and was no proof. I agreed with him that it had no evidence in itself of being genuine, but I told him that the various accusations against him pointed to some irregularity on his part, and had shaken my confidence in him. I added that I was bound to report what I had heard to Peking and that the result would possibly be that he would be discharged, in which case he would be handicapped in ob-

(6)

taining other employment. I advised him to resign, ~~in which case~~ saying that, if he did this, there would be no official stigma attached to his name. The same day I received his written resignation, copy of which was enclosed in my despatch No.3154. As I said in my last letter, ~~that~~ Stocks denied the charges against him. ~~The only evidence in support of them various statements made in the case is~~ (that furnished by) the documents received from Ma Pao-ch'ing. ~~That~~ The one giving the list of shops with ~~pay~~ money received from them, seems to me conclusive as far as it goes, and the books of the steamer hong. These first seems to be conclusive as far as it goes, while the books testimony of the ~~books cannot be disputed.~~

Well, there is nothing I have seen that conclusively proves them. But there would hardly be so much talk about him for nothing, and for a man ~~employed~~ whose duty it is to keep others straight (to have this name of not being straight himself) ~~having a bad name completely unfits him for his employment.~~ destroys confidence in him and so unfits him for his employment.

With regard to the other Native Customs employes implicated, I have allowed the Maritime Customs Weigher, Yen Po-chuang to resign also, and have discharged the Watcher Yang Ming who, I feel certain, made out the first named account. And I have made a general shift of the Examiners. I have not discharged any of these, as they are, one and all, as corrupt as they can possibly be, and to duscharge any one of them, except on proof that he could not possibly deny,

(7)

possibly deny, would probably lead to his accusing others and might end in a general recrimination that would make confusion worse confounded. I told Yen that I made him resign because he was a member of the Maritime Customs staff, the rules for which are specially strict, and also because his name appeared in the accounts of the steamer agency as having received money from it, all in addition to appearing in the list of the shops as having received part of what had been collected from them.

The only way to prevent the Native Customs staff from levying fees from the merchants is to prevent their doing anything for them. A foreign officer who is proof against any improper influence and who is energetic in his work will see that cargo is not passed that has not paid its proper dues, and if this is the case, the merchants will not be able to reap any advantage from paying fees to the staff, and will probably not pay any.

Of course, there would still remain the possibility of junks taking in cargo at down river places after they had left Wenchow. This we cannot, with our present equipment, do anything to prevent. And then there are the down river stations which also have to be supervised. From here to Ningtsun is over twelve miles. With our present means of getting about, the quickest way to get there is to drift down with the tide. It takes about four hours to do this, and the round trip will need the most of two days, ex-

cept when the tide suits early in the morning. It is quite
an easy matter for a messenger sent from here on foot

(8)

as soon as the officer begins preparation for a down river inspection, to arrive at any of the stations hours before he gets there and warn the staff at it of the impending visit and thus render the visit useless. As I said in my last letter, we want a launch—not a steam, but a motor launch that could start at once and without waiting this power ready. This would give us a control that I feel sure would result in benefit to our revenue and, in three or four years, pay or nearly pay initial outlay. But I had better leave the matter to my successor. I have all along wished to have a launch, but the present disturbed period did not seem an opportune time for putting the matter forward. However, the recent occurrences have impressed on me the importance of having our supervision of the staff extensive and complete as well as strict, and so I give you my ideas on the subject.

       I remain
       Yours faithfully,

INSPECTORATE GENERAL OF CUSTOMS,

S/O

PEKING, 15th August, 1916.

Dear Mr Acheson,

      I have duly received your S/O No. 50 of 7th August.

<u>Resignation of Mr C. W. Stocks, Second Class Tidewaiter, charged with malpractices.</u>

      Seeing how very shorthanded we are I think you were unduly precipitate in the matter of Mr Stocks. If the charges were not proven, it would have been better to report instead of forcing resignation.

                  Yours truly,

.cheson, Esquire,
    WENCHOW.

NO. 52

CUSTOM HOUSE,
Wenchow, 16th August 1916.

DEAR MR AGLEN,

NATIVE CUSTOMS Staff.

My reply to Circular No.2533 goes with this. *The despatch* is not much of a confidential report, but I have nothing to say personally about the members of the Native Customs staff, or rather *what* is true of one is true of all. Each is quite capable of doing his work, but not one can be trusted to do it honestly, and a perfectly reliable foreigner to over-see them *for* is a sine qua non. From the documents that Ma Pao-ch'ing produced, I calculate that sowhere about $300 a month *has been* paid by the merchants in squeezes to the ~~staff~~. This possibly represents as much as $600 of duty evaded. If we had a motor launch, we would probably reduce the $600 to $100, and thus enrich the revenue by about $500 a month. But the net profit would not be as much as this. Because, if we cut down the squeezes of the staff to a minimum, they would likely demand more pay or seek other employment. The Examiners--Ssushih--get now from $16 to $25 a month as salary, and their pickings amount to between $30 and $40 more, total $50 to $70 a month. It can be seen *Thus* ~~from this~~ what ~~cutting~~ effective supervision would mean to them. But we ~~should~~ *notwithstanding* should gain by it, and the sooner it is instituted the better. I have already made a rule that a list of all junks, steamers or rafts cleared in any one day *is* ~~are~~ to be *sent* ~~reported~~ the same

The list of the staff which it encloses is corrected to the 31st of July. Since the Stocks affair I have shifted the individuals at the various Examiners, so the stations are not just as the list states. But it had been already made out and, as no list would be correct for any length of time--next month I intend to shift all the Watchers--I have not had it re-written. ~~It is quite good for all the purposes the Circular mentions.~~

(2)

day, ~~day~~ by the officer in charge of the Native Customs work, to the Tidesurveyor, who will now and then re-examine one. This will constitute a check that has not before existed. And if the Tidesurveyor had a launch in which he could pursue a junk down river and ~~check~~ go over her cargo after she had left the port, the effect would be very good for the revenue, I feel certain.

I would like to add to what I have said about Stocks that, ~~for~~ after I had first heard about his not being straight, I frequently asked ~~Kaneko~~ concerning him, But Kaneko always said that he saw nothing suspicious ~~about~~ in ~~his~~ the way he did his work. So in time I ~~gave up suspecting him and~~ began to think he had possibly been maligned. and ~~regained confidence in~~ him.

The Superintendent ~~writes me~~ that he was about to go on leave to Peking and that the head of one of his yamen departments ~~will~~ act in his absence. I believe ~~he is~~ his object in visiting the Capital is to secure his position here which is some danger owing to the death of the President and the consequent change of officials at head quarters. I presume his absence will be short, so I am not reporting it officially.

During the last month the weather has been very hot and for the last two days we have been having hot winds from the north-west. But three weeks more should see us into cool autumn temperature.

I remain Yours faithfully,

Inspectorate General of Customs,

PEKING, 25th August, 1916.

Dear Sir,

I am directed by the Inspector General to acknowledge receipt on the 20th Aug. of your S/O No. 51 dated 14th August.

Yours truly,

For Private Secretary.

—cheson, Esquire,

WENCHOW.

INSPECTORATE GENERAL OF CUSTOMS,

S/O

PEKING, 31st August, 1916.

Dear Mr Acheson,

I have duly received your S/O No. 52 of 16th August.

<u>Native Customs</u>. Frequent inspections by the foreign staff from the Commissioner downwards would do much to check irregularities. If I were Commissioner at Wenchow I would spend a large part of my time at the different stations.

Yours truly,

Acheson, Esquire,
   WENCHOW.

NO. 53.

CUSTOM HOUSE,
Wenchow, 5th September 1916,

DEAR MR AGLEN,

I have duly received your S/O letter of 15th August. Since writing it, however, I presume you have received my S/O No.51 which gives full particulars regarding the case against Stocks. The proofs against him may not have been conclusive, but they were so strong that they made him impossible here as an overseer of the Native Customs staff. The Superintendent is ~~now~~ at present in Peking, and will, no doubt, call upon you. If he do, I shall be very glad if you will talk to him about how the work is carried on here ~~in the Native Customs~~ and also about Stocks. ~~I have~~ But in future the Tidesurveyor at the Native Customs will not hire now made it the rule that a list of all junks and inland steamers cleared on any day shall be sent to the Tidesurveyor on the same day. The list ~~gives~~ will particulars regarding the cargoes and the names of the officers engaged in the clearing. The Tidesurveyor will occasionally take a vessel and turn out her cargo, and in this way check the doings of the staff. But the turning out of a vessel's cargo is not always an easy job. A few days ago Stevens set to work to check a timber junk. She had on board over 20,000 planks, and it took two days to transfer these to cargo boats and the coolie hire amounted to over $20. The cargo ~~had been~~ was found

— 243 —

(2)

~~correctly declared.~~ — all right. I hardly expected to find anything wrong, as the ~~resignations~~ clearing out of Stocks and the Weigher had (made it) ~~put~~ pretty certain that the Examiners and Watchers would be more ~~some fear into the Examiners and Watchers for the time being~~ careful for a while as to how they passed cargo. ~~and made them more careful as to how they did their work.~~

In fact ~~&~~ my chief object in having the junk turned out by Stevens was to show ~~the shipping people and the staff~~ all concerned that under the new rule the work of the staff was at any time liable to be overhauled by the Tidesurveyor and that even the Tidewaiter ~~on Native Customs duty~~ would be ~~was~~ subject to check. ~~I will recommend to my successor that the rule be continued.~~

ce for stant.

Hitherto the Assistant in the Native Customs has had his desk in the same office with the Lushih and Examiners and the Tidewaiter has sat opposite him at the same desk. I never thought it quite right, but when the Stocks affair was on I was unable to talk privately with Kaneko when I went to ~~the place~~ see him. So I got an estimate for boarding off a corner of the office, so as to make a small room for the Assistant. I wanted it done at once and therefore did not ask for authority in advance. But the cost is only $22 and I hope you will not disapprove of the work. It should have been done long ago.

CUSTOMS.
to
t Wong.

I have given Mr Wong Haiu Geng, 4th Assistant A, four weeks leave to visit his home in Foochow. Kaneko comes to the Maritime Customs for a portion of each day and puts through some General Office work and I do the rest.

(3)

IVE CUSTOMS.
Power.

Tidewaiter Power has not arrived yet. Stevens has had a letter from him in which he says that, on account of the illness of his child, he was unable to catch the first steamer from Shanghai for here. But he says he will take the next. I expect him therefore at the end of the week. The delay is not causing much inconvenience, as the native staff are not likely to relapse into malpractice for a while yet, especially as the Tidesurveyor is hanging over them all the time.

I remain
Yours faithfully,

[signature]

NO. 54

CUSTOM HOUSE,
Wenchow, 9th September 1916.

DEAR MR AGLEN,

Tidewaiter Power arrived yesterday evening. But this morning he handed me his resignation. He said that, in passing through Shanghai, he received an offer from the China Mutual Insurance Company of a situation with a salary of Tls 226 per month and that, being a man with a family, he thought it right to accept the offer. He says he is going to live in Moukden. I have sent you a telegram today asking for a man to replace him. I regret very much that you should have such trouble over the Customs here, but I do not see any help for it. The Tidesurveyor has not time for the continuous supervision of the staff and their doings which is necessary to keep things right, and the services of a special man for the Native Customs cannot be dispensed with.

Towards the end of August it became quite cool and we thought the summer was over. But it has got hot again and the autumn weather is still to come.

I remain
Yours faithfully,

CUSTOM HOUSE,

Wenchow, 14th September 1916.

DEAR MR BOWRA,

If you could kindly let me know, by telegram, as soon as decided, who my successor is to be, and when he is likely to arrive here, I should feel very much obliged. I cannot engage my passage home till I have an idea as to when I can get away, but to secure good accommodation in the steamers or trains, it is necessary to engage berths well in advance. I have resigned from the 16th of next month, but of course I shall be willing to remain after that date as long as it suits the convenience of the Service.

If my successor be a married man and accompanied by his wife, I shall not be able to put the both up. The Commissioner's house here is all right as a residence and quite suitable for a man with a faily; but the bathroom arrangements are very awkward and I could not possibly put up a lady guest. Stevens, however, has quite good accomodation in the Consulate and the new Commissioner, if accompanied with a wife, could stay with him. Or the new man could come here alone and be joined by his wife later. I shall feel obliged if you will kindly let my successor know this.

Kind regards, Yours very truly,

James Acheson

Inspectorate General of Customs,

PEKING, 19th September, 1916.

Dear Sir,

I am directed by the Inspector General to acknowledge receipt on the 12th Sept. S/O No. 53 dated 5th Sept.

Yours truly,

Acheson,
Private Secretary.

...eson, Esquire,

WENCHOW.

Inspectorate General of Customs,

PEKING, 26th September, 1916.

Dear Sir,

I am directed by the Inspector General to acknowledge receipt on the 17th Sept. of your S/O No. 54 dated 9th Sept..

Yours truly,

L. Acheson,
Private Secretary.

—————— Matheson, Esquire,

WENCHOW.

NO. 55

CUSTOM HOUSE,

Wenchow, 27/75 September 1916.

DEAR MR AGLEN, See Back

QUARANTINE.

In the beginning of the month I received a despatch from the Superintendent's yamen stating that there was cholera at Nagasaki and that instructions had been received from Peking that precautions were to be taken to prevent the disease being brought here. I have done nothing in the matter except tell Stevens to give the pilot a note to the captain of any steamer from Japan he goes to pilot in north, stating that, if there is any sickness on board his ship, he must anchor below the limits and prevent any communication between the ship and the shore till he has been boarded by the Customs ~~the doctor has visited him and reported what should be done.~~ This is about the best I can do, and I think it will meet all requirements. It is only on a very rare occasion that a steamer comes ~~here~~ to Wenchow from Japan (since I have been here there has not been one ~~the beginning of 1914 there only been~~) And any outside steamer visiting the port is almost sure to ask in advance for the pilot. Besides ~~At the time I~~ received the above despatch ~~cholera~~ there ~~had already been~~ was already ~~several cases of~~ cholera in ~~Wenchow~~ the place that country in well, so a vessel, ~~even if she had~~ cholera on board, could hardly ~~be considered as~~ having introduced it. The ~~establishment of precautions here for~~ carrying out in this port of proper quarantine regulations could not be done with our present staff or equipment. ~~From the Cus~~

Many thanks for your telegram of 21st. The end of October will suit me all right, as I wish to leave by the French Mail of 7th of November.

(2)

We have no signal station and only one gig to get about the harbour in. The doctor is not always in the place, especially in the summer, when the Missionaries are in their bungalows up the mountains or on the sea shore. Of course he can always be sent for, but on occasions it may be a good many hours before he comes.

K'o Yu-p'ing.   I should like to bring to your favourable notice Mr K'o Yu-p'ing ( ), Third Clerk C, who has been here since last October. He is a first class man, capable, willing and pleasant mannered. I have had him at Accounts and Secretary's work the whole time and have not wished for a better assistant. When he came he knew almost nothing about typewriting; but I put him in the right way of learning it and in a very short time he had mastered the touch system, and can now use the Underwood rapidly and accurately. He types all the despatches that go to Peking from him and I presume you find them fairly well done. He has an excellent knowledge of the Accounts and keeps his records well up to date, and is always ready to do any bit of extra work I give him. He deserves to get on and I think it is only fair to him for me to say these few words for him before I leave Wenchow.

yet.   Mr Kabbert has not arrived yet, but he will likely be here by the next steamer. The Native Customs work is going on all right, but of course the oversight of a foreigner is necessary to keep the Chinese staff from re-

(3)

lapsing into old ways.

The summer is finished, but we have still an odd hot day and a warm night, and the true autumn weather is still to come.

I remain

Yours faithfully,

James Acheson

Inspectorate General of Customs,

PEKING, 11th October, 1916.

Dear Sir,

I am directed by the Inspector General to acknowledge receipt on the 2nd Oct. of your S/O No. 55 dated 27th Sept..

Yours truly,

L. Ackson,
Private Secretary.

...neson, Esquire,

WENCHOW.

N°. 56

CUSTOM HOUSE,
Wenchow, 14th October 1916.

DEAR MR AGLEN,

NATIVE CUSTOMS.

  I have received a telegram from Currie that Kabbert will not be here till the end of the month. Stocks resigned on the 9th of August, so by the time his successor gets here, we shall have been without anyone for about three months. I will say, however, that the revenue has not suffered from the want of a special man to superintend the work. For the last three months it has been a good deal ahead of last year. The collection on fish especially is very good, and the end of the year will likely see a record total. Now that Stocks has gone, people talk about him. His appearance was prepossessing and his manner was pleasant. But there is no doubt he slacked a lot. One thing he did was to allow the inland steamers to ship their exports without any examination. After they had been shipped he gave them a look over on board and that was all. Since I have been here I have gone constantly to the Native Customs and I constantly asked Stocks if he studied my Memorandum with the Rules and the Order Book and carried out the routine therein laid down and he always told me that he did. But I know now that he did not. However, the Tidesurveyor is now exercising a supervision over the doings of the Native Customs

(2)

247

staff, and ~~the man who succeeds Stooke~~ Kalbert will be subject to a check which ought to keep things going right. The superindendence of Stevens has worked very well so far, but a special man to be with the native staff the whole time is necessary all the same, and when ~~Kabbert~~ comes there will be lots for him to do.

Tanant.   I have heard from Tanant that he ~~has been appointed my successor~~ succeeds me. His appointment will give pleasure to the community here generally, as the people are all English and French, except ~~two~~ Americans.

Isko.   Wong Haiu Geng is back from leave. I should like to say that, during his absence, Kaneko ~~did~~ attended at the Maritime Customs almost daily for a longer or shorter time and did nearly all the work, while attending also at the Native establishment and doing all that was to be done there. He is a very capable and a very willing Assistant and I am only doing him justice in putting in a good word for him.

P.S.   My telegram ~~to~~ of the 28th September about soldiers carrying arms was consequent on a letter I had received from the Superintendent's yamen stating that the troops stationed here were being transferred to another part of the ~~same~~ Chekiang province. You will find the letter in the Non-urgent Correspondence for Septmber. Circular 2508 ~~did away~~ seemed to exclude arms from the list of articles which the provincial authorities could authorise the movements of within the ~~with the freedom of the provincial officials to as regards movements of arms within the~~ province, and I sent you the

— 256 —

(3)

telegram as I thought there might be a bare possibility that arms carried by soldiers for their own use were included. In June I received from the Superintendent copy of a despatch from the Shui-wu Ch'u stating that articles carried by soldiers for their own use were to be passed without formality, but I had not received a Circular on the subject and, in view of paragraph 4 of ~~the Circular~~ No.2508, I considered it best to make sure.

Weather here now bright, cool and dry.

I remain

Yoursfaithfully,

NO. 57.

CUSTOM HOUSE,

Wenchow, 21ˢᵗ October 1916.

DEAR MR AGLEN,

mination work.
    I send you with this my reply to Circular 2561 regarding the examination of cargo. There is evidently a lot of false declaration going on in connection with Chinese goods of foreign type. I am perfectly certain that considerable quantities of yarn spun in China are declared, on exportation coastwise to be foreign re-exports. How to deal with such abuses is a difficult matter. It is impossible to tell from inspection of the yarn itself where it has been manufactured, or from scrutinising the labels where they were affixed. If Shanghai will give ~~us~~ the marks examination can be done better however, ~~we can get along better~~, but so long as things are slack generally in China, so long will there be difficulty in doing anything in proper style.

tric light.
    I regret that, in my despatch about electric fittings, I understated the sum that Stocks paid for his installation. He gave me his bill, which amounted to $26.26. As the 22 lights put up in my house only cost $9.69, it did not seem possible that less than half the number could cost nearly three times as much, so I took it for granted that the $20 deposit on the meter was included. The Company have informed me, however, that the sum Stocks

(2)

paid them was $46.26, and that the $26.26 was only for the lamps and wiring. They said that the reason of the great increase in cost was that at the beginning installations were put up for almost nothing, in order to induce people to use the light.

Native Customs. The Native Customs is doing very well; the collection to the 20th is about Tls 3,000, or nearly as much as that for the entire month of October last year. Kabbert has not yet arrived, but Stevens is keeping a good look out and the staff have not yet got over the exposures of three months ago and are still afraid to attempt resumption of their old tricks.

I remain
Yours faithfully,

INSPECTORATE GENERAL OF CUSTOMS,

PEKING, 24th October, 1916.

Dear Mr Acheson,

I have duly received your S/O No. 56 of 14th October.

<u>Staff : slackness of Mr Stocks : supervision of Native Customs Staff by Tidesurveyor instituted.</u> Surely the Tidesurveyor ought to have seen before that Mr Stocks was doing his work properly.

<u>Staff : good work of Mr S. Kaneko, 2nd Assistant, A.</u> I am glad to hear that he is doing well.

Yours truly,

Acheson, Esquire,
WENCHOW.

INSPECTORATE GENERAL OF CUSTOMS,

PEKING, 31st October, 1916.

Dear Mr Acheson,

I have duly received your S/O No. 57 of 21st October. <u>Examination Work : suggested marking of Native Yarn at Shanghai to prevent fraud.</u> It ought to be possible to prevent actual loss of revenue by this means. The Chinese yarn only pays one duty in any case so there is no loss of Coast Trade Duty and original exports are still examined carefully at Shanghai. I hardly think that if fraud on a large scale were

‑son, Esquire,
  W E N C H O W.

were being practised, we should fail to receive information.

Yours truly,

N°. 58

CUSTOM HOUSE,
Wenchow, 21 November 1916.

DEAR MR AGLEN,

Yesterday ~~To-~~day I ~~have~~ sent you a telegram saying that Kabbert had resigned. He arrived here on ~~Friday~~ Saturday, the 28th. One of the first questions he asked Stevens was if he would be allowed to keep his woman in the quarters. Stevens said it was against the rules, but that he would mention the matter to me. He did so and I said it could not be allowed. When he told this to Mr Kabbert, the latter ~~then~~ said he would resign. Another thing was that he brought with him two large dogs, which Stevens told him would be objectionable if he had them on the premises. ~~I need hardly explain that~~ The Tidewaiter's quarters consist of three rooms above the Post Office, and ~~that~~ the entrance to them is direct from the Examination Shed, on the opposite side of which is the entrance to the various Customs offices. Dogs kept by an officer would, therefore, be more objectionable here than at other ports. Not being allowed to have his woman and his dogs in his rooms is the reason that Mr Kabbert has put forward for leaving the Service. However, I feel sure it not the real reason. Stocks has been to Changsha and ~~they~~ he and Kabbert have seen eachother ~~and Kabbert has got stuffed~~ and the latter has doubtless been given a picture of Wenchow

(2)

that has just him against the place and made him come here in a discontented frame of mind and ready to take offence at any interference with his habits or mode of living. I have said in my telegram that there is no need for his immediate replacement. I have said so because I wish to make the resignation as little inconvenient as possible. The Native Customs has been doing very well of late and the revenue promises to be quite good this year. For a month or so longer we can still do without the special man to oversee the work. Stefens keeps an eye over what is going on and Kaneko does a little outdoor overseeing also. But the port cannot do permanently without the extra man and he should be appointed as soon as convenient.

Tidesurveyor and Native Customs. I have duly received your letter of 24th October. With regard to the Tidesurveyor looking after Stocks and keeping him straight, I should explain that, the Commissioner took over effective charge of the Native Customs, until the Stocks affair occurred, the Tidesurveyor had nothing to do with the working of the establishment, and, as things are, he could not possibly control the staff in the same manner as he does that of the Maritime Customs. The is too far away for him to keep track all the time of what the staff are doing. The daily work has been done by the Assistant in charge, who gives orders to the Tidewaiter direct. This is the way

(3)

at some other ports: Stevens says he had nothing to do with the Native establishment at Amoy. He can continue to do what he is doing now--visit the places where examination is going on and board junks from time to time--but he can hardly do much more.

  I believe Tanant has arrived in Shanghai. I hope he will be here about Monday, so that I can catch the French Mail of the 17th.

      I remain
      Yours faithfully,

NO. 59.

Custom House,
Wenchow, 8th November 1916.

ge handed
  to
.E. Tanant.

DEAR MR AGLEN,

    I have handed over charge to Mr Tanant, in accordance with the instructions of your despatch No.679. Things are going all right here, and I have a clean desk to my successor.

    I thank you for the good wishes contained in your despatch. In return, I beg to express the hope that the Customs Service may, under your able guidance, continue to be a mainstay of Chinese national credit and a leading light in the administration of the country.

    With kind regards,

    I remain

    Yours very truly,

INSPECTORATE GENERAL OF CUSTOMS,

PEKING, 14th November, 1916.

Dear Mr Tanant,

    I have duly received Mr Acheson's S/O No. 58 of 1st November.

<u>Staff</u> : vacancy caused by resignation of Mr Kabbert. We shall have to give you a man, but it may be a Japanese!

    Yours truly,

Tanant, Esquire,
WENCHOW.

CUSTOM HOUSE,

S/O No. 60.

ack

Wenchow 18. November, 1916

Sir,

As already reported by despatch I took over charge of this Office on the 8th from Mr Acheson who left Wenchow on the 12th after receipt of your telegram of 9th.

The SUPERINTENDENT who had been away to Peking returned on the 9th. He did not complain to me, but I heard indirectly that all his luggage had been searched at Shanghai, and one of his Secretaries who expects his own family with a lot of luggage from Yangchow, wanted me to issue him some kind of a document to avoid this search at Shanghai, but I referred to the Shanghai Superintendent - an advice which will not be acted upon, I am told.

Yours respectfully,

S/O No. 61.

Custom House,
Wenchow, 7. December, 1916.

Sir,

NEW LORCHA : REGISTRATION OF.

A lorcha having been built and her owner having applied for issue of a Customs Register, I referred him to the Superintendent to first obtain a Certificate of Registration from the Board of Communications (I.G. Circ. No. 2346); but, strange enough, the superintendent replied that he had not received from the Shui-wu Ch'u the instructions transmitted by that Circular. However he issued a temporary Register and is going to apply for the Board's Certificate. In the meantime the lorcha has been allowed to begin her runs and I collected the Customs Registration Fee on deposit. Copy of the correspondence is going forward in the November Summary of non-urgent Chinese correspondence.

In this connection I beg to call your attention to my despatch No. 3172 which shows a want of uniformity in the rules and fees for the issue of Customs and Board of Communications Registers.

STAFF

STAFF : APPOINTMENT OF TIDEWAITER.

I duly received your S/O of 14th November. I mentioned its contents to Mr. Stevens who remarked, and perhaps justly, that a foreign Tidewaiter, if procurable, would do better 1o. because of the difficulty for the Tidesurveyor to watch him, and 2o. for the O.D. Staff who have so little society to associate with here. On the other hand Mr. Kaneko to whom I also mentioned the possibility of a Japanese Tidewaiter's appointment, was delighted, for the question of society also affects him and his wife. There are only 3 Japanese merchants here, two country people and a Tokyo dentist, and he does not seem very keen of their company. But his other argument that a Japanese Tidewaiter who could read Chinese documents would be preferable, particularly for N.C. work, to a Foreign Tidewaiter who does not know Chinese, has something good in itself... so long as the man keeps straight.

CHANGE OF TIDESURVEYOR.

Mr. Stevens has been rather startled by his transfer for it looks as if the leave which he had just applied for will not be granted. On receipt of your telegram instructing me to arrange with Foochow to enable me to keep Mr Stevens until Mr. Lloyd's arrival, I wired to Mr. Ferguson, quoting your telegram, and I hope that owing to the comparatively big staff at his disposal he will see his way to

S. No. 62.   Wenchow   9. December, 6

Sir,

PACKING MATERIALS : WOODEN TUBS USED TO PACK ORANGES : dutiability of, questioning.

I find that there is a very large trade in Wenchow Oranges here, all sent North, specially packed in strongly built tubs on which no duty is collected, and I am forwarding to your address C/o Transport Office, Tientsin, one such tub not so much for the oranges - which may perhaps be useful in your or Staff households to make marmalade - as for getting your opinion as to the advisability to charge duty on the tubs. I don't think the duty amounts to much, after all, perhaps 3 to 400 Taels (both Export and C.T. Duties) a year. However should you think duty should be collected I will submit my proposal with figures of exportation. The " Poochi " is specially sent to Tientsin this trip with a cargo of 3540 tubs.

Yours respectfully,

/O No. 63.   Wenchow 11. December, 6

Sir,

NEW YEAR PRESENTS ~~AND GRATUITIES~~ T

I am told that it is still the practice at this port to exchange presents with the Officials at New Year. It is a useless and costly ceremony as well to themselves as to ourselves (Commissioners) and is only profitable to the Official servants who not only expect a tip but even may appropriate some of the presents. Do you see any objection to my stopping the practice here?

Yours respectfully,

DEC 1916

Inspectorate General of Customs,

PEKING, 12th December, 1916.

Dear Sir,

I am directed by the Inspector General to acknowledge receipt on the 25th Nov. of your S/O No.60 dated 18th Nov.1916.

Yours truly,

Acheson,
Private Secretary.

E. Tanant, Esquire,

WENCHOW

Inspectorate General of Customs,

PEKING, 18th December, 1916.

Dear Sir,

I am directed by the Inspector General to acknowledge receipt on the 4th Dec. of S/O No. 61 dated 7th Dec.

Yours truly,

L. Acheson,
Private Secretary.

C. Tenant, Esquire,
WENCHOW

INSPECTORATE GENERAL OF CUSTOMS,

PEKING, 18th December, 1916.

Dear Mr. Tanant,

I have duly received your S/O No.62 of 9th December.

<u>Duty treatment of tubs used for packing oranges: sample tub of oranges sent to Inspector General.</u> The oranges will be most acceptable. As for the tubs, report officially if you think there is a case after studying all the analogous questions on which decisions have been given!

Yours truly,

Tanant, Esquire,
WENCHOW

INSPECTORATE GENERAL OF CUSTOMS,

PEKING, 27th December, 1916.

S/O

Dear Mr. Tanant,

I have duly received your S/O No.63 of 11th December.

Suggested abolition of local custom in connection with New Year presents.

There is no official sanction for this practice. It is entirely a private matter and you must do what you think right.

Yours truly,

Tanant, Esquire,
WENCHOW

1917 年

CUSTOM HOUSE,

/O No. 64.　　　　　Wenchow 9. January, 1917.

Sir,

A curious case has occurred concerning the VALIDITY OF INLAND TRANSIT PASSES.

The Standard Oil Co on 15th December, 1916, took out some transit passes at Shanghai to cover Kerosene Oil destined to Yotsing, a small town on the sea shore between Ningpo and Wenchow, but comparatively close to Wenchow with which City it is connected by an Inland Canal. The local Acting Agent of the S.O.Co reported a few days ago the arrival of a Shanghai junk carrying the Oil covered by the Transit Passes, saying that the junk drawing too much water, it had been found more safe to bring the junk here, tranship the cases and drums into smaller boats and send them to yotsing by canal instead of by sea. From the conversation my impression is that this is only an excuse and that the junk was bound to Wenchow because it had a large cargo (1800 tins and 267 barrels of 30 gallons each) and the S. O. Co was afraid to consign such a big lot to a small country agent, and it would prefer to keep it here in its godown and release it gradually.

However,

However, I replied that the case was abnormal, but considering that Transit Dues had been paid, and being in doubt as to the possibility for the Junk to reach Yotsing direct without coming this round about way, I would this time grant the permission asked for. 400 tins and 102 barrels were at once reshipped to Yotsing and I instructed the N.C. Office to detain the Transit Passes and issue them according to re-exportations. But a new factor then stepped in, the Tungchuan Chü, which claimed payment of its dues on the Oil landed and stored here in the Company's godown under pretext that oil thus landed here loses its right to further Transit privileges and must pay what is practically Loti shui. As this is outside of my sphere I have not done more, only mentioning the case to the Superintendent in conversation. I think, though, if Yotsing cannot be reached from the sea direct, that the S.O.Co is entitled to store its Oil here for it has 13 months to carry the Oil to destination. I would like to have your instructions on the question.

In this connection I should add that I represented to the Agent the difficulties his Company puts itself in with its action, that we are willing to help it but not so far as to transgress our

our own Regulations, and I advised him to ship his oil here by ships under Maritime Customs control instead of by junks, and he said he would ask his Shanghai Office to act accordingly in future. But I am not sure he told me the whole truth. Wenchow is connected with Shanghai by only one through steamer line (the China Merchants S.N.Co.,) which on account of its arrangements with B.& S.and J.M.&Co rulees steamers freights practically as it likes. Besides there are 5 or 6 lorcha which on account of their foreign status share with the C.M.S.N.Co the monopoly of the Shanghai trade. There is already a marked difference between lorcha and C.M.S.N.Co's rates of freight, and it remains to know whether ordinary junks which report to the N.C. Office are not cheaper than the lorcha. The S.O.Co which has large shipments to make is quite aware of these differences and up to the present all its shipments for Wenchow were practically made by lorcha. As there are no more risks on shipments by junks than by lorcha it remains to know whether this Company is going to use junks in future.

STAFF.

I enclose copy of a confidential letter which

Mr. Verner, Assistant Examiner, received a few days ago from the Ningpo British Consul. Mr. Verner having his wife and 2 children here and some dependents at home replied that he does not care to enlist unless compulsory service be enacted, and would like then to join the coolie corps.

Mr And Mrs Lloyd arrived on the 7th having been kept for 7 or 8 days in Shanghai for want of a steamer and also on account of Mrs Lloyd being sick Mr Stevens left for Shanghai on the 29th December.

Yours respectfully,

Sir,

I have received instructions from His Majesty's Chargé d'Affaires stating that His Majesty's Government desire to obtain a list of those men living in foreign countries who are ready to place their services at the disposal of the Government should they be required. I have therefore to request you to furnish me with answers to the questions in the enclosed list.

I have to make it clear that men need not be deterred from taking this preliminary step by considerations such as uncertainty as to whether they can leave their present employment, because such questions will receive the fullest consideration, when necessary in conjunction with the heads of British firms or the foreign heads of Chinese Government Departments, before they engage themselves definitely to home if and called upon by the War Office.

I have to state that the actual cost of travelling expenses home will be given to any men called up, but not those of their family or dependents.

     I am, etc.,

1. Full name
2. Date of birth.
3. Married or single; Children - number, age, and sex.
4. Occupation.
5. Correct Postal address.
6. Length of residence in China
7. Can you speak Chinese (dialect and degree of proficiency)
8. Can you read Chinese?
9. Have you applied for a commission in the Coolie Corps or would you accept one if offered at a later stage
10. Are you willing to go home and serve in H.M. forces if called upon. If not willing, give reasons, or conditions on which you would be willing.
11. Any other particulars likely to affect question of service - previous military training training, etc.

Note. CONFIDENTIAL. It is hoped to recruit coolie corps of Northern Chinese to serve in France and elsewhere, the object being to release able-bodied British subjects for combatant service. The labour battalions are not to be employed under fire, and the work will be purely non-combatant. The Officers, warrant and non-commissioned officers and medical Officers are to be selected from British subjects in China. Candidates should be within the ages of 20 and 45, energetic, and of active habits. Knowledge of the Northern Dialect is very desirable, though men without this qualification may be accepted if otherwise specially qualified.
Further particulars will be sent on application.

CUSTOM HOUSE,

/O No. 65.

Wenchow, 16. January, 1917.

Sir,

I must apologise in advance for worrying you with a small affair like that of N.C. Examiner Feng Chen-hsi reported in my despatch No. 3181 mailed with this letter, but I could not help protecting this man though he may to a certain extent be guilty, if not of malpractice, anyhow of neglect. Shortly after my arrival I received an anonymous petition accusing both South Gate and Ningtsun Examiners of malpractice, but as there has been so much of these local anonymous denunciations I took no notice of it, thinking it must be the work of some one anxious to get a position, and I think my surmise is fairly right. As I was not moving, the Ningtsun affair now reported then took place.

After I had reported the theft to the Superintendent he sent his Weiyuan to the N.C. Office to enquire from Mr. Kaneko whether any petition had been received against Feng and what action I had taken. The Weiyuan also mentioned that Feng was liable to a fine of $50. for each missing document. I waited a few days thinking the Superintendent would reply to my letters, but as he did not, I called on him and in the conversation he handed me the rules for misuse of Official documents (Enclosure 4 in despatch 3181). He also asked me whether I had reported the case to you, and I replied I thought it was not worth while. He then told me there were bad rumours about Feng and he showed me a copy of the petition which I had received over a month ago. On leaving him I had made my mind to ask Feng to resign, but on enquiring about him Mr. Wong Haiu Geng, my Assistant, (also a Fookienese) who was placed in charge of the N.C. Office at the beginning of the Commissioner's control in 1913, assured me there was nothing very wrong against Feng except that he must have powerful enemies, and this changed my mind. It is indeed very strange that a thief or thieves should enter the Ningtsun station - a miserable house in a remote country corner, where nothing very valuable is stored - and should be satisfied in stealing a tobacco pipe and an ink box and Customs documents when Feng and the Watcher's trunks and bedding were lying close by. Again, the return of all the documents but 5 rather points out to a premeditated intent to have Feng incriminated for a loss of documents.

I

I also questioned again Mr. Kaneko who pointed out that Feng had been re-appointed by Mr. Bowring in 1913 (possibly at Mr. Wong's recommendation) without consulting the Superintendent, and all these details led me to believe that spite - and may be inter-provincial animosity - are parties to this affair, and that Feng is its victim. But in the meantime I am myself the victim of all those machinations, for I was greatly worried by the desire to be just, and it is only reluctantly that I decided on referring the case to your decision.

Having come to this conclusion I sent word to the Superintendent that I would call, but he said he preferred to come to the Office, and I then told him that after careful reading of the Regulations he had handed me it seems necessary to punish Feng, but as the Regulations had not received your sanction - and were perhaps unknown to you - I thought it would be better to report the case to you. He did not say I was wrong, but he replied that I could settle the case myself being authorised by the last sentence of the Regulations.

Yours respectfully,

INSPECTORATE GENERAL OF CUSTOMS,

PEKING, 22nd January, 1917.

Dear Mr. Tanant,

I have duly received your S/O No.64 of 9th January, 1917.

<u>Native Customs Treatment of Shanghai Transit Pass covered Kerosene Oil transhipped from Shanghai Junk at Wenchow for retailed shipment inland.</u>

I do not quite understand how you treated this Oil at your Native Customs. A Transit Pass exempts from Native Customs Duty and it seems to me that all you had to do was to allow the goods to go on to destination under protection of the pass. We are not concerned with the route followed and the pass protects the goods and not the means of conveyance!

Yours truly,

E Tanant, Esquire,
WENCHOW

CUSTOM HOUSE,

No. 66.

Wenchow 25. January, 1917.

Sir,

N.C.Staff : Mr. Wu Ch'i-ta's resignation.

I have now reported (Wenchow No. 3183) the resignation of the old (73) N.C. Examiner Mr. Wu Ch'ita against whom I received the same anonymous petition as against the Ningtsun Examiner Feng, mentioned in my last S/O and Wenchow No.3181. There was no hurry to get rid of this old man for after all I think he did his work like the rest of his colleagues; however, seing how things turned in the Ningtsun case I was not going to be caught napping and have a new case raised, so I called Mr. Wu, informed him of the petition having been received, and suggested that he should resign, for if he did not some one would easily find fault with him, and then he would run the risk of being discharged or dismissed, while resigning now of his own would entitle him to the issue of a fractional Retiring Allowance. He naturally objected that he performed his duty as well as young men, that he had no money, etc., but finally he saw his advantage to follow my suggestion.

There

There was therefore an Examiner's vacancy, and according to instructions it should be filled by my appointing one of the Superintendent's nominees, and that is exactly what was expected by the senders of the anonymous petition; but to disappoint them I promoted the best Watcher, Tung Chiu, to be Examiner and I appointed as Watcher in his place the son of the retiring Mr. Wu, and in order to forestall possible Superintendent's objections, I informed him of Mr. Wu's son's appointment as a solatium to the old man for good services.

<u>N.C. Examiners : recruitment, position, and retiring allowances or bonuses of.</u>

With reference to the last paragraph of Circ. 2590 announcing the coming issue of instructions regarding treatment and classification of N.C. Staff for "Service List" purposes, I seize this opportunity to mention that there is no correspondency as regards N.C. Examiners between Mar. and N.C. Customs Employés of this rank. From the time we assumed control we entered their names at the head of the N.C. Out-door Staff Pay sheet, but socially they are regarded as superior to the O.D. Staff, not so much by knowledge as by social standing, and the fact that they should be appointed on the Superintendent's nomination goes to prove

prove that the position is somewhat analogous to that of Lushih who we make rank as In-door.

In view, however, to stimulate the watchers flagging zeal, I take leave to suggest that these Examiners be in future recruited, when possible, amongts suitable Watchers. This would promote Service interests and at the same time stop official interference, for it must be borne in mind that any man recommended by a Superintendent for a position has to pay for it, if not to the great man himself, anyhow to his subordinates, and therefore the more appointment there are and the more profit to one or the other. All this works to the Service detriment, for the money paid either in coin or in presents to purchase a recommendation has to be found somewhere once the nominee has been appointed.

I must also point out that no New year gratuities were issued to N.C. Examiners having served for three years while we issue them to Mar. Customs Weighers. If this is wrong it can be altered at once and I presume they will rather prefer the issue of a month pay now than to have to wait for 12 years for a years pay.

Yours respectfully,

No. 67.

CUSTOM HOUSE,

Wenchow, 27. January, 1917.

Sir,

K'anmen and Juian Fish duty question.

My despatch No. 3184 informs you of an attempt by the Superintendent to collect duty on fish at K'anmen, one of his stations, instead of letting the fish, as of old, pay duty here. I think my action in refusing to honour the K'anmen duty receipts knocked the scheme on the head, but your intervention with the Shuiwu-ch'u is necessary, not only to give it the last blow, but particularly in order to replace the Juian fish collection under our control. The Ch'u and Board's sanction which, the Supt's despatch of 22nd January says, was obtained on the 3rd and 5th moons of 1915 was never communicated to this Office, nor probably to you, and it seems it may be a fitting opportunity to remonstrate with the Ch'u for thus sanctioning without obtaining your assent such proposals which encroach on our rights.

The case, anyhow, is worth while studying in its outlines. First comes the proposal that the stations under the Commissioner's control should adopt

Quadruplicat

Quadruplicate Duty Receipts (Vide Subject 3 - Duty Receipts - in January 1915 Summary of non-urgent Chinese correspondence; Subject 3, February 1915 Summary; Subject 2 (Quadruplicate Duty Certificates), April 1915 Summary) to which Mr. Acheson rightly objected (Wenchow despatch No.3087). Then, on the sly, while his attention is directed to this question the Juian Weiyüan begins issuing Quad. Duty Receipts for fish. Some are brought to the South gate and accepted by us, may be simply tolerated (the question of fish being overseen) on account of the Supt's request that they be accepted when presented and returned to him. The precedent is thus established ; gradually more fish is imported, and the Staff which have been instructed on their first report to let go, do not object any longer, and after a few months when the collection is well started the matter is reported to Peking as succesfully experimented, is approved, and the affair is settled, and we have thus lost our Juian fish collection. Then follows a rest. For some reason or other the same Weiyüan who plotted this duty-grabbing is transferred to K'anmen, and it so happens that there is at the same time a change of Commissioner, and the same process begins again : K'anmen issues its Quad. Receipts without warning. Our Puchow station as a matter of fact accepts them only charging duty on difference

difference in weight, and it is due to the refusal of our Examiner at the fish station (possibly for private reasons) to recognise these Quad. Duty Receipts that the whole affair falls through. Had we not objected it is more than probable that within a short time the Ch'u and Board's sanction would again have been requested to register a new " fait accompli ".

In my despatch I mention that the N. C. Weiyüan brought me himself the Superintendent's despatch of 20th and gave oral explanations. Indeed he asked whether I could not give instructions to recognise temporarily the duty receipts already issued on account of the difficulty for the Supt to recover the Receipts which we would not honour, but I refused to have anything to do with them.

I have further to add that when Mr. Kaneko reported this case he mentioned that the K'anmen and Juian stations were farmed and that some arrangement must have been arrived at between the Weiyüan and the Wenchow merchants, but after fruitless enquiries he was unable to obtain substantial proofs. In fact, the Supt's N.C. Weiyüan to whom I put the question abruptly denied that the collection was farmed. But I have no doubt it is, and my conviction is strengthened by the

the enclosed statement prepared for me by Mr. K'o Yu-p'ing, 3rd Clerk, C, my Secretary, who obtained all this valuable information from a former superseded or discarded Weiyüan. It is interesting to note that it is the same Weiyüan, Mr. Shih Hsin-ju, who had farmed the Juian collection in 1914 and 1915 for $1700 and 2700 respectively, and was in 1916 transferred to K'anmen (farmed to him for $ 650), who now wants to " resume the duty collection " at K'anmen The actual Juian farmer, Mr. Sung, is said to be a relative of Supt Mao. Unfortunately all this information lacks of official confirmation, and therefore I could not avail myself of it as an argument against the Weiyüan's proposal.

Yours respectfully,

	Name of Farmer	Amount $	Name of Farmer	Amount $	Name of Farmer	Amount $
Juian	Shih Hsin-jü	1,700	Shih Hsin-jü	2,700	Sung	—
Ao Kou	Ch'ên K'ê-chai	4,400	Ma Chu-tsun	6,500	Ch'ien	6,500
Ta Yü	Wang Wei-chung	6,500	Ch'ên K'ê-chai	6,500	Wang	10,000
Pu Ch'i	Yuan Yao-fu	1,800	Yuan Yao-fu	2,200	Yuan Yao-fu	2,200
Kanmên	Nan Mao-yung	520	Chang Yü-lin	650	Shih Hsin-jü	650
Ning Kang	about $70 to $80 a year.					

三年至五年數目

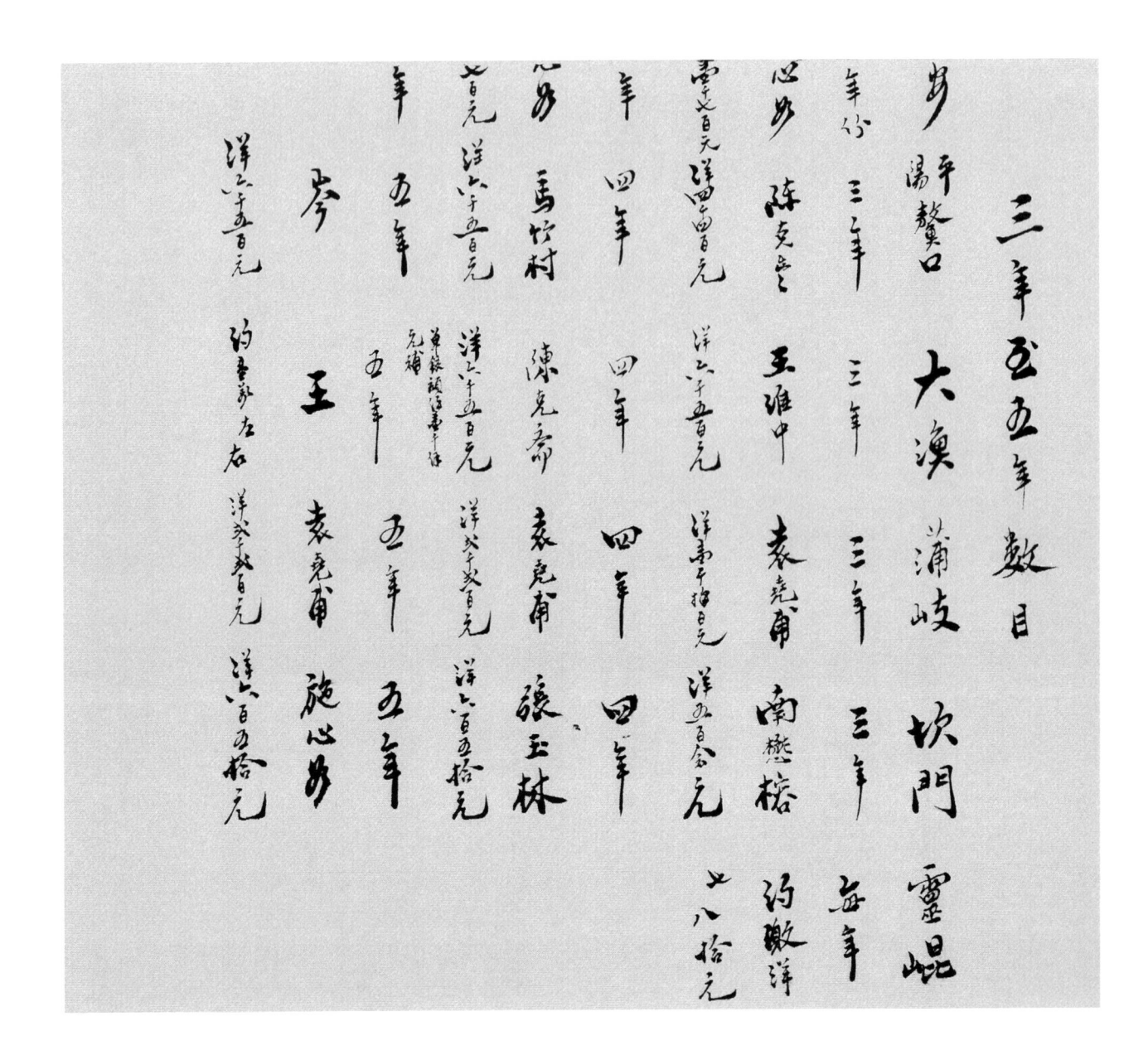

岁 平陽鰲口 大澳 蒲岐 坎門 靈崑
年份 三年 三年 三年 每年 四八拾元
每岁 陳克宣 王淮中 袁亮甫 南麂礁 汀敬洋
壹仟壹百五拾元 洋六百五拾元 洋五百元 洋五百參拾元
年 四年 四年
壹仟元 洋六百元 洋五百五拾元
年 馬竹村 陳克齋 袁亮甫 張玉林
四年 五年
叁 王 袁亮甫 施心乡
洋七百元 約壹百元左右 洋參百五拾元 洋壹百五拾元

INSPECTORATE GENERAL OF CUSTOMS.

PEKING, 30th January, 1917.

Dear Mr. Tanant,

I have duly received your S/O No.65 of 16th January, 1917.

<u>Theft of documents at Ningtsun Station; treatment of case.</u>

You must treat the case like any other staff case according to the evidence and your sense of justice!

Yours truly,

Tanant, Esquire,
WENCHOW

CUSTOM HOUSE,

Wenchow, 5th February 1917

No. 68.

SIR,

With reference to my S/O No. 64 and your S/O of 22nd January, in reply :

<u>Native Customs treatment of Shanghai Transit Pass-covered Kerosene Oil transhipped from Shanghai Junks at Wenchow for retailed shipment inland</u>

in which you say : "I do not quite understand how you treated this oil at your Native Customs", I beg to add the following information :

Yotsing, the destination stated on the Transit Passes is an inland town close to the coast between Ningpo and Wenchow, 80 li from the latter. It is said to be connected with the sea by a creek or canal and therefore the cargo brought by junk and covered by Shanghai Transit Passes should have been carried to Yotsing direct without coming to Wenchow, as Wenchow is 80 li farther South. The Standard Oil Co's argument to explain the oil's arrival here is that the creek linking Yotsing to the sea is too shallow to admit of a junk of the size of the one used to proceed to Yotsing direct, and therefore

the

the junk came here so as to tranship the cargo into several small boats going from Wenchow to Yotsing direct by an inland canal. Acting on the precedent established by Circular 805 I replied : "if you have to tranship you may as well tranship close to Yotsing and not come here at all, since in doing so you are beyond the place named on your Certificates". I consider, I (rightly think,) that it is no concern of ours to know whether the creek linking Yotsing to the sea is navigable or not. Circular 805 seems to me clear on that point and besides the principle was reiterated by Circular No. 1,734, No. 259 : "A transit Pass, by treaty, only protects from port to place". Anyhow as far as my N.C. Office is concerned I informed the S.O. Co. that I would exceptionally allow, this time, the transhipment at Wenchow.

But at the same time and quite independently of my action the Tungchuan Chü claimed payment of its dues. As I told you I mentioned the case verbally to the Superintendent and I was a few days ago informed by the S.O. Co's Agent that he had had to pay the Tungchuan tax here but was granted

a

a receipt which would exonerate him from further taxation at Yotsing.

If my argument is wrong please let me know so that I instruct my N.C. Office to alter its practice.

Smuggling of mails and parcels.

I enclose copy of correspondences which I exchanged recently with the Chekiang Postal Commissioner re smuggling of mails and particularly parcels, and also of a letter and its Enclosures received by my predecessor from the local Postmaster a few months ago. When this man admits himself as he does in his letter to Mr Destelan that the parcels (which he complains of as being smuggled) bear no address I do not see what claim he may have against smuggling. The parcels which I handed over to the Postmaster recently bore addresses giving the name of the Minchü through which they were forwarded, but they were not in a Minchü bag, being carried "à découvert" by a Minchü runner. As there was no doubt that they were smuggled by that runner I handed them over to the Postmaster.

Gun powder explosion.

The local military Authorities sold some time ago

ago all their useless arms and ammunition to a Company styled An Lan Kung Ssu (安瀾公司) at the condition that they should be broken into pieces before exportation. So, all the old iron guns on the city wall were broken into 3 or more parts, and old rifles, bayonets, swords, scabbards, etc., were properly broken. There was also a lot of damaged old cartridges and while workmen - mostly women - were busy separating the bullets and powder from the cartridge cases an explosion occurred killing outright 2 and wounding some 20 people. The total dead now amounts to 11. The firm promptly indemnified the families - $130 per head, I am told, for indemnity and funerals -. The temple in which the work was done and which was badly damaged received $500. Now the Company instead of paying its workmen $0.40 per day pays them $0.80 and makes them sign an agreement by which they bind themselves not to claim anything in case of another explosion.

Yours respectfully,

C O P Y.

POSTAL COMMISSIONER'S OFFICE.
POST OFFICE.
Hangchow, 20th December 1916.

Dear Mr. Tanant,

Mr. To Tzu-pei, the Wenchow First Class Postmaster, in his Charge Memorandum to his successor, reports that smuggling of mails by Minchü, especially on board the Haimen steamers, is rampant and suggests that I should approach you with a view to obtaining Customs co-operation in searching steamers. As I have no reason to doubt the correctness of Mr. TO's statement may I take the liberty and kindly request your help in the matter by issuing instructions to your searching staff to keep an eye on Minchü runners and try to effect seizures of Minchü and other smuggled mails.

Yours truly,
(Signed) E. A. Schaumlöffel.

for reply, vide No. 809 (General) of 2. Feby. 1917.

TRUE COPY:

Commissioner.

Copy of correspondence with Chekiang Postal Commr. re rifling of mails, and inefficiency of Postal Service between Ningpo and Wenchow.

C O P Y.

POST OFFICE,
Wenchow, 11th October 1916.

S/O

Dear Mr. Acheson,

I beg to enclose herewith copies of S/O letter No. 19 which I sent to Mr. H. Picard Destelan, the Associate Director General, at Peking, and S/O letter No. 37 which I received from Mr. E. Schaumloffel, the Postal Commissioner, at Hangchow, on the subject of silk parcels being smuggled on board of steamers of the C.M.S.N. Co., for your perusal. This Office will be grateful if steps can be taken to protect our parcel traffic.

Your obedient servant,
(Signed) To Tzu pei.

(2)

hire from the sender's house to the steamer, 25 cents for steamer employés, and 2 cents for coolie hire from the steamer to the addressee's house at Shanghai, in all 29 cents. Parcels forwarded in this manner bear no address on the wrapper.

On the 30th August the Customs at Shanghai seized a lot of silk parcels on board of S.S. Poochi arrived from Wenchow to the value of about $150.00 and the same confiscated.

Your obedient servant,
(Signed) To Tzu-pei.

POST OFFICE,
Wenchow 6th October 1916.

S/O No. 37
Wenchow

Dear Mr. To,

The A.D.G. has forward to me copy of your S/O No. 19 to him. With reference to the latter the A.D.

Received 13/1/02

Copy of Wenchow Postmaster's letter to Wenchow Commr. re Smuggling of parcels.

CUSTOM HOUSE,

S/O No. 69.　　　　　　　　　Wenchow, 10th February 1917.

Sir,

With reference to my S/O No. 65 and yours of 30th January :

Theft of documents at Ningtsun station :

I beg to report that the case has been settled as reported in my despatch No. 3187 now posted. As said in my letter No. 65 I did not like worrying you with that affair which I intended for lack of proof of complicity on the Examiner's part, to pigeon-hole, but Mr. Mao's (Superintendent) interference obliged me to take up the case, and as I could find no trace of the rules concerning misuse of Official documents having received your sanction, I had no option but to submit you the case. After receipt of your instructions and my personal visit to Ningtsun I felt, though I cannot convict Feng of complicity, that some sanction must be taken against him for remissness, and I fined him one month's pay, viz. $ 25.

Mr. Werner, Asst-Examr, has been laid up for a few days on account of trouble with his lever.

We have had very cold weather at New Year and again quite recently. Two days ago all the mountain tops were snow-capped.

Yours respectfully,

INSPECTORATE GENERAL OF CUSTOMS,

PEKING, 14th February, 1917.

Dear Mr. Tanant,

I have duly received your S/O No.66 of 25th January, 1917.

<u>Native Customs Examiners: recruitment, position and Retiring Allowances or Bonuses of.</u>

"Examiner" does not seem a very appropriate name, and as they do outdoor work of a kind it is certainly desirable that they should not be appointed by Superintendent. Would "Ssu Shih" (司事) describe them adequately? In order that we may be able to decide, please apply for a ruling officially making your own suggestions and giving an accurate description of these men's standing and the work they do for comparison with other ports.

Yours truly,

Tanant, Esquire,
WENCHOW

INSPECTORATE GENERAL OF CUSTOMS.

S/O

PEKING, 14th February, 1917

Dear Mr. Tanant,

I have duly received your S/O No.68 of 5th February, 1917.

<u>Native Customs Treatment of Shanghai Transit Pass-covered Kerosene Oil transhipped from Shanghai Junks at Wenchow for retailed shipment inland.</u>

If you want an official ruling please officialise with map!

<u>Smuggling of mails and parcels: copies of correspondence on subject forwarded.</u>

Please do not send enclosures in S/O correspondence. Either send such documents officially or embody them in your letter!

Yours truly,

C.E. Tanant, Esquire,
WENCHOW

No. 70.

CUSTOM HOUSE,
Wenchow, 16th February, 1917.

Sir,

Dutiability of Inter-treaty ports cargo carried by I.W.S.N. Steamers.

I have had in my despatch No.3189 to ask for your instructions as regards the Ningpo Superintendent's action in trying to issue Fen Yun Tan to cover Shanghai-Ningpo cargo. This, at my point of view, is a gross malpractice, and when in all their reports to Peking the various Superintendents speak of malpractices which nearly reflect on our Service, I think the opportunity should be taken to point out to the Ch'u that its Superintendents are the originators of the malpractices. This question had already been reported to you by Mr. Acheson in his S/O No. 42 of 6. March 1916, replied to by yours of 21st March 1916. Upon receipt of your letter Mr. Acheson wrote to Ningpo and as a result no cargo was shipped any longer per Inland steamers from Ningpo to Wenchow, but it was all declared for Taichow (Haimen), and it was then that the Kuan Tan were if not instituted, anyhow substituted to Hungtan to cover original Ningpo cargo

remaining

remaining on board and taken on by the same ship to Wenchow. I should say that this a clear case of malpractice ! As this case concerns as well Shanghai and Ningpo I thought it advisable to inform the Commissioners of my action, and I enclose copy of my despatch.

Strange enough in the present case the matter was first brought semi-officially to my notice by the Wenchow Superintendent who handed the Ningpo Superintendent's despatch to the N.C. Weiyüan with a slip sealed by himself :" The N.C. Weiyüan is to see the Commissioner and ascertain his views how this procedure is going to affect Customs trade ". I told at once the Weiyüan that I thought the proposal objectionable as affecting our Maritime Customs Revenue and liable to cause a demand for the abolition of Coast Trade Duty. I still wonder what caused the Superintendent to inform me in advance. Would it be that he is in bad terms with his Ningpo colleague, or is it bluff to show his zeal to increase the Customs revenue ? There is a rumour that he has been accused by a former Weiyüan (farmer) of one of his N.C. stations of selling the station farm at a higher figure than that officially reported, and various other "crimes", and I am also told that an investigating

investigating Weiyüan has arrived to go into the case.

The S.S."Haean" has been the first C.M.S.N.Co's steamer to come after the old style New year Holiday (25 days without Maritime Customs Steamer). She brought and took away good cargoes, but unfortunately it is reported that there is little cargo for this port now at Shanghai and this may affect the running of the steamers.

The new China Merchants Agent, formerly the "Kiagwah" compradore, has arrived. He is a brother of Mr. Alfred Sze the Chinese Minister to London.

Yours respectfully,

O No. 71.

CUSTOM HOUSE,

Wenchow, 19. February, 1917.

Sir,

Currency : new subsidiary coins.

With reference to your Circular No. 2619 I have to report that the Superintendent sent me through his Weiyüan a despatch embodying the Shui-wu Ch'u's instructions enclosed in your Circular, and at the same time two copies of a joint proclamation in his and my name to inform the public of the circulation and compulsory acceptance at par of the new subsidiary coins.

As your Circular and the Ch'u's despatch referred to the coins being only circulated in the Northern Provinces for the present I felt like refusing to sign the proclamation. However as there is no harm in warning the public in advance I signed it and had the copies posted at this Office and at the Native Customs, but I thought better to mention this to you, for after all later on should these coins become depreciated, there might be some difficulty in refusing them or accepting them only at their market value.

Yours respectfully,

Inspectorate General of Customs,

PEKING, 27th February, 1917.

Dear Sir,

I am directed by the Inspector General to acknowledge receipt on the 12th Feb. your S/O No.67 dated 27th Jan. 1917.

Yours truly,

Acheson,
Private Secretary.

E. Tanant, Esquire,

W E N C H O W

Inspectorate General of Customs

PEKING, 27th February, 1917.

Dear Sir,

I am directed by the Inspector al to acknowledge receipt on the 25th Feb. r S/O No. 70 dated 16th Feb. 1917.

Yours truly,

L. Acheson,
Private Secretary.

E. Tanant, Esquire,

WENCHOW

Inspectorate General of Customs,

PEKING, 27th February, 1917.

Dear Sir,

I am directed by the Inspector General to acknowledge receipt on the 25th Feb. of S/O No.71 dated 19th Feb.1917.

Yours truly,

L. Acheson,
Private Secretary.

. Tanant, Esquire,

W E N C H O W

1 8 MAR 1917

Inspectorate General of Customs.

PEKING, 9th March, 1917.

Dear Sir,

I am directed by the Inspector al to acknowledge receipt on the 19th Feb. S/O No.69 dated 10th February.

Yours truly,

Acheson

Private Secretary.

E. Tanant, Esquire,

W E N C H O W

CUSTOM HOUSE,
Wenchow, 12 March 1917

S/o N° 72.

Sir,

Revision of Agreement with Bank of China.
(Wenchow despatch No. 3196).

Clean Mexican dollars are the local medium of exchange and I have not heard of the local or Taichow made dollars referred to in "Hai Kwan Banking System" by Mr. Mackey. If we were to raise the Hk.Tl. dollar exchange from 152 to 155.63 $ I fear there would be strong objection, for we have been satisfied with $152 or about for 40 years, and it is in this view that I suggested the adoption of the Ningpo system though itself objectionable. However it would be a step to lift us out from that rut, the 152 rate, in which we are still embedded.

Kanmen and Juian Fish Duty question.

I duly received your despatch No. 700/64017 in which you say you are addressing the Shui-wu Ch'u on the subject. I have since received a Superintendent's despatch informing me that he had been instructed to stop his intended collection at Kanmen, but recognising

on

on the plea of established practice, his right to collect at Juian.

<u>Ling kun Barrier : illegal levy of duty at.</u>
There is a Superintendent's barrier just outside my sphere of control, called Ling kun, established to search junks but not to collect duties. However lately it collected duty to which I objected. It has even been admitted by the Superintendent that it is farmed! I think that my objection has very much annoyed the Superintendent. He has been writing twice asking my opinion about the transfer of the station to me or its abolition. I really know nothing about it except that its upkeep would mean extra expenditure probably wasted, so I carefully guarded myself against giving any opinion and I referred him to his archives to see the result of the station's work. He would have liked me to express an opinion and then would have memorialised the Ch'u screening himself behind me. Copy of the correspondence will be sent with the March return of non-urgent Chinese correspondence.

<u>Superintendent</u>. The special investigating Commissioner sent from Hangchow to investigate the accusations

against

against the Superitendent has left. It is said that it might cost him $5000 to square up with his accus accuser and the investigator.

We have had snow three times on the hills all round last month, a rare occurrence here.

Yours respectfully,

INSPECTORATE GENERAL OF CUSTOMS,

PEKING, 20th March, 1917

Dear Mr Tanant,

I have duly received your S/O. No. 72 of 12th March, 1917.

Kanmen and Juian Fish Duty question. Superintendent's intended collection at Kanmen stopped, and right to collect at Juian recognised, by Shui-wu Ch'u :

I have not been instructed yet, but I think it is the line the Ch'u may be expected to take.

Yours truly,

E. Tanant, Esquire,
 WENCHOW.

CUSTOM HOUSE,

Wenchow 30. March, 1917.

No. 73.

Ack.

Sir,

<u>Native Customs : malpractice at Haimen N.C. Office.</u>
With reference to my despatch No. 3199 reporting that I had to inflict a fine to stop the malpractice caused by the Haimen N.C. Office in issuing Ssu lien tan short of the real weight of cargo, I have to add that two similar cases have since occurred and that I continued inflicting the same fine. The three Steamers Companies thus fined (they seem to include Customs duty in their freight and apply for the goods) approached me on the subject and said they had heretofore been granted a 10 % allowance on weight but I replied that in the actual cases the difference in weight amounted from 15 to 30 and more per cent. To-day one of the Companies argued that on arrival it declared itself - which is true - that there was a discrepancy between the actual weight and the Ssu lien tan, and for having thus warned us of the difference of weight, it claimed to be exonerated of fine, but I declined, for I said if they knew of the discrepancy they should have insisted on being provided

with

with regular papers at Haimen.

I sent Mr. Wilzer a copy of my despatch 3199 so that he be acquainted with the case should his Superintendent happen to mention it to him. In fact it might perhaps have been the regular way to stop this malpractice to ask Mr. Wilzer to mention the case to his Superintendent, but I thought better not for two reasons : 1o. It is always rather unpleasant to go and tell a Superintendent that his Staff commits malpractices, for, at a Chinese point of view, the Sup't must take it as a personal affair since the Staff at the Stations forms part if not of his family, anyhow of his retinue. 2o. The Haimen Weiyüan, and indirectly the Ningpo Sup't, really deserve that their action be reported to the Ch'u They already ignored us in trying to put in force the Fen Yun Tan system which your despatch No. 702 authorised me to ignore; now not satisfied with this rebuke they go on with another evil practice. This is taking things rather too easy, and I cannot see any other way to stop it but by report to and sanction by the Shui-wu Ch'u.

The Taoyin, Mr. Chao Tseng-fan, has arrived. Mr. Verner, Asst-Examr, returned to duty yesterday after a fortnight's illness (lever).

Yours respectfully,

CUSTOM HOUSE,

S/O No. 74.   Wenchow, 3rd April 1917.

SIR,

GERMAN PASSENGERS' LUGGAGE: EXAMINATION OF, ETC.

I duly received your Circular 2642 transmitting the Shui-wu Chu's instructions concerning search of German passengers' luggage, and issued an order to the staff accordingly. I must however ask you to kindly let me know how we are going to ascertain the nationality of passengers. The proper way would be to ask them to show their Pass ports. But this is more within Police than Customs attributions; besides, foreigners have hitherto been travelling without passports, and a good many may not possess one. Also, suppose that in the doubt about a passenger's nationality we happen to unsuccessfully search a Britisher's luggage: though we have the right to search nevertheless that man is bound to complain. It would be therefore better that we be assisted by the Police who would first make sure of the passenger's nationality, or else that the instructions be amplified, and that we be authorised to ask for passports and to search all passengers irrespective of nationality.

In this connection I have to report that a German Missionary and his family arrived from the interior on the 30th March in the morning and boarded at once the I.W.S.N. steamer

steamer "Paohua" for Ningpo, on their way to Shanghai. The steamer was to leave about noon. At quarter to one while I was at tiffin in my house the N.C. Weiyüan called to request me to stop the "Paohua" at the Superintendent's request. I told him I required a written authority to do so, for if I delayed the steamer she may accidentally ground on the bar or should she go ashore somewhere else there would be a complaint that the accident was caused by my delaying the ship and I added that if it meaned a short delay he might as well arrange himself with the captain. The weiyüan did not give the reason for the search but I have some suspicion that it was on account of formalities with the departure of this German - I had not received then your Circular -. Anyhow I refused to detain the ship. The Superintendent whom I saw the next day told me he thought I could have detained the ship to oblige him. I said yes if it is only an affair of half hour or so, but the Weiyüan thought it might be an affair of 3 hours and cannot take on myself to detain a ship here so long on account of tides. I don't think he was very satisfied, though I told him that if he had any business he had only to send me a written demand and that I would comply with it at his own risks.

After a fortnight's illness Mr. D. Verner, Asst-Examr, A, returned to duty, but I cannot say he looks well. A Medical Certificate recommending his transfer to a Northern port is attached to the March return of Service movements. That Certificate is rather non-committal, but nevertheless the Doctor verbally gave Mr. Verner a warning that he may have another attack and might have to be operated, and he told me the same thing; so, on this account, and in view of the short staff at my disposal I hope you may see your way to transfer him to a better climate.

Yours respectfully,

Inspectorate General of Customs,

PEKING, 10th April, 1917

Dear Sir,

I am directed by the Inspector at to acknowledge receipt on the 7th April n S/O No.73 dated 30th March, 1917

Yours truly,

L. Acheson,
Private Secretary.

E. Tanant, Esquire,
WENCHOW

INSPECTORATE GENERAL OF CUSTOMS,

S/O

PEKING, 10th April, 1917.

Dear Mr Tanant,

I have duly received your S/O No.74 of 3rd April, 1917.

<u>Examination of German passengers' luggage. Difficulty of ascertaining foreign travellers' nationality.</u>

There can hardly be so many foreign passengers in Wenchow that it would be difficult to ascertain the nationality of those who come!

Yours truly,

Tanant, Esquire,
   WENCHOW

CUSTOM HOUSE,

No. 75.

Wenchow, 11. April, 1917.

Sir,

Steam vessels employed by Military and Police Administrations.

There is a Govt. Gunboat " Chao-wu ",1200 tons, occasionally calling here, and flying a flag different from that prescribed by Circ. 2518, although the Commander's card reads : 浙江外海水警超武兵艦砲隊員盧志安. She has heretofore been allowed to ply as she likes without interference from this Office. She arrived a few days ago from Ningpo with 140 men of the Chekiang Gendarmerie for Wenchow. I instructed the Tidesurveyor to enquire whether she had any Customs papers. The reply was : " No, we do not report to the Customs at Ningpo ". In view of the instructions of Circ. 2518 I wrote to the Superintendent referring him to the Regulations, and asked him to inform me of the status of that ship. No written reply has been received, but the Sup't whom I saw afterwards said that in

the

the present juncture it would be better not to enforce the Regulations (which he gave me the impression to scorn), and he added that he would write to the Governor. I replied that I would wait. Since the above occurred a smaller gunboat "Hsin Pao Shun", about 200 tons, arrived from and returned to Ningpo. She had on board a Maritime Police Official.

<u>Arrest of, and sentence passed on Assistant's</u> Chair bearer. (<u>Vide</u> Subj. 3, March Non-urgent Chinese Corresp.)

One of Mr. Kaneko's chair bearers fought with, and wounded by a blow on the head, one of his neighbours. The affair was reported to the Police and the Chien Cha Ting issued an order to the chair bearer to report for judgement. The Chair bearer not satisfied with this struck the Official messenger. However Mr. Kaneko ordered him to report to the Court and finally he got 3 months gaol. Mr. Kaneko while informing me pointed out that a foreigner's servant should not be arrested without the Employer's consent, and in the case of Customs Employés
without

without due notification to the Commissioner. I took up the case verbally with the Sup't, and also sent Mr. Kaneko to argue with the Sup't's Weiyüan, and it was admitted that the Chien Cha Ting should in future inform me should it be necessary to arrest any of the Staff. The chair bearer has been duly dismissed.

<u>Revenue Collection : raising of dollar rate</u>.

On receipt of your Desp. No. 705/64227 authorising the raising of the dollar rate, I called for the Supt's assistance, for I am afraid there will be serious objections on the part of the merchants. After I had explained the case he asked me to write so that he may inform the Chamber of Commerce. I did so and at the same time issued a Notification that the dollar rate would be raised from 1st May. I am discussing with the Bank of China to arrive to a settlement of its commission. I am afraid that instructions must have been received from the Hangchow Head Office to get everything they can from us, which I don't think is very fair, considering the great favour we confer on that bank by recognising it as Customs Bankers.

Yours respectfully,

No. 76.

CUSTOM HOUSE,
Wenchow, 19. April, 1917.

Sir,

Revenue Collection : raising of dollar rate.

I have now telegraphed to you as follows : "Chamber of Commerce objecting to raising of Haikwan Tael rate to dollars 155.63 informed me verbally yesterday that it petitioned by mail on seventeenth Ministry of Finance and Shui-wu Ch'u to adopt Ningpo system. They wanted me to postpone enforcing new collection rate from 1st May to 1st June pending instructions. I replied difficult postpone and suggested they should wire for reply by telegram. I take leave suggest you impress on Ministry and Ch'u necessity adopt standard rate otherwise we shall have to adopt Ningpo system. Revised Bank agreement posted seventeenth Tanant "

The Banker when discussing the new agreement had already said he heard objections would be forthcoming. I replied it is inevitable but our reasons are good and the standard rate is lower than the Treaty rate, so there should not be so much objection after all. I have an idea that he, too, would prefer the Ningpo system

system he would gain more by it.

I told the Chamber of Commerce representatives that it would not be wise to reject the standard rate, for, if we follow Ningpo, all the increase will go into the Bank's pocket instead of the Government, and this they saw well enough.

Yours respectfully,

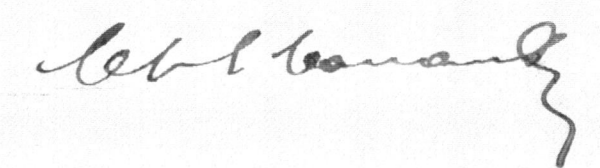

INSPECTORATE GENERAL OF CUSTOMS,

S/O

PEKING, 24th April, 1917.

Dear Mr Tanant,

I have duly received your S/O No.75 of 11th April, 1917.

Status of steam vessels employed by Military and Police Administrations. Superintendent written to and referred to existing instructions.

Having got the matter on record you need do nothing more for the present.

Yours truly,

Tanant, Esquire,
WENCHOW

CUSTOM HOUSE,

Wenchow, 25 Apr. 1917

No. 77

Sir,

Revenue Collection : raising of dollar rate.
After they had promised me on the 18th to wire to the Ministry of Finance and to the Ch'u to obtain an early reply to their petitions, the Chamber of Commerce wrote to the Sup't who transmitted their letter on 21st to say we had better continue to collect at the old rate until the raising of the dollar rate becomes a general measure enforced at all the ports. I called at once on the Sup't and met at his place the Chairman of the Chamber of Commerce who would not change his decision. It was then proposed by the Sup't that he would report the matter to the Ch'u and ask for a speedy settlement. My despatch No. 3204 now mailed informs you of all this.

It is unfortunate in this business that the Sup't be a quasi local man : He married here has resided here for years, owns property, and

is

is practically a native of the place, and such being the case he is bound by his own interest to foster the merchants demands. From the beginning he has objected to the standard rate. He wanted the Ningpo system. He even wanted to keep the Ku Ping taol rate as it now stands at $151. under pretext that he collects at $150. while *pro rata* to the new Hk.Tl; rate it will be $153.114. I told him there could not be any difficulty over that as the N.C. rate has a fixed correlation to the Hk. Tl. Anyhow he has not yet issued the joint proclamation to be posted at the N. C.

So long as exchange remains high merchants by the Ningpo system will have to pay as much as by the standard rate, and the gain would all go to the Bank which, under pretext that it worked at a loss ever since it signed the agreement, will not consent to a reduction of its fee.

It seems to me it would be time for the Central Government to affirm its authority and uphold your decision. In any case if we are not to collect at the standard rate I beg leave to suggest that as a transitory measure the

the rate be made, say $154.50 for a year and afterwards $155.63. I did not suggest it as it would have been taken as an acquiescement on my part that the standard rate is too high. It would be more easy to substitute such a fixed rate in the revised bank agreement than to start bargaining again with the bank if we were to follow the Ningpo system.

The merchants are down on the Manager of the Bank of China for having applied for a revision of the agreement. He called two days ago to enquire, in view of the local opposition whether we were determined to collect at the standard rate. I told him the matter was being referred to the Ch'u and he would be informed later on. He mentioned that one of the merchants reasons to raise such opposition to the change of rate is that the tea season is just going to begin, and as the tea trade has been exceptionally bad last year (owing to adulteration of local teas) it is felt that an increase of over 2 % in the duty payment rate will again affect profits adversely.

Yours respectfully,

INSPECTORATE GENERAL OF CUSTOMS,

S/O

PEKING, 1st May, 1917.

Dear Mr Tanant,

I have duly received your S/O No. 77 of 25th April, 1917.

Dollar rate for revenue collection: Central Government should assert its authority.

No doubt: but we must fight our own battles as far as we can. There is no hurry and as our position is fundamentally sound, sooner or later things will come right! The standard rate is not too high: do not suggest any such half measure as a $ 154.50 rate!

Yours truly,

Tanant, Esquire,
WENCHOW

CUSTOM HOUSE,

No. 78.

Wenchow, 4th May, 1917.

SIR,

<u>Revenue Collection: Raising of Dollar Rate.</u>

I duly received your telegram of 27th ult. saying you have no objection to postponement till 1st June. I duly informed the Superintendent asking him to notify the Chamber of Commerce. I also wrote to the Bank of China which reluctantly agreed to the postponement for one month as will be seen by the copy of its reply (Case 2, April Summary of Chinese Correspondence). The Banker, I am informed, is particularly annoyed as May is supposed to be our best month it being the time for the exportation of Tea.

<u>Inter-treaty Port cargo by I.W.S.N. Steamers: recognition of Fen Yün Tan.</u>

I also received your telegram of 2nd May instructing me to refund Maritime Customs duty collected on cargo under Fen Yun Tan, and gave the necessary instructions. As you will see by my despatch No. 3209 I

had

had not waited for your telegram to order the refund of those duties, but acting upon the instructions of your despatch No. 711/64,454 I had made it subject to production of Import Ssu Lien Tan, so as to oblige the Haimen N.C. Office to issue Ssu Lien Tan which it might otherwise not issue, pocketing the duties thus not officially recorded, and I hope that when replying to my despatch you will see your way to sanction my action as now established.

<u>Lorcha Chin Yung-fu detained by Maritime Police at Tinghai and part of her cargo taken delivery of by Standard Oil Co. with Police permission.</u>

A troublesome case has occurred which is being investigated and which I shall have to report later on. A Shanghai Lorcha bound to Wenchow, carrying 100 drums and 500 cases Kerosene Oil for the Standard Oil Co., and other shippers' sundries, was detained recently by the Maritime Police at Tinghai, close to Ningpo. In the meantime, while his ship was detained, the owner, a Wenchow resident, petitioned for assistance in in obtaining release of his ship. I informed the Superintendent who wrote to Tinghai and the Police replied stating the ship had been detained on account of smuggling of 1 catty of opium by the crew. Subsequently the ship was released (the supercargo and one of the crew having been sentenced to 3 months gaol) and arrived here short 2 cases clocks detained by the Police and the Standard Oil Co's Kerosene Oil which was said to have been landed by the Tinghai (may be Ningpo) Agent of the Standard Oil Co. with the Police permission under pretext that on account of delays the tins would get rusty and the oil would leak.

Upon hearing of this I informed the Superintendent verbally and we made the owner hand me a promissory Note for Tls. 500 in case it would become necessary to inflict a fine for breach of Customs Regulations, and I wrote to the Ningpo Commissioner to enquire whether his permission had been requested for the landing, and he wired he knew nothing of the case. I have now written to the Superintendent asking him

to

to obtain the Police vertion of this new procedure.

The Superintendent admitted that the Lorcha, apart the smuggling of opium, could not well be made responsible for the landing of cargo at Tinghai if it was allowed by the Police; but although this may be taken into consideration I think a nominal fine must be inflicted to establish the irregularity and after receipt of the Police reply I intend objecting 1° to its searching of the lorcha, and 2° to its interfering with the destination of the cargo on board.

<u>Status of steam vessels employed by Military and Police Administrations</u>

I duly received on 1st inst. your S/O letter of 24th April telling me to do nothing more for the present. Reference to Subject 1 of the April Summary of Chinese Correspondence will however show you that the case was reopened by the Superintendent himself sending me on 21st a despatch (No. 89) informing me of the detachment of four cruisers for patrol duty on the Chekiang Coast, and a letter (No. 90) admitting the Chaowu was now a Police patrol boat and asking

asking me to issue her a Certificate freeing her from Customs Examination. I replied (No. 63) that the Chaowu when employed as a transport would have to submit to Customs Regulations. I also took advantage to point out that she did not fly the flag, design of which was appended to your Circular. No reply has been received.

Staff :

Mr. D. Verner, Assistant-Examiner, has again been obliged to rest for 3 days on account of his lever, and with the advert. of the hot weather I am afraid he will get worse.

Yours respectfully,

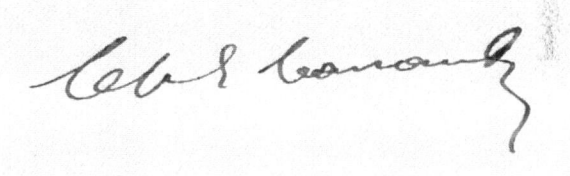

21 MAY 1917

Inspectorate General of Customs,

PEKING, 15th May, 1917.

Dear Sir,

I am directed by the Inspector General to acknowledge receipt on the 11th May, S/O No. 78 dated 4th May, 1917.

Yours truly,

L. Acheson,
Private Secretary.

. Tanant, Esquire,

W E N C H O W

OUSTOM HOUSE,

Wenchow, 23rd May, 1917.

S/O No. 79.

SIR,

REVENUE COLLECTION : RAISING OF DOLLAR RATES.

I have duly received your S/O of 1st May, and your despatch No. 720/64,876 in which you tell me that should the instructions therein contained call for modification of your previous despatch No. 714/64,687 concerning the Bank Agreement I am to withhold action until I have reported further. This despatch (720) having reached me just after I had transmitted you (Wenchow despatch No. 3,213) the revised Bank Agreement re-arranged as per instructions of your despatch No. 714, I withheld action as directed, and in order to dissipate all possible doubts about the local currency I wrote on the 16th to the Chamber of Commerce to enquire about local taels - currency - and market rates (how and where they are fixed and whether they are posted for public information). I also asked as regards remittances by drafts to Shanghai in which currency they are made, how the exchange rates for these remittances are fixed,

posted.

posted, and generally made known. Receiving no reply I wrote again on the 21st and was informed that the question had been referred to the Money market guild (Chien Yeh Kung So 錢業公所). The short and the long of all this is that they (Chamber of Commerce) fearing that your rate must be enforced from 1st June are taking advantage of every opportunity to delay.

In the meantime I received a visit from the Manager of the Bank of China who came to enquire whether the question had been settled I said "No, and I am to further report about market rates etc.", and I took advantage to ask him whether or not there is a local Tael: the reply was "No, the currency are clean Mexican Dollars", about market rates they are the rates of exchange between this and Shanghai which are fixed daily by the bankers. He went on saying that in ordinary circumstances each banker fixes his rates from the information received by mail from Shanghai, allowing a small percentage for local small rises or falls of exchange, but if there are important

important fluctuations at Shanghai, then the Shanghai Agents telegraph the Shanghai dollar-tael rates. These local rates are not posted and he (Bank of China) added that he does not go to the daily meetings, but waits for the bankers to come with their offers.

This should dispose of the Chamber of Commerce arguments about market rates being posted. However I must wait, before reporting, for the Chamber's reply. The Banker also mentioned that the adoption of the Ningpo system would cause much trouble on account of the fixation of a rate and of the various calculations it would involve, and for this I strongly support him. It is very unfortunate that the dollar-tael exchange at Shanghai fell down a little these last few days as this might be a further argument by merchants to insist on the adoption of the sliding Ningpo system. However as regards the principle that a fixed dollar rate should be adopted at ports where sycee is not customarily in use in trade transactions and where consequently market rates are not quoted, I think there

cannot

cannot be any doubt about its application here. The Chamber practically plays on words when it argues that the dollar rate was fixed 40 years ago according to the Shanghai Tael. That may be so, but actually there are no taels and no sycee current here. Transactions are in dollars and when speaking of rates they mean exchange rates between Wenchow and Shanghai, quite a different thing.

What annoys me in all this are the delays. The Banker in the conversation said that if necessary he could wait if the fixed rate is established, and in view of his letter of 29th April saying that his old agreement must terminate on 31st May (case 2, April Summary of Non-Urgent Chinese Correspondence) I asked him to confirm this change of attitude by letter, but this conversation took place a week ago and the letter has not come. While all this is going on our collection is fairly good. (Tea begins to be exported) and the larger the collection is and the more the Banker objects to the actual $152 = Hk.Tls. 100 rate while merchants cling to it.

Yours respectfully

CUSTOM HOUSE,

S/O No. 80.

Wenchow, 25th May, 1917.

Sir,

REVENUE COLLECTION : raising of dollar rate.

I am now posting my reply to your despatch No 720/64,876, having received the Chamber of Commerce reply to my enquiries re market rates, etc., and the Banker's proposal to postpone the change of rate mentioned in my last letter.

As I said before the Superintendent being connected by family ties with this place is largely responsible for not stopping the objections to the adoption of the Standard rate, and I must say of him as of most Chinese Officials that they only see their private interest. Now, for instance, you gave instructions by telegraph on 25th April to allow export of wheat free for one year. There is still here in force a local prohibition to the export not only of Rice, but of wheat and all other cereals including sweet potatoes which dates from several years and has not been cancelled. I wrote on the 26th April to the

the Superintendent to notify your telegram and ask whether the prohibition would not be cancelled. Up to now no reply has been received. In the meantime, on the 16th, the Chamber of Commerce wrote that the matter had been referred to it and that it was of opinion that 5,000 piculs could be exported, but the Superintendent's reply has not yet reached me, and as I now hear that exportation was if not officially allowed, anyhow tolerated at the Superintendent's stations I presume that my request to cancel the prohibition upsets all calculations and some means must be devised to make good for the loss. The Chamber itself has no reason to recommend more the export of 5000 piculs than of 10000 as no wheat is consumed locally while most flour consumed is imported, but I am told the Chairman of the Chamber itself is interested in the export of the 5000 piculs.

  Yours respectfully,

CUSTOM HOUSE,

S/O No. 81.   Wenchow, 4th June 1917.

SIR,

OPIUM :

We seized recently on a passenger a small box prepared opium, probably about half a tael, and on being caught the man threw it in the river, but it was picked up and the man was arrested and I had him sent to the Police with the box. The case was tried by the Shen pan ting who inflicted 3 months gaol.

A few days ago a Formosan Chinese, who claims Japanese protection, was arrested in an inn for smoking and having in his possession 40 taels of opium. On his case being investigated he unfurled a special permit from the Japanese Governor of Formosa allowing him to smoke $3\frac{1}{2}$ mace a day. The officials would not recognise this permit as valid in China, but as the man's papers were otherwise in order he was sent to Shanghai to be sued before the Japanese Consul. In this connection I was requested by the Superintendent (at the last moment

as

as usual) to have his luggage searched, and a list of contents made out, so as to use it as proof should the man or the consulate put up a claim later on for shortage in his luggage. This list I declined to make out, saying the whole case was one of police and not within Customs attributions.

RICE, WHEAT, AND CEREALS:

The prohibition to export which still existed when your Circular No. 2661 was received, has not been rescinded, and the Superintendent wrote a week ago as will be seen in the May Summary of Non-Urg. Chinese Correspondence to still enforce it as crops are not promising.

DUTY COLLECTION:

The Maritime Customs show a loss of about Tls. 900 as compared with last year. Fortunately it has been more than compensated by an increase of over Tls. 1,700 of the N. C. Collection.

YANG KWANG CHÜAN (洋廣捐):

Messrs Slowe & Co., a Shanghai firm, wrote a fortnight ago to complain that hoglard which they pack here in a factory of their

their own and export in big quantities is being taxed by the Yang Kwang Chü, and asked me to have this levy stopped I replied that it didn't concern me and referred them to their Consul. I nevertheless mentioned the case to the Superintendent's Wei Yüan and said I am of opinion that once goods are in town it is difficult to oblige the exporter to pay dues which should have been collected before the goods reached the open port. I now hear the Consul has written to object to the levy of the tax. If this firm or its local agent were to apply for the steam factories privileged treatment they would in any case only pay 5 % ad valorem, the same as they pay now, and therefore the more reason, it seems to me, they have to object to pay the Yang Kwang Chüan.

PROVINCE SECESSION FROM CENTRAL GOVERNMENT.

A proclamation was issued on the 1st June by the Magistrate by order of the Provincial Governor and Tuchun saying that

that the Province had ceased to follow the Central Government's orders on account of the President and National Assembly's wrong doings People were exhorted to carry on trade as usual.

SUPERINTENDENT.

Is it the anticipation of impending trouble or the result of accusations referred to some time ago? It is difficult to guess, nevertheless the Superintendent has begun to remove part of his family to his native place. Some 20 of them, including servants, are leaving to-night with 150 packages luggage, and the rest - 30 more persons and some 600 luggage will follow by batches. It would seem from this that the Superintendent evidently thinks it is time for him to move. The Tao-yin who has only been here two months is said to be ready to start at a moment's notice.

STAFF.

Mr. Werner left a week ago, and Mr. Singer arrived yesterday.

Yours respectfully,

S/O.

INSPECTORATE GENERAL OF CUSTOMS,

PEKING, 5th June, 1917.

Dear Mr Tanant,

I have duly received your S/O. No. 79 of 23rd May, 1917.

Revenue Collection : Raising of Dollar Rates : If the dollar-tael rate is based on Shanghai, the Bank of China should have no difficulty in establishing it.

Yours truly,

E. Tanant, Esquire,
Wenchow.

S/O.

INSPECTORATE GENERAL OF CUSTOMS,

PEKING, 5th June, 1917

Dear Mr Tanant,

I have duly received your S/O. No. 80 of 25th May, 1917.

<u>Local reluctance to cancel prohibition of export of wheat</u> :

Central Government instructions, unless countermanded, should overrule provincial arrangements.

Yours truly,

G. E. Tanant, Esquire,
  <u>W e n c h o w</u>.

No. 82.

CUSTOM HOUSE,

Wenchow, 9. June, 1917.

352

Sir,

<u>Revenue Collection : raising of dollar rate.</u>
The Superintendent sent me two days ago through the N.C. Weiyüan a joint proclamation to sign and issue at the Native Customs informing the public that henceforth the duty rate of the dollar would be fixed according to the Ningpo system. The Weiyüan said that the Sup't had just received instructions from the Shui-wu Chü approving his (Sup't's) proposal (referred to in my despatch No. 3204 and my S/O No.77). As the matter was again referred to you in my S/O Nos. 79 and 80 and my despatch No.3217 I replied that I had not received your instructions, and I returned the proclamation to the Weiyüan.

As explained in the above quoted letters and despatch our position to insist on a fixed dollar rate is strong and I think you should this time assert your authority. You gave way to the Superintendent sneaking of the

Juian

Juian fish duty; you similarly assented to the recognition of the Haimen Fen Yun Tan which establish a preferential duty in favour of Inland steamers, prejudicial to Maritime Customs duty collection, and which might be claimed by Foreign Powers as a precedent for the abolition of the Coast Trade Duty; if you, this time, allow the Ch'u and other parties to interfere with this important question this will gradually undermine our position. You might think from this that I make it a personal affair and that there is spite on my part, but I can assure you there is nothing of the kind as I always mentioned in these dealings that the questions would have to be reported to you for your decision, so my own personality is shelved, but at a Service point of view I cannot help seeing that on a gross collection of about Hk.Tls. 100,000.(Foreign and Native Customs) we collect $152,000. while at the Standard rate we should get $155,550., viz. 3500 more dollars. According to the Ningpo system we should not get so much, but as on the whole the public will blame the Customs it seems it would be just as well, if we have to be blamed, to reap the whole benefit.

In any case the moment seems inopportune to effect the change, and if you have not issued any new instructions I think that we should let the matter stand until the banker presses again for a solution. His move in writing the letter transmitted in my despatch No. 3217 seems to indicate that he is willing to temporise.

REVENUE REMITTANCES.

Owing to the actual political uncertainty I am remitting the Revenue at once to Shanghai as soon as funds in Bank amount to over $1000.

   Yours respectfully,

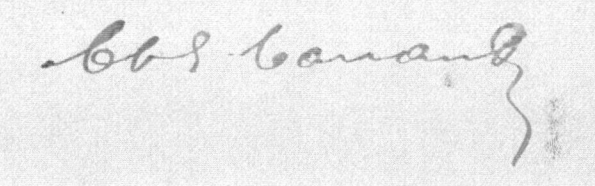

INSPECTORATE GENERAL OF CUSTOMS,

PEKING, 19th June, 1917.

Dear Mr Tanant,

I have duly received your S/O letter No. 81 of 4th June, 1917.

<u>Japanese Government permits for opium smoking.</u> These permits give Japanese subjects no authority to introduce opium into China.

Yours truly,

— Tanant, Esquire,
—NCHOW.

INSPECTORATE GENERAL OF CUSTOMS,

PEKING, 19th June, 1917.

Dear Mr Tanant,

I have duly received your S/O letter No. 82 of 9th June, 1917.

<u>Dollar rate for Revenue collection.</u>

The Ningpo system does not conflict with principle and it is to be tried. The Ch'u does not interfere with these matters or overstep in any way and did not issue instructions until I had acquiesced. Don't you worry about our position! it is quite safe!

Yours truly,

nant, Esquire,
N C H O W.

No. 83.

CUSTOM HOUSE,

Wenchow 28. June, 1917.

Sir,

Revenue Collection : raising of Dollar rate.
I am glad to report that the matter is progressing well. The Bank agreement has been revised. The Banker pretended that the Ningpo Office allows an addition of $0.25 per 100. Taels to the monthly average rate for the Banks benefit. The matter was referred to Ningpo who replied that nothing of the kind was granted and I consequently refused to grant it. The Superintendent has instructed the Chamber of Commerce to furnish daily market rates to the Bank, and we shall collect at the new rate on the 1st July.

Property.

Mr. Dick visited the Port on the 11th and left on the 12th after having examined the Customs properties and inspected desirable sites for possible buildings, but nothing was

decided

decided for he would have liked to know which of the lots I showed him could be purchased and at their cost. I subsequently made a rough plan which I communicated to the Sup't with request to say whether they could be purchased and at which price.

Revenue Collection.

Our Collection for June is good and we already exceed last year's by Hk Tls 2000 for Maritime Customs, and shall exceed it by 1000 for Native Customs.

Yours respectfully,

No. 84.

CUSTOM HOUSE,

Wenchow, 5th July 1917.

STAFF. MR. SINGER, EXAMINER B: APPLICATION FOR TRANSFER TO SHANGHAI.

Mr. Singer whose application for transfer to Shanghai I transmitted in Wenchow despatch No. 3223 has not been on duty ever since, and Dr. Stedeford issued him on the 2nd a Certificate of "Chronic Dysentery". Such being the case I am afraid it is no use waiting for his recovery for some time, and I shall be obliged if you will replace him.

CHANGE OF GOVERNMENT.

The Shanghai papers which arrived this morning brought news of the change of

government

government in Peking. At the same time the local Officials (Taoyin, General, Chih-shih) issued a notification informing the public that they were instructed by the Chekiang Tuchün to say that Chang Hsün and others had plotted against the Republic but that he was not ready to support them. Otherwise quiet here and very hot.

REVENUE COLLECTION:

The Ningpo procedure has been put in force as reported in despatch No. 3227 of 4th instant. June collection has been very satisfactory; we have an excess of Tls.3,369 over the 1916 figures for Maritime Customs and Tls. 1,827 for Native Customs.

500 TROOPS. arrived on 30th June said to be necessary to protect the country in case

China

China should go to war with Germany.

Yours respectfully,

INSPECTORATE GENERAL OF CUSTOMS,

PEKING, 10th July, 1917.

Dear Mr Tanant,

I have duly received your S/O letter No. 83 of 28th June, 1917.

<u>Bank agreement for revenue collection revised and dollar rate raised.</u>

Good!

<u>Transfer or leave for Mr H. Singer, Examiner B.</u>

If Mr Singer is sick, he should forward a medical certificate!

Yours truly,

nant, Esquire,
ENCHOW.

Inspectorate General of Customs,

PEKING, 17th July, 1917

Dear Sir,

I am directed by the Inspector to acknowledge receipt on the 14th July S/O No. 84 dated 5th July.

Yours truly,

R. Acheson,
Private Secretary.

Tanant, Esquire,

WENCHOW.

No. 85.

CUSTOM HOUSE,

Wenchow, 17. July, 1917.

Sir,

CONFISCATED CHINESE COINS.

I duly received Circular 2692, and as it is not given a Native Customs series number I beg to ask whether the same limitation as to the quantity allowed to any one passenger is not to be enforced by the Native Customs

As to the disposal of the cash through the Sup't, I beg to point out that here where so far cash are still in current use and where there is no Official Bureau for the purchase of cash and their subsequent smelting by the Govenment, the adoption of the Ichang practice — where it seems that there is a purchasing Office — means simply a present to the Sup't. For instance, we seized recently a lot of 24,000 spurious cash weighing 55 catties. Those cash though spurious are nevertheless accepted on the market at a low value, about 3 to 4000 to a dollar. The whole lot would therefore be worth at least from 6 to 8 dollars. Acting

upon

upon the instructions of your Circular I sent them to the Sup't and claimed 2 tenths of their value (at the Gov't rate 1 Tael weight = $ 0.01) = $ 1.76, so this leaves a balance of over $ 4; presented to the Sup't who will, besides, later on again receive his share of the one tenth carried to account, when the proceeds are divided at the end of the quarter.

UNREST. Some of the 500 troops which recently arrived have been sent to Chüchow where it is said there is some unrest. The Chüchow Magistrate has warned the Taoyin of the intended importation of 36 rifles by rebels, and the Superintendent has notified me to stop the importation.

STAFF. Mr. Singer, Examiner, B, is still sick, now absent for over two weeks. Mr. Lloyd, Tide-surveyor does his work but there is really too much out door work for one man alone.

WEATHER. A typhoon has been blowing on the 13 and 14th; fortunately it does not seem there has been too much actual harm done in our neighbourhood, although I understand there has been too much rain and the rice crop might suffer.

Yours respectfully,

CUSTOM HOUSE,

O No.86.

Wenchow, 21. July, 1917.

Sir,

STAFF : Mr. H.P.Singer, Examiner B 's application for leave.

Despatch No. 3229 now mailed transmits a Medical Certificate and a new application for leave instead of transfer. Dr. Stedeford rather recommends leave for though Mr. Singer might find better treatment and food in Shanghai, the Docter fears it is also an affair of climate, and he would have liked to see Mr. Singer go to a more bracing climate than Shanghai.

STAFF HOUSING ARRANGEMENTS.

In my last letter while mentioning a typhoon I forgot to say that Mr. Lloyd was unable to cross the River on those two days Fortunately ships movements were out of question with such weather, but nevertheless it is one of my arguments to have the Staff housed on this side of the River instead of on the Island.

Another typhoon is now coming up the Formosa Channel.

Yours respectfully,

INSPECTORATE GENERAL OF CUSTOMS,

PEKING, 24th July, 1917.

S/O

Dear Mr Tanant,

I have duly received your S/O letter No. 85 of 17th July, 1917.

<u>Confiscated Chinese Coins.</u>

It is not so much a question of the money as having a regular procedure and adhering to the principle that contraband is not disposed of by sale.

Yours truly,

—— nant, Esquire,
—— ENCHOW.

Inspectorate General of Customs.

PEKING. 31st July, 1917.

Dear Sir,

I am directed by the Inspector to acknowledge receipt on the 27th July S/O No. 86 dated 21st July.

Yours truly,

Jackson,
Private Secretary.

Tanant, Esquire,

WENCHOW.

CUSTOM HOUSE,

No. 87.

Wenchow, 4. August, 1917.

Sir,

DIVERSION OF DUTY BY SUPERINTENDENT'S N.C. STATIONS.

There has been some activity of late by various Sup't's Weiyüan to issue D.P.C.s for goods not entitled to them, and I have had to object.

1o. In the May Summary of non-urgent Chinese correspondence (N.C.case No.1) you will find letters *re* levy of duty by the Pingyang Sup't station on Fookien Lungngan destined to Wenchow.

2o. In the same Summary (N.C. case No.2) other correspondence objected to the reported export of wheat and potato cuttings by canals while their export is prohibited at the Head Office.

3o. In the July Summary you will again see in case No.1 that I had to complain of duty collection on Salt Fish by the Puchi station (a case somewhat similar to the Kanmen case settled in your despatch No.706/64,229 - N.C.69) while my staff assert that heretofore that station

station only collected duty on dried shrimps and fresh cockles and clams. The case is not closed and in further correspondence I refused to make any concession for goods not heretofore recognised as passed by that station.
4o. Now my despatch No.3230 (N.C. 174) has informed you of the Sup't's complete disregard of my objections to the export of potato cuttings by his station at Juian.

All this is very unsatisfactory and I hope that when you have the opportunity you will point out to the Shui-wu Ch'u the false position it puts us in by if not actually farming to the Sup't the Revenue collection of the stations outside of the 50 li radius, anyhow by allowing him to farm those stations All the trouble comes from that, for the Weiyüan who has paid for a term of office is bound to take steps to make good his money, and the Sup't must fight for him.

I have another case to bring to your special notice : it is that referred to as case No. 2 in the July Summary of non-urgent Chinese correspondence : PADDY : attempted exportation of. A chinese of the literati class
attempted

attempted to export from Ningtsun over 100 piculs paddy. He was not present when the seizure was made, The Ssu shih fearing the junk on which the paddy was loaded might escape at night had her brought up to Wenchow by a crew of villagers. The owner called the next day at the N.C. Office together with the Superintendent's brother in law, Chief of Division in the Sup't's Office, and the latter explained that the rice was the property of his friend who though residing in an Island close by owned extensive rice fields in Ningtsun's neighbourhood. Mr. Kaneko referred them to me, but the owner came alone, and although his case had all appearances of one of smuggling I told the man that upon receipt of a Sup't's official letter informing me of his right to export the paddy I would allow the exportation. But the next day the villagers who had helped bringing the junk here petitioned against the man and asked for protection in case he would seek to take revenge against them. I then transmitted the petition to the Sup't and asked him to investigate the case. My letter was sent on the 6th

6th and finally on the 19th I received a Superintendent's letter telling me the ownership had been successfully proved before the Magistrate and the exportation could be permitted. This in itself is a violation of the prohibition to export grain, for, according to Treaty no grain whatever should be exported while the prohibition is being enforced, but I did not think worth while argueing this special point. But I must particularly call your attention to this Sup't's brother in laws visit to Mr. Kaneko which might be taken as a kind of intimidation or interference. Besid if the case was so clear it is rather strange that it would take 13 days to clear it, and to speak frankly my opinion is that this was a clear case of smuggling in which the Sup't's brother in law was mixed up.

TRADE is not as good as it promised lately. Our M.C. collection for July shows a decrease of Hk.Tls.769 as compared with July 1916. Fortunately the loss has been made good by the N.C. which show an increase of about 900 Tls. The China Merchants S. N. Co having but little demand for freight are occasionally removing

removing the S.S. "Loochi" from her regular run and sending us only the "Kwangchi". Of the small Ningpo - Haimen - Wenchow steamers two are now out of run for repairs and, it is reported, eventual sale, and our mail service is rather disorganised.

The weather in July has been exceptionally wet. We had 6.70 in. of rain one night.

Mr. Singer, Examiner B, left on the 2nd rather dissatisfied that he was not granted full pay while on leave considering that he never had any leave during his 20 years service.

Yours respectfully,

O. No. 88.

CUSTOM HOUSE,

Wenchow, 7th August 1917.

374

of foreign
ers luggage
ditious papers.

SIR,

I was going to write S/officially to report my action in issuing 2 Certificates to the Superintendent to enable his delegates to search incoming ships for seditious papers, etc. But as I see that the matter was already reported on officially though not exactly on the same lines by my predecessor I thought better to imitate him and I only write this letter to bring the case to your immediate notice - vide Wenchow No. 3232/I.G. of this day.

Yours respectfully,

CUSTOM HOUSE,

89.　　　　　　　　　　　Wenchow, 9. August, 1917.

Sir,

　　PADDY : Exportation of with Police assistance.

With reference to that part of my letter No. 87 dealing with : "Paddy : attempted exportation of" I have to report a new case at Ningtsun in which after having been told to stop a junk with paddy not covered by Huchao, the Police allowed her to go under pretext that it knew the owner and would be guarantor for him. I reported the case to the Sup't but again refrained from referring to the Treaty prohibition, and shall await your instructions. Nevertheless I asked for a severe punition for the Police for releasing cargo without my permission.

　　　　　　Yours respectfully,

S/O.

INSPECTORATE GENERAL OF CUSTOMS,
PEKING, 14th August, 1917

373

Dear Mr Tanant,

I have duly received your S/O. Letter No. 87 of 4th August, 1917 : Diversion of duty by Superintendent's Native Customs Stations :

In any particularly glaring case it may be necessary to charge our duties and leave it to the merchants to bring on the pressure. The Shui-wu-Ch'u can do very little and naturally is always disposed to support the Superintendent.

Yours truly,

Tanant, Esquire,
Wenchow.

Inspectorate General of Customs.

PEKING, 14th August, 1917

Dear Sir,

I am directed by the Inspector General to acknowledge receipt on the 13th Aug. of S/O. Letter dated 7th Aug. No. 88

Yours truly,

G. Acheson,
Private Secretary.

Tanant, Esquire,

Wenchow.

Inspectorate General of Customs,

PEKING, 21st August, 1917.

Sir,

I am directed by the Inspector to acknowledge receipt on the 16th Aug. S/O. Letter dated 9th Aug. No. 89

Yours truly,

Acheson,
Private Secretary.

Tanant, Esquire,

Wenchow.

CUSTOM HOUSE,

No. 90.

Wenchow, 23. August, 1917.

Sir,

With reference to my S/C No. 87: DIVERSION OF DUTY BY SUPERINTENDENT'S N.C. STATIONS:

and particularly case 3o. mentioned under that heading (duty collection on Salt fish by the Puchi station) - Vide also Subject 1 in July Summary of non-urgent Chinese correspondence - I have to add that the Superintendent in a letter which he handed himself to me on the 10th, submitted 4 butts of Hungtan, three years old, showing that some fresh fish had then been passed by the Puchi station. Those butts cannot well be recognised as proof that the cargo was really passed by our stations so much the more as it is commonly known that such butts were specially filled up formerly by Weiyüan to accompany their accounts , and this was so much objected to that the Superintendent himself replaced the Hungtan

by

by Ssu-lien-tan. However after enquiring from Mr. Kaneko and the N.C. Ssushih who declared that with one exception to which they objected no such fish had been passed by them, I replied on the 18th to the Sup't that unless he could show the Hungtan themselves instead of the butts I was put in a wrong position having either to disbelieve him or my Staff. I added that leaving aside the question of documents, enquiry into the real origin of the goods would prove that with the exception of cockles and clams, which might claim local origin, all other fish products, including shrimps, were imported from the sea at various places where the Puchi station has opened sub-stations, to be there dried or salted and re-exported, and that following the principle of the settlement of the Kanmen case it seems that the duty should not be collected at those sub-stations. I took advantage to point out that those sub-stations which are within the 50 li radius should be under my control. I went on asking why they were not handed over to my predecessors

predecessors or were established subsequently. However as they are not stated in the Shui-wu Ch'u's list of Custom Houses, etc., they should not exist, or, if needed, should be handed to the Commissioner, and I finally said that the case was too important for local settlement. I have had no reply so far.

SEARCH OF FOREIGN PASSENGERS LUGGAGE FOR SEDITIOUS PAPERS.

I reported in my S/O No. 68 having issued 2 Certificates to the Superintendent to enable his delegates to search incoming ships. The Maritime Police took advantage to follow the Weiyuan and 8 Policemen boarded and searched the I.W.S.N. Steamer on arrival from Ningpo via Haimen. I objected to this to the Sup't who asked me to write to him and he transmitted my letter to the Police, and passengers are now searched on shore. I noticed in a Shanghai paper that the Japanese to whom this measure referred to were arrested just as they were leaving for Hangchow.

Paddy

PADDY : EXPORTATION OF WITH POLICE ASSISTANCE.

With reference to my S/O Nos. 87 & 89 I have to report that the last case has noy yet been replied to by the Superintendent, but I am told that a Magistrate proclamation was posted yesterday at the City gate to the effect that persons residing outside while owning ricefields within this district will be given a Huchao allowing them to export their paddy on due production of land tax receipts. This solves the case in one way, but what of the prohibition, and of the possible fraud on the part of the Magistrate's staff who might sell Huchao ?

AUTHORITIES TO SIGN CUSTOMS DOCUMENTS.

My despatch No. 3235 mailed yesterday mentions that no official reply was sent to Circular No. 2232. There was, however, a reference to that case in Mr. Acheson's S/O No. 7. It seems the real motive of the Ch'u's instructions to the Sup't was then misunderstood by Mr. Acheson as the Sup't could not help asking him his opinion, and even investigating behind his back.

WAR.

WAR.

The Sup't informed me on the 15th of the declaration. The Telegraph Office notified at once various restrictions in the despatch of telegrams. Censors have been sent to the Post Office. The Sup't told me that the few Germans in the China Inland Mission at Chü-chow would be sent to Shanghai.

Mr. Kaneko left yesterday. Your telegram transferring him was received on the 15th only a few hours before the departure of the Steamer, and for 8 days we have had no steamer.

The Tidesurveyor has been somewhat disappointed not to be moved as he expected that the removal of so many German Tidesurveyors might be a chance of transfer to a more important port.

Yours respectfully,

Inspectorate General of Customs,

PEKING, 5th September, 1917.

Sir,

I am directed by the Inspector to acknowledge receipt on the 1st Sept. S/O No. 90 dated 23rd August.

Yours truly,

Acheson,
Private Secretary.

Tanant, Esquire,

WENCHOW.

S/O No. 91.

CUSTOM HOUSE,

Wenchow, 10th Sept. 1917.

SIR,

REMOVAL OF POST OFFICE WITHIN THE CITY:
EXAMINATION OF PARCELS.

Some time ago the Postmaster told me the two rooms we rent the Post Office are insufficient, and he asked me to rent him the Tidewaiter's Quarters above his Office. I replied it was impossible. On thinking over the question, however, I came to the conclusion that it being unlikely that we should, for some time at least, have more than one Tidewaiter, we might as well rent one of the 3 rooms to the Post Office, thus leaving two for the Tidewaiter's use, and I informed the Postmaster accordingly. He referred my proposal to the Hangchow Postal Commissioner and the latter has now replied that the extra room would not be required as they want to build or rent a house in the city for the Head Office,

keeping

keeping the actual office rented from us as a Sub-office. As most business is transacted here by Chinese merchants living towards the South Gate I think the idea is a good one. But as regards Customs co-operation that is quite different. We are very short of Staff and on this account it has been the rule - several times objected to by the various Postmasters - not to examine parcels after noon on days of clearance of steamers. If the central Post Office is removed within the city I am afraid the Postmaster will also remove the Parcel Office to his new premises. This would mean sending our Examiner to that office for the examination of parcels, which cannot well be done in actual circumstances. I therefore beg to ask you to note this, and if you have an oppertunity to see the Associate Director General to mention him the desirability to let the Parcel Office at the Custom House as heretofore.

POST OFFICE RENT.

While on this question I beg to point

point out that we only charge $5.00 rent to the Post Office for the 2 rooms we lease it, which is far too cheap. $10.00 would be a fitting rent, rather below than above local demands from neighbouring house owners, and I beg to ask for your anthority to raise the rent to $10.00 a month.

<u>Mr Matsubara placed at the General Office and Mr. Wong Haiu Geng at the Native Customs</u>

Mr. Matsubara has arrived, and owing to his limited knowledge of Customs work - only General Office - I have thought it advisable to place him in charge of the General Office and Returns to begin with, and sending Mr. Wong Haiu Geng to the Native Customs. I think Mr. Wong's presence at the N.C. will be the best check I can place on that Staff's doings, for being Chinese he can hear more than us foreigners. There is only one thing I regret for Mr. Matsubara, and that is that he loses thus the use of the chair which has been granted to the Assistant detached to the Native Customs. ~~In thi~~

Discontinuance

<u>Discontinuance of chair for Weigher detached to Native Customs.</u>

In this connection I must report an abuse which to me appears as grotesque, and which, with your permission, I want to stop. A chair with 2 bearers was formerly granted to the Tidesurveyor when he used, at the beginning of the N.C. control in 1903, to spend all his time at the N.C. Time passed on, the Tidesurveyor was removed, an Assistant was put in charge, while the Tidewaiter was sent daily to the N.C. for out-door control, and he was given the Tidesurveyor's chair. It seems to me already rather objectionable to thus provide a Tidewaiter with a chair; there were, however, extenuating circumstances : long distance, heat climate, health, etc. But it appears that when the Tidewaiter did not or could not go over, one of the weighers was sent there in his place. Thus, since the last Tidewaiter resigned, over a year ago, the senior Weigher has been detached to the N.C. and has been granted the use of the chair. As this man is regularly transferred and

does

does not any longer do duty at the M.C. I do not see more reason to grant him a chair than to any other employé either of the M.C. or the N.C., and I therefore wish to stop this. The re-appointment of Mr. Wong to the N.C. seems a good occasion to re-transfer the senior weigher to the M.C. and replace him by his junior, and do away with the chair entirely. It is not so much in my opinion an affair of saving - though it represents $192. a year + as of face for the Assistant and other men above the Weigher who have to pay for chair when using them.

Yours respectfully,

No. 92.

CUSTOM HOUSE,

Wenchow, 13. September 1917.

Sir,

SMUGGLING BY CHINA MERCHANTS S.N.Co's Ships. My despatch No. 3238 calls your attention to this smuggling, and it may look strange that I should call for your assistance to stop it. But I do not see what else I can do. The foreign staff of those ships is inadequate to efficiently supervise the shipment of cargo. They themselves complain of no support at head quarters. They repeatedly gave us hints of the smuggling going on. They dare not do anything else : if they give away information they will have all the staff against them, and that means a terrible time for them ; if they are too strict with the crew complaints go to head quarters and they are advised by the foreign Marine Superintendent to go slow.

I am told that in view of this smuggling which is not limited to Charcoal and Firewood the crew canvass for it. They undertake, at shippers risks, to deliver goods in Shanghai, and

and do not charge any commission until the cargo has been duly landed. If we confiscate or fine all the loss is supported by the shippers; the crew only swear at us and laugh in their sleeves and begin again next trip. So if we want to stop this the only chance is to find a way to fine the crew.

In this connection I must ask your view upon a point of difference of opinion I have with the Tidesurveyor. He tells me it is current out-door staff practice to see particularly that there be no smuggling in the cargo space, because such smuggling takes the place of duty paying goods. My opinion is that it is immaterial where smuggled goods are concealed as long as we stop them. Of course we lose duties when the cargo space is occupied by non-paying-duty goods, but in any case goods which cannot be shipped to-day will have to be shipped to-morrow, and we shall then collect the duty.

The August collection has been bad, resulting in a loss of Hk.Tls.1700.(3159 Tls in 1917 as compared with 4948 in 1916). The N.C. collection was fortunately only 232 Tls short. Slack season, typhoons, political uncertainty.

Yours respectfully

To. No. 93.

CUSTOM HOUSE,

Wenchow 15 Sept. 1917.

Sir,

N.C. Tariff : Hemp and Hempskin : rates of.
With reference to my despatch No. 3241 I have to add that before answering me the Superintendent sent me the N.C. Weiyüan to say that the N.C. Tariff was going to be revised and that the case had as well to wait. I replied that there is a talk of revision of the M.C. Tariff, but as regards N.C. we might have to wait several years. I added that it was unimportant whether the alterations of the rates which I proposed could or not be effected, but that the error in the interversion of the actual rates should be corrected, and from what the Weiyüan said I saw that the Sup't was unwilling to admit officially that Mr. Mao had made a mistake.

Now his reply shunts the responsibility on the Chamber of Commerce, which seems rather abnormal; but in the meantime there is a publis grievance against the N.C. which, I think, should be remedied.

Sliced Potato: prohibition to export.

The

The Weiyüan also asked what was the yearly exportation of sweet potato. I replied: How can I know when for several years we enforced the prohibition? You had better enquire from your Juian station which passed it. He then said the crop was very good this year at Juian, to which I replied then have the prohibition withdrawn, for if any goes out otherwise I shall also allow exportation. I took advantage to make the Weiyüan read Art. XIV of the MacKay Treaty.

Mr. Ehtman, our recently arrived Examiner is sick - Buboes (groin)- otherwise the Tidesurveyor is very satisfied of him and particularly of Mr. Singer's removal, and though the latter is on this Office Paysheet while on leave we hope he may not be re-appointed here when his leave expires.

Yours respectfully,

No. 94.

CUSTOM HOUSE,

Wenchow, 18. Sept. 1917.

396

Sir,

DIVERSION OF DUTY BY SUPT'S PUCHI STATION AND OPENING OF SUB-STATIONS WITHIN COMMR'S RADIUS.

The case of diversion of duty and existence of Supt's stations without, apparently, the Ch'u's sanction, now reported in my despatch No.3243 has been hanging on for two months as is shown by reference to my S/O Nos. 87, 30., and 90.

I cannot refrain from laying too much stress on the Supt's mischievous and unfair action ever since he has been appointed he All his, and his Weiyüan, ideas and work have had only for object to reduce the Commr's collection. If it were solely for the Govern't's benefit, one might admit it though reluctantly for we also collect for the Govt, but Mr. Mao and consorts' activities have in my mind and my predecessors - if not Mr. Acheson, at least Mr. Bowring- been only due to their greed and nothing else in his S/o N° 95 of 28 April, 1913,

m?

Mr. Bowring reported: "I discussed the question of duties being levied at a place called Puchi just outside the 50 li radius on goods for Wenchow. He (Supt.) affected to be unaware of this fact and would remove the delinquent Officials.

As a matter-of fact I have learnt that he is endeavouring by lowering of duties to allow goods to and from Wenchow to fulfill their duty treatment at places where he has sole control."

In another S/O. No. 97 of 3rd May 1913, Mr. Bowring again reported:" As I pointed out to you the Supt. is enticing merchants to pay lower duties outside the 50 li radius. I found out however that according to an old ruling, copy of which is not extant but well known that cargo for Wenchow carried by canal from Juian cannot acquit itself of its duty en route but at Wenchow alone. I sent for the Weiyüan and requested him to get a Notification issued by the Supt. jointly with myself informing the public of this fact".

Again

Again in his next S/O (he 98 of 10th May, 1913,) Mr. Bowring said:" The Notifications I referred to in my last S/O viz. a/. payment of Tonnage dues, b/. duties on goods to and from Wenchow not to be collected outside 50 li radius, etc., have been jointly issued by the Supt. and myself and are satisfactory".

Such being the case the Supt's attempt to collect at Puchi, as he did at Juian is so much the more reprehensible. Once he has given his word to the Commr. that he agrees with him about the illegality of the collection, it is expected that he will not start again collecting on the sly. I very much regret not having been acquainted with these facts when I had to write about Juian.

There is, however, one point of doubt with these S/O statements : there is no Chinese correspondence to corroborate them, and that is where Mr. Mao scores again. As you will see in my despatch he told me " there is no use writing so much about all those petty cases which we might settle *vivâ voce*". Well that would be all *right with a man one can trust, but the* fact remains that there is nothing whatever on record of the cases referred to by Mr. Bowring, and with his downright effrontery Mr. Mao would probably have denied having said or done anything including the issue of the joint proclamations. He sends them by his Weiyüan who makes the Commr. sign a receipt and that is all. Nothing is left in our archives. With a man of this type I see no other way but to put everything down on paper. I have done my best to refute his arguments without coming to this question of verbal agreements with Mr. Bowring for I feel it is about useless, and I shall be thankful if you will take up the case with the Ch'u.

The opportunity might at the same time be seized to show the Ch'u that the introduction of the Quadruplicate D.P.C., also in use in the Ningpo N.C., although theoretically an excellent measure, is a failure in practice, as too expensive if special employés have to be kept and even their work scrutinised in order to compare the parts of D.P.C. received with the *butts and enquire from the various offices about missing*

missing documents. Those Quadruplicate D&P.C. could only be made use of in a Service like the Maritime Customs where there is only one head superintending all the Mar. Customs Offices of the country, but in the N.C. where each district on account of the dual collecting system is absolutely independent of each other with but the nominal control of the Board at Peking, it is but waste of time and money.

Yours respectfully.

CUSTOM HOUSE,

S/O NO. 95.

Wenchow, 22nd Sept., 1917.

SIR,

I have to report a <u>Supt's visit on the 17th to try and settle various pending cases</u>:

<u>Paddy: exportation of from Ningtsun with Police connivance</u>: (August Summary, N.C. Subject 3 and S/O letters Nos. 89 and 90).

On the 14th, I transmitted to the Supt a petition from the villagers who had helped us to stop the Junk (which the Police subsequently allowed to clear) claiming for my assistance as they were accused by the paddy owner of having stolen 16 piculs while the Junk was in our custody. In a lengthy letter of the 17th the Supt. replied that the case was still undecided the police denying that the Junk sailed with its connivance. This was received in the forenoon and when the Supt called in the afternoon he informed me he had seen the Magistrate and

and that the paddy owner and Police were wrong, and he asked me what would be the proper fine. I said the case as regards disregard of Customs regulations was one for us to decide and that the Magistrate had better limit himself to punish the Police, and that I proposed obliging the owner to pay the value of the smuggled paddy which should really be confiscated, and that besides for the making a Junk go and thus ignore us ~~that~~ I would impose a 10 Tls. fine. The Supt agreed. The owner has since come and I informed him accordingly, taking his own figures to estimate the quantity and value of the Paddy ($60.). He had no money and promised he would pay within a week. I informed at once the Supt by letter to instruct the Magistrate not to close the case until I inform him.

    The second subject discussed with the Supt was the <u>Potato Cuttings Case</u> (vide Wenchow desp. No. 3230 (N.C. 174) and your reply No. 747/66,278/82). The Supt said his Juian Station was powerless to stop this
                          smuggling

smuggling as the people are too turbulent and said all it can do is to collect duty when it seizes some potato cutting. He begged me to find a way to help him as he said the Taoyin was unwilling to remove the prohibition. I gave him Art. XIV of the Mackay Treaty to read and said it was for the Governor to decide, that the prohibition could not go on for ever, and finally that if I obtained proof that this collection of duty goes on, I would have to allow exportation here. In my opinion this prohibition is a source of Revenue to all the officials concerned who must receive bribes to close their eyes; otherwise they would not in a year of plenty, as is presently the case, impose a prohibition. If I had means at any disposal. I would soon search the junks leaving Juian but this means a sea going launch which is not worth the amount of duty at stake, and therefore we have only to wait for our luck in catching some shipment accompanied by Duty Receipt.

We

We then came to the <u>Diversion of duty on Salt Fish by the Supt's Puchi Station</u> (vide Wenchow desp. No. 3243/178 and S/O Letters 90 and 94). The Supt referred to the last 2 cases mentioned in my letter No. 127 and said he had punished his Weiyüan on account of the case of false declaration of value; but as regards the fish imported by 4 junks and seized while transhipped into 9 small boats and found to be 157 instead of 71 piculs as per 2 D.P. C. handed in by the Junks, he produced the <u>butts</u> of 4 D.P.C. covering the 157 piculs issued by his station and asked me what I had to say against the Weiyuan. I simply told him I could not understand how the smugglers only handed me 2 D.P.C. if they paid for four, and that as regards the smugglers they had paid the $100 which I fixed as value of the confiscated excess, and I thought if they had thus paid without difficulties there must be something wrong somewhere. I also pointed out the lack of entries, repeatedly, on those Puchi documents.
To

To this the Supt replied by showing me some of my stations documents which seem improperly filled up, and he added his Stations were doing the same. I do not think he was satisfied and he told me he was going to reply but his letter has not reached me yet.

I then asked him what progress had been made about the cost of the building sites recommended by Mr. Dick and he replied that the question was a very difficult one and was still in the Magistrates hands. This, I must admit, is true, and with a very backwards population as that of Wenchow I am afraid it will take months to settle.

The Supt also mentioned the arrival of a special delegate appointed by the Governor at the Board of Communications request to investigate a dispute which has been going on for upwards of 20 years on account of the anchorage of Ningpo Junks in the Harbour and the question of access to

a

a certain jetty by country boats and he said he was going to ask me to join with the Harbour Master in the investigation.

Yours respectfully,

Duplicate.

INSPECTORATE GENERAL OF CUSTOMS,

PEKING, 26th September, 1917.

Dear Mr Tanant,

I have duly received your S/O. Letter No. 91 of 10th September, 1917 :—
<u>Removal of Post Office within the City at Wenchow : difficulty anticipated in the examination of parcels</u> :

The Post Office will have, I think, to send the parcels to us for examination ! <u>Commissioner proposes to discontinue the practice of granting a chair to Weigher detached to Wenchow Native Customs</u> :

Do so !

Yours truly,

E. Tanant, Esquire,
<u>Wenchow</u>.

Duplicate.

INSPECTORATE GENERAL OF CUSTOMS,

PEKING, 26th September, 1917.

Dear Mr Tanant,

I have duly received your S/O. Letter No. 92 of 13th September, 1917 : Smuggling by crew of China Merchants S. N. Co.'s ships :

Organised smuggling by the crew can only be stopped by getting at the crew and incidentally delaying the steamer. You should, if the case warrants it, get the Superintendent to arrest the responsible Chinese members of the crew and have them punished !

Yours truly,

Tanant, Esquire,
Wenchow.

Duplicate.

Inspectorate General of Customs,

PEKING, 26th September, 1917

Dear Sir,

I am directed by the Inspector to acknowledge receipt on the 22nd Sept S/O. Letter dated 15th Sept. No. 93

Yours truly,

C. Acheson
Private Secretary.

— anant, Esquire,
Wenchow.

CUSTOM HOUSE,

O No. 96.

Wenchow, 1. October, 1917.

Sir,

STAFF : Mr. Ehtman, Examiner, sent to Hospital at Shanghai.

In continuation of my S/O letter No.93 I regret to have to inform you that upon the Doctor's advice I had to grant 3 weeks leave to Mr. Ehtman to go to the Shanghai Hospital for treatment. It is not that the Doctor could not treat him here, but the man had practically nobody except his boy to attend to him, while in Hospital if, as is presumed, an operation is necessary, he will have all medical and material assistance handy. I should add that the Doctor made no objections to crossing over to the Island to visit Mr. Ehtman, but as it takes him at the lowest over one hour to go and return, and as he is rather busy not only with his own hospital but with occasional outdoor patients and classes which he has

to attend at the Methodist College in the
absence

absence of Missionaries to whom the British Government refuses Passports, all his time is more than amply taken, and I am sure this loss of time in crossing over to the Island must have been for some thing in his so readily endorsing Mr. Ehtman's application.

About STAFF I would like to know who, in case of emergency, should be left in ~~the~~ charge of the port, viz : Mr. U. Matsubara, 4th Asst. B, or Mr. Wong Haiu Geng, 4th Chinese Asst. A? It is not that I want a leave, but accidents may happen. Besides I think it would be better that a question like that be settled would it be only for precedence in social functions, occasional official calls, etc.

HARBOUR. Just as I was writing my despatch No. 3245 showing a discrepancy in Customs and Port Regulations concerning Harbour limits, I received Printed Note No.462 calling for the text of Regulations for the intended new issue of III.- Misc. Ser. : Regulations, so I shall have to wait for your reply

before

before answering the Stat. Sec.

At the same time I received a telegram from the Coast Inspector referring me to your despatch No. 666/62098 and saying he was sending the "LIKIN" to make a survey of the Harbour. That despatch, I regret to say, does not give me any authority for disbursements for the work and party, etc., and if I am to pay anything or advance funds in that connection I would like to have an authority.

Yours respectfully,

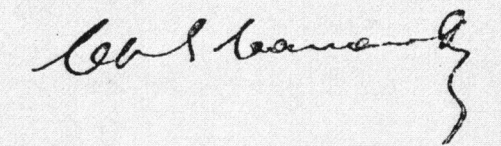

No. 97.

CUSTOM HOUSE,

Wenchow, 2. October, 1917.

Sir,

I duly received your despatch No. 755/66518/83 on the Puchi Salt fish duty collection question, and as this despatch and mine (No. 3243/178) crossed each other I have taken the liberty to wire as follows : "Your despatch 755 and my 3243 crossed each other: as the latter replied fully to your queries must I still endeavour to arrange settlement locally or will you first reply Shui-wu-Ch'u on the light of my despatch The whole affair is one of principle and if any concession is made it will mean further encroachments". I can assure you there is nothing private in all those questions which I have had to take up with the Supt. In fact they were thrown upon me volens nolens as a result of Mr. Acheson's indifference or inaction in not nipping in the bud the attempt - which proved so successful - to steal the Juian

collection

collection from us.

 The Weiyüan who has now attempted to grab the Puchi collection was already before employed in the N.C. and subsequently in the Supt's Office, and is a clever man from all reports ; but it seems he has just met with an accident on account of over charging duty, and it is said he was arrested by local people and handed over to the Yoching magistrate, and that he has been dismissed. So, the question will perhaps resume its former undecided state. The Supt whom I saw 3 days ago (before I received your despatch) had already received the Ch'u's instructions to collect as before and seemed rather indifferent; nevertheless I saw he was not satisfied not to have gained his point. He tapped me on the sleeve and told me now the case is settled and we must be friends like two arms in one sleeve, but I am afraid of this outburst of friendship when I see that all this trouble comes from his not keeping

his

his promises to Mr. Bowring, and that is why I think it would be better that you claim the whole fish duty collection to finish with these local squabbles.

The September collection shows a loss of 666 Tls for the Maritime Customs, but fortunately a gain of 250 Tls for the N.C. on respective totals of Tls 3857 (M.C.) and about Tls. 4000 (N.C.)

Yours respectfully,

INSPECTORATE GENERAL OF CUSTOMS,

PEKING, 3rd October, 1917.

Dear Mr Tunant,

I have duly received your S/O letter No. 94 of 18th September, 1917.

<u>Diversion of duty question : Superintendent's previous undertakings not on record.</u>

What about the notifications themselves? Could not copies be obtained from somewhere?

<u>Diversion of duty question : Commissioner asks that the case be taken up with the Ch'u.</u>

The Superintendent got in first word officially and the Ch'u did not wait for me to take up the case, but, as you will see, took it up itself and supported the Superintendent.

<u>Uselessness of H.C. Quadruplicate D.P.C.</u>

I quite agree with you but your predecessor's recommendation that the Tsuliantan be adopted by us, which is on record, is rather in the way.

Yours truly,

INSPECTORATE GENERAL OF CUSTOMS,

PEKING, 3rd October, 1917.

Dear Mr Tanant,

I have duly received your S/O letter No. 95 of 22nd September, 1917.

<u>Paddy Export case settled locally with Superintendent.</u>

I think that you are more likely to get local difficulties settled by trying to cultivate friendly relations with the Superintendent – unsatisfactory though he may be – than by me taking up such questions, which here do not assume great importance, with the Shui Wu Ch'u, more especially as the Ch'u will always back the Superintendent if it can.

<u>Prohibition of Export of Potato Cuttings a source of profit to officials.</u>

The prohibition should be withdrawn as soon as possible!

Yours truly,

t, Esquire,
CHOW.

/O No. 98.

CUSTOM HOUSE,
Wenchow 8. October, 1917

Sir,

PUCHI SALT FISH DUTY COLLECTION QUESTION:
Two despatches received from the Supt. on the 3rd, after I had sent you my telegram of 2nd inst., but prior to receipt of your telegram of 4th telling me to try to settle the question locally, made me change my mind and I decided to report once more before doing any more in this connection.

In the first despatch the Supt informed me of the Weiyuan's discharge which would be quite a success and a kind of acknowledgement of our right had the measure been taken specially as a result of my complaints, but there is a rumour that the people's action in handing the Weiyuan to the Magistrate forced the Supt. to act, so I cannot attach much importance to the Weiyuan's discharge, though we shall be enabled to claim it as a kind of acknowledgement of our right. I have now reported this incidental case as settled in my despatch No. 3248/179.

The second Supt's despatch received was about the POTATO CUTTINGS PROHIBITION, and I thought better to forward it at once for I think your intervention is urgently needed. I take leave to refer you to my despatch No.3249/180 which will give you the details of the case. As well as I can see the Supt has not yet made his mind to accept the CHU's verdict about Kanmen, and now to make good for that loss he wants to get hold of the Potato cuttings export duty. He represents Juian as the center of the exportation, which may be true, but nevertheless there is a large trade in it here also, and had we allowed the export I am sure that trade would have developed for the shippers would not have been compelled to send their potato cuttings to Juian, such a round about way, to be thence smuggled out, and that is what makes the Juian export so flourishing.

In this connection I must not omit to point out the doubtful position of the Tao-yin. He answered a few months ago the Supt's

queries

queries saying it would be necessary to await the result of the crop; however the crop has been gathered, is admitted to be a good one, and yet the prohibition is not withdrawn. Why ? because it gives the Taoyin's representative a chance if not to allow the exportation anyhow to close his eyes - for a consideration - when export takes place. Seeing this coming move of the Superintendent I thought better to report first and await your decision for if you refer the potato cuttings case to the Ch'u I think it would be as well to settle also at Peking the Puchi Salt fish duty question. If I have to settle the question as given in your despatch No.755/66518/83, viz. that fish dried and salted at Puchi must pay there, we entirely give way to the Supt. The old practice prior to the discharged Weiyuan's appointment was not to collect there even on fish salted there but to send it all to Wenchow to pay duty here. Besides my predecessors and myself have done our best to impress honesty on our N.C. staff, and giving way now would not exactly be an encouragement. They know better than we do what was former practice, and when I see all the misstatements not to call them otherwise - in the Supt's despatches I have as well believe my staff than the Supt.

My argument that only goods shipped to Nanhui should pay duty at Puchi (which you do not think a tenable one) was forced upon me by the Supt proving that some small lots of shrimps, cockles and clams had paid at Puchi and had been imported at Nanhui. However he was unable to prove that fish paid at Puchi and was imported at either Head Office or Fish station.

As to obliging applicants to state their real destination at Puchi and have it filled in on the D.P.C. + which the Supt refuses - I beg to say that Chili (Puchi Weiyuan residence) is only 60 li from Wenchow, and considering that we have three stations at Wenchow, viz. Head Office, Fish station, and Nanhui, I cannot admit it is a hardship on merchants to declare their real destination. The case reported as settled in despatch No. 3248 clearly shows that the Weiyuan knew the destination of the fish in question; nevertheless he entered on his D.P.C. Wenchow, which
allows

allows of all sorts of tricks by the smugglers.

On the whole I should say that the Supt took advantage of my weakness and desire to meet him to claim more and more. Had I refused point blank to recognise any Puchi documents matters would not be worse As a matter of fact I gave way on his exhibiting his few D.P.C. passed by Nanhui and this was a mistake for I could as well have replied those were clerical errors.

I regret very much that my despatch reporting the whole affair was forwarded so late. I thought I was doing well to have the case complete. In any case I think that the correspondence about the discharged Weiyuan should be shown to the Ch'u with explanationas that the whole affair was started by this man ignoring the old practice.

The R.S."LIKIN" arrived two days ago.

Yours respectfully,

CUSTOM HOUSE,

No. 99.   Wenchow, 11. October, 1917.

Sir,

Superintendent's: removal of.

In my last letter I informed you that owing to the evident difficulty to have the Potato cuttings prohibition settled, I had postponed seeing the Supt to try and arrange the Puchi Salt fish duty collection question. It seems I was right for the Supt must have then already been informed of his removal from office.

In my S/O Nos. 70 and 72 of February and March last, respectively, I informed you of an investigation into the Supt's doings by a Weiyüan appointed by the Governor. Nothing seems to have come out from it, the Weiyüan having obviously been "squared". However new accusations were made and another Weiyüan appointed by the Governor at the Ministry of Finance's request came recently without warning and left on 30th September after having

having ascertained by inspection of shops' books that certain payments debited to official account by the Supt had not been made and that the seals on the vouchers were forgeries. It is also said that afterwards the same Weiyüan went into the Supt's office showing his special mandate, and, without asking for the Supt, inspected various documents.

It is now rumoured that on the 8th or 9th the Supt received a private telegram informing him that a Presidential Mandate had been issued calling him to Peking for explanations. No other details seem to have come and I am told the Supt's people say he is called to Peking for another appointment as his local tenure of Office has expired. Whatever be the case he has not informed me. I called yesterday (Chinese National Festival) but did not meet any of the Officials who were said to have gone to some school sports, so I don't know more than hearsays.

If this is true - and we shall know it in a few days on receipt of the mail - then

all

all the discussion and writing about those Puchi salt fish and Potato cuttings prohibition cases will be time wasted, and in that case I beg to ask whether it would not be advisable for you to take up the two cases with the Shui-wu Ch'u. If Mr. Mao is really discharged it might perhaps be an opportunity to represent to the Ch'u that he reported falsely on the Juian case when he said that the collection by his Juian office was old practice. You have Mr. Bowring's S/O letters proving that the practice was only started in Mr. Acheson's time. The Ch'u very reasonably decided that it was inadvisable to oblige merchants to ship their fish from Juian by sea and that as they had taken to send it by canal they should be allowed to go on. But as regards payment of duty at Juian we could argue that the principle is the same as at Kanmen and at Puchi: no collection on fish was heretofore allowed at those stations (except at Puchi exceptionally, and even then not on every kind of fish) the duties being,

according

according to old practice, payable at Head Office, and as we thus collect duty on fish imported through Kanmen and Puchi we should similarly collect on fish imported via Juian at the Nanhui (South Gate) Office. If there are fears of fraud the first Superintendent's station passed by should issue a kind of way bill (kuo tan as it is termed locally). It must not be forgotten that this collection by the Supt's Juian Office is highly detrimental to us, for, that office inaugurating the practice which the Kanmen and Puchi stations wanted to establish, obliges all junks fishing in Juian's neighbourhood to report and pay duty there, and once duty is paid there is no more talk to take it by sea to the Head Office. Besides there are arrangements to induce merchants to pay at Juian. Of this, of course, we have no proof, but it is obvious. Another point is that this collection at Juian creates a precedent and future Supts and their Weiyüan are bound sooner or later to try and enforce it at other stations.

If the three cases now referred to could be settled before the arrival of Mr. Hao's successor, and if he was specially instructed by the Ch'u to respect old practice, it would greatly facilitate matters.

Yours respect--

INSPECTORATE GENERAL OF CUSTOMS,

PEKING, 16th October, 1917.

Dear Mr Tanant,

I have duly received your S/O letter No. 96 of 1st October, 1917.

Emergency charge of port: Mr Matsubara or Mr Wong Hsiu Tong to take precedence?

Neither: both are too junior to have charge. In case of necessity somebody will have to be sent!

Coast Inspector's survey of Wenchow harbour: no authority received for disbursements in connection with.

You had better first see what arrangements the Coast Inspector has made. He has probably arranged about expenses!

Yours truly,

─── Tanant, Esquire,
WENCHOW.

Inspectorate General of Customs,

PEKING, 16th October, 1917.

Dear Sir,

I am directed by the Inspector General to acknowledge receipt on the 8th Oct. your S/O No. 97 dated 2nd Oct.

Yours truly,

L. Acheson,
Private Secretary.

— anant, Esquire,

Wenchow.

No. 100.

CUSTOM HOUSE,

Wenchow, 16. October, 1917.

Sir,

I beg to acknowledge receipt of your two S/O letters of 3rd instant, in reply to mine Nos. 94 and 95.

Uselessness of N.C. Quadruplicate D.P.C.

You tell me that my predecessor's recommendation that the Ssulientan be adopted by us is on record and that it is rather on the way: I read again the English and Chinese correspondence and I regret to say I fail to find that Mr. Acheson recommended the adoption of those Ssulientan. On the contrary he strenuously opposed them and up to now we do not use them in the Commissioners radius. Mr. Acheson's despatch No. 3087 transmitting copy of the Chinese correspondence is clear on this subject. By reference to Enclosure No.1 (Chinese correspondence) you will see that in his despatches Nos. 135 and 158 he said: the idea is good, but useless in practice as involving more labour, additional staff, and consequently increased

inadvisable

inadvisable expenditure considering that the collection tenth does not pay expenses. His admitting that the idea is good cannot be claimed as an acquiescement as he subsequently deprecates it. Similarly the Superintendent in his despatch No. 145, previously received, referring to Mr. Acheson's order to use Import Duty receipts at all stations, also praised the idea but finally found fault with it, and reiterated his demand for the introduction of Ssulientan. If a precedent is claimed for use of Ssulientan by our Offices it can only be, to my knowledge, that established by the Shanghai Customs in allowing their use at Woosung as stated in the Supt's despatch No. 145.

<u>Diversion of duty question : Commissioner asks that the case be taken up with the Ch'u.</u>

No doubt, the Supt got in first word officially, and I deeply regret my delays, but how can the Ch'u take a decision without first hearing both parties ? The removal of Mr. Mao and his delays in settling the Potato Cuttings Prohibition, are, I think, a good oportunity to take up again the case, so insignificant

it

it be, simply on account of the precedent it established. It is no question of face for me, for, for that matter, the Supt felt more annoyed than myself of the Ch'u's decision.

About intercourse with the Superintendent I must try and correct an impression which you seem to have that I am not in good terms with him. I have done my best to keep in good terms, but as everything with most Chinese Officials is simply an affair of money Mr. Mao cannot see me with an equal eye as I stopped his Kanmen collection and prevented him, at least for the present, to transfer his collecting propensities to Puchi (Chili) which is perhaps in a better location than Kanmen to stop all incoming junks and make them pay there. That is simple enough, but it means a loss to himself personally of several thousand dollars a year. Just the same about the Potato cuttings. He admits they are exported from Juian notwithstanding the prohibition, and this again is all gain to him, and if we can stop it it will mean a further loss not only to himself but

to

to the Taoyin and to the Juian Magistrate. After that the Commissioner cannot be persona very grata. Another Supt, unless the Shui-wu Ch' stops all those attempts, will do the same, or if not himself, his Weiyüan.

Our mail connections with Shanghai are most deplorable. Of the two China Merchants ships only one now comes regularly, and the three small steamers between this and Ningpo have ceased running, one sold to the Japanese for 250,000$ when she was hardly worth 50,000 before the war, and the two others being docked, may be prior to being also sold. So we have only one mail a week and everybody grumbles because the last parcel mail was left behind for want of room on board the ship.

Yours respectfully,

INSPECTORATE GENERAL OF CUSTOMS,

PEKING, 23rd October, 1917.

Dear Mr Tanant,

I have duly received your S/O letter No. 98 of 8th October, 1917.

Puchi Salt Fish Duty Collection Question.

I think that the appointment of a new Superintendent will give you perhaps an opportunity of settling the matter on a better footing. Any way it will be as well to have a try.

Yours truly,

— t, Esquire,
— CHOW.

CUSTOM HOUSE,

S/O No. 101.   Wenchow, 25th October 1917

SIR,

DIVERSION OF DUTY QUESTION: SUPERINTENDENT'S PREVIOUS UNDERTAKING NOW ON RECORD.
(reference to my S/O No. 94 and to your S/O letter of 3rd October in reply)

You asked whether the copies of proclamations issued in Mr. Bowring's time could not be obtained from somewhere. It was impossible to find them in our archives. Moreover Mr. Acheson when framing his Memo on the working of the N.C. applied verbally to the Superintendent or to the Weiyuan for a copy of all proclamations heretofore issued and copies of eight proclamations were handed him but not of the very one referred to by Mr. Bowring. On receipt of your letter I sent word to the Weiyuan that I would like to have a copy of a proclamation issued in May 1913, while he was already here. The reply was all copies were already given to Mr. Acheson. I said no, there must have been others. Then he
replied

replied the Superintendent is sorry but archives are already packed up for his successor. I then wrote to the Superintendent and said I had been directed by you to send a copy and I could not much wait longer. The reply brought me a copy of the proclamation about timber of 5th May 1913. I replied this is not the one wanted. There came a copy of a proclamation of 11th July 1913 - which had not been communicated to Mr. Acheson - stating that all imports from Juian must report to our Nanhui (South Gate) Station and pay duty there. I replied again it was not that and finally I received the wanted document 2 days ago. I am preparing my despatch and the correspondence will be forwarded by the next steamer.

PADDY EXPORT CASE SETTLED LOCALLY WITH SUPERINTENDENT BUT FINE STILL UNPAID.

In my S/O Nos. 89, 90 and 95 I reported about a case of export of paddy from Ningtsun with Police connivance and that the owner had promised to pay the fine. Unfortunately

Unfortunately he didn't keep his word and never returned. So, I wrote on 4th October to the Superintendent to ask him to urge the District Magistrate to make the man pay up, and as no reply was received I wrote again on the 18th and am still waiting for the money.

Yours respectfully,

[signature]

CUSTOM HOUSE,

No. 102.

Wenchow, 26. October 1917.

Sir,

<u>Diversion of duty : Puchi and Juian cases</u>

I transmit in my despatch No.3252 the text of the proclamations issued at Mr. Bowring's request on 5 May, 1913, and that of another one issued on 11 July, 1913. Strange to say nothing whatever can be found in despatches S/O letters, and Chinese archives about the latter which, though inferentially establishing that goods from Juian can be conveyed by canal, nevertheless maintained the old ruling that imports must pay duty at our South gate station. So, after all, the main principle cannot be denied that up to Mr. Acheson's time we collected on fish imported <u>via</u> Juian

About Puchi although Mr. Bowring referred to it in his S/O letters Nos 95 and 98 it is not specifically mentioned in the proclamations which deal only with
Pingyang

Pingyang and Juian cargo; but as it is in about the same position to the left of the River as Juian and Pingyang are on the right, it may be inferred that the rule then re-affirmed applied as well to Puchi.

There is still a point which, I notice, I omitted to mention in despatch No. 3152, and that is the limitation of the "small lots" permitted to pay duty at Puchi. This will again sooner or later be cause of friction with the Supt. for the Weiyuan instead of issuing one receipt say for 200 piculs will issue four of 50 piculs each and pre-date or post-date them according to requirements. If you could have the whole question settled it would remove causes of bickering which otherwise must inevitably exist.

Mr. EHTMAN, Examiner, writes at last that he will be allowed to quit the Hospital to-day. Mr. Lloyd out of 9 months stay here has been doing Examiner's work for four months during the successive illnesses of Messrs Verner, Singer, and Ehtman.

Yours respectfully,

Inspectorate General of Customs,

PEKING, 30th October, 1917.

Dr Sir,

I am directed by the Inspector General to acknowledge receipt on the 26th Oct. your S/O no. 99 dated 11th Oct.

Yours truly,

L. Acheson
Private Secretary.

E. Tanant, Esquire,

Wenchow.

INSPECTORATE GENERAL OF CUSTOMS,

PEKING, 30th October, 1917.

Dear Mr Tanant,

I have duly received your S/O letter No. 100 of 16th October, 1917.

<u>Diversion of duty question: Commissioner asks how the Shui Wu Ch'u can take a decision without first hearing both parties.</u>

It is an incurable habit of the Ch'u and invariably gives trouble.

Yours truly,

anant, Esquire,
WENCHOW.

CUSTOM HOUSE,

S/O No. 103. Wenchow, 3rd Nov. 1917.

SIR,

CURRENCY: NEW DOLLAR ONLY CURRENT AT A DISCOUNT.

I have to inform you that the Banker who collects our Revenue does not accept the new dollars - Head of Yuan Shih Kai, 3rd year of the Republic - at par with the Mex. Dollars. As the Mex. Dollar is the recognised local currency, and as our agreement for duty collection says: "7. - The Bank undertakes to receive duties which are payable in Hk.Tls. and Kpg.Tls. in the recognised local currencies of the port, etc." I do not object and leave it to the public - if not satisfied - to agitate the question with the Chamber of Commerce.

In this connection I beg to refer you to your Circular No. 2550, "4. - x x x The Chinese Government has for the last two years been minting a Standard Dollar of Mint K'up'ing Taels 0.72 weight and 90 per cent

cent fineness". I now read in an article on "Coins of the Republic of China" published in the Journal of the N. C. Branch of the R. H. Society, 1917, page 141: "118. Dollar - Silver (gr. 27, 88 % fine), etc." As the author, a Dr. Giuseppe Ros of the Italian Consular Service, got his information from the Head Engraver of the Tientsin Mint it seems this should be correct, but it does not agree with your Circular. Our Banker adds that these new dollars do not sound as well as the Mex. Dollars and are more easy to imitate and he even tells me that they are already successfully imitated at Pingyang in this district and that the authorities are trying to stop this. The actual depreciation is 30 cents per 100$.

WHEAT: EXPORT OF.

I received a petition from merchants asking, owing to a good harvest and to over production since the prohibition to cultivate poppy was established, to help them in having the local prohibition to export wheat cancelled. Following the instructions of your despatch

despatch No. 759/66574/84 re error in N.C. tarification of Hemp I referred them to the Chamber of Commerce. But nevertheless I transmitted the petition and my answer to the Superintendent who has informed me that he passed them on to the Taoyin and that he will let me know his reply.

While thinking over this question I see one way to do something to stop the prohibition. As you are aware by my February and May, 1917, Summaries of Non-Urg. Chinese Correspondence and my despatch No. 3230/174 the prohibition has only been renewed by the local Officials without, apparently, the Governor's sanction. Such being the case could we not allow the export at the Maritime Customs, the prohibition being illegally established? This would come to about the same treatment which you instructed me to grant at the N.C. to Potato Cuttings if I find that more is exported through the Superintendent's Stations (I.G. No. 747/66278/82). Nothing more has been head from the Superintendent than what

I

I wrote in my despatch No. 3249/180 in reply to your despatch above quoted.

Staff.

Mr. Ehtman has at last returned from the Hospital and resumed his duties cheerfully.

Mr. Lloyd asked my opinion about the opportunity to send you a statement showing that owing to successive illnesses of Messrs Verner, Singer, and Ehtman he has been doing Examiner's work for 4 months out of 9 which he has been stationed here. I told him that I did not think advisable to write specially as I had already mentioned it to you and he withdrew his statement. If I am not to have more than two men on my O.D. Staff I would as well prefer to have an Examiner with a slight knowledge of River work, and one Tidewaiter, than a Tidesurveyor and an Examiner for it is rather hard to ask the Tidesurveyor to do Tidewaiter's work, i.e. board, search, and clear steamers and look after N.C. junks.

Yours respectfully,

INSPECTORATE GENERAL OF CUSTOMS,

PEKING, 6th November, 1917.

S/O

Dear Mr Tanant,

I have duly received your S/O letter No. 101 of 25th October, 1917.

<u>Diversion of duty question: Superintendent's previous undertaking now on record.</u>

This may help matters somewhat.

Yours truly,

—— Tanant, Esquire,
WENCHOW.

Inspectorate General of Customs,

PEKING, 6th November, 1917.

Dear Sir,

I am directed by the Inspector General to acknowledge receipt on the 3rd Nov. of your S/O No. 102 dated 26th Oct.

Yours truly,

L. Acheson,
Private Secretary.

. Tanant, Esquire,

Wenchow.

CUSTOM HOUSE,

S/O No. 104.   Wenchow, 12th Nov. 1917

SIR,

<u>STANDARD OIL CO'S TANK INSTALLATION.</u>

    When reading over my predecessor's correspondence I found the following letter dated 3rd October 1916 addressed to the Standard Oil Co's agent: "I believe you are intending to construct tanks for oil here. In case you should be unaware of it, I write to say that there are certain conditions which have to be observed regarding the establishment of such. The site for the tank or tanks must be approved for the purpose by the territorial authorities and before oil can be stored licence must be obtained from the Customs. If you would like any further particulars on the subject, I shall be glad to furnish them. I only write this to tell you in a general way what is required.". No reply seems to have been received. But, nevertheless, work has been progressing. That Company purchased a large site on the north side of the River,

River, some two miles below enchow, at a place where it seems there will be constant access, unobstructed by sand banks, for their ships. The site consists half of flat surface land and half of the spur of a hill, and stones are quarried therefrom to fill up and face the River front. A large wall is also being erected all round the property.

I took advantage of the "Likin"'s presence to have a rough plan made, and the property is given thereon as 600 feet frontage x 500 depth, the flat frontage filled up measuring about 500 x 150 feet.

This is all I know of the Co's intentions. Nothing was mentioned to me, nor do I know what kind of an installation will be put up, i.e. tank or simply godowns, but the rumour is tanks, and I now think better report in advance and ask whether you have any special instructions to give me. I presume the purchase must have been done regularly otherwise the Chinese authorities would have objected; but it seems to me me rather strange that the Customs were not, if not consulted about the suitability of the place for shipping arrangements, anyhow informed of the officials' decision, for after all the matter concerns the Customs also on account of supervision.

LAND FOR COMMR'S AND STAFF QUARTERS.

Some progress seems to have been made: Mr. Mao, the Supt. professes to be very eager to see the question settled before his departure, so, following Mr. Dick's recommendation I am urging for the sale of the two hills Hai Tan shan and Tzu shan, but it is doubtful whether I will be able to get both. About Commr's neighbours one of them who refused outright to sell is now reported to be ready to bargain. One of the heads of the Shanghui is, at the Supt's recommendation, acting as my intermediary.

NINGTSUN PADDY CASE.

(My S/O Nos. 89, 90, 95, and 101, and your S/O of 3rd October).

The fine is still unpaid. I wrote again to the Supt. on 18th October for speedy payment. To-day I called again to renew the demand. The excuse is: no answer from the Magistrate.   Yours respectfully

INSPECTORATE GENERAL OF CUSTOMS,

PEKING, 13th November, 1917.

Dear Mr Tanant,

I have duly received your S/O letter No. 103 of 3rd November, 1917.

<u>Currency: non-acceptance by banker of Yuan Shih-kai dollar in payment of revenue: apparent discrepancy between fineness of standard dollar of Circular No. 2550 and that given by Dr Ros in printed article.</u>

My information came from the Canton Mint and I have no reason to suppose that it was inaccurate at the time. The dollars may of course have deteriorated. Unless the mints are under proper foreign supervision, they are bound to do so. That is the curse of Chinese mints and what makes currency reform so hopeless. We shall only accept Cheng Yang dollars as standard dollars so long as they are up to standard!

Yours truly,

ant, Esquire,
NCHOW.

CUSTOM HOUSE,

S/O No. 105.　　　　　Wenchow, 19th November 1917.

SIR,

THEFT OF CARGO.

One package arrived recently from Shanghai declared on Manifest, Cargo Certificate, and Application "Dyes", but on examination it was found that the Dyes had been removed and replaced by ashes. The cargo was covered by Shanghai E. C.. I understand the owners are claiming refund of the value of the goods from the China Merchants S.N. Co., but I don't know what to do as regards Customs treatment of the case.

We may claim that the goods presented for examination do not agree with the documents and confiscate, but the ~~possession~~ of a box of ashes will not make any difference to either owner or transporting Company. On the other hand I don't think we can claim a case of false manifest for the package was duly brought from Shanghai and submitted for examination. There is, though, a danger that cargo not being examined at Shanghai

Shanghai on re-exportation, the package though declared "Dyes" might have contained tins of opium which could have been removed on board before arrival of the ship at destination. The easiest way would be to ignore the case and drop it but before doing so I would like to have your advice.

POSTAL COMMISSIONER'S VISIT : POSTAL PARCELS.
The Postal Commr. for Chekiang, Mr. Arlington, arrived on the 10th by the Poochi and left by the same ship on the 13th. He told me he had come about the possibility to purchase a lot of land in the City for the building of a central Post Office, and in this connection he asked whether we could examine parcels there. Basing myself upon the wording of your S/O letter of 26. Sept, I replied it could not be done for the present as we have not the necessary staff. He then said that when at Changsha he had arranged with the Customs to have parcels examined by his staff, and he suggested the same arrangement.

I

I replied that I did not care for it for his staff know nothing of examination work. It seems to me a very objectionable principle to admit that men without proper training could do our own specialists' work. In any case there is really no hardship in having parcels examined here at the Custom House which is not far from the center of the City.

Mr. Arlington then asked me to extend the actual examination hours of outward parcels. My predecessor finding that occasionally our Examiner was too busy on a steamer's day had put up a notification restricting the examination of parcels to noon on mail days. In order to please the Post Office I replied that I would have again parcels examined in the afternoon, and after a few months we would see how this works. But if the public returns to the habit of waiting to 3.55 p.m. to bring in parcels for examination I shall resume Mr. Acheson's practice.

Mr. Arlington left without having been able to purchase his lot. While here he also investigated

investigated various anonymous charges against the actual Postmaster, none of which could be substantiated. He notably called on the local newspaper to apologise for a paragraph against the Postmaster and threatened to take official action if due apology was not published, but as he left next day it is to be feared the paper will not apologise.

 Yours faithfully,

CUSTOM HOUSE,

Wenchow 22. November, 1917.

No. 106.

Sir,

SUPERINTENDENT.

The new Superintendent has not yet arrived but is said to be due on 1st December. But again political changes in Peking may possibly delay him. I think the old Supt. is rather glad of the political change which makes him hope that Liang Shih-i, his protector, will be recalled to Peking to assist the Government on account of his wealth, and I am the more convinced of it that the Supt. speaks of visiting some known temple in this district before leaving, may be to await political developments.

CUSTOMS AND PORT REGULATIONS.

I duly received your despatch No. 766 in reply to mine No. 3245 pointing out an error in the printed Customs and Port Regulations book affecting Harbour limits, in which

which you say that " the latest sanctioned regulations are those in force ". This is all very good in theory; but in practice when those sanctioned regulations have been amended, and the amendment has been given effect to for several years although it does not seem from Office records to have received the I.G.'s or Tsung-li Yamen's sanction, can we ignore the "<u>fait accompli</u> " ? and when I am asked where are the Harbour limits, am I to answer : the North Water Gate (sanctioned regulations), or the village of Chupopu (amended regulations) ?

The Stat. Sec.'s Printed Note No. 462 calling for copies of regulations now in force in view to republish III.-Miscellaneous Series : No.25 says :" Obsolete rules are not to be sent, and where modifications have been introduced it is the amended rules in force at the time of despatching your manuscript that are wanted ". This seems to me rather at variance with the reply of your despatch No. 766, and I would like to have more definite instructions so that an error as the one published in the old book be not repeated.

In my opinion we should admit that the amendment--made in 1878 and enforced to our knowledge at least until 1882 (Wenchow despatch No. 99 of 1882) if not until 1890 when the error was made in the printed book of Regulations--is the actual Rule. This is so much the more necessary as it gives us control over that part of the Harbour reserved to Native shipping, after which we did not care in 1877 when the Regulations were first framed, but which now should revert to us if we want to have a proper control of Native Customs shipping. If we were to limit ourselves to the sanctioned rules of 1877 then the question of extension of Harbour limits would have to be considered! I must repeat that the two pontoons of the Ningpo I.W.S.N. steamers and the Standard Oil Co's godown with river frontage (not the intended tank installation mentioned in my S/O No. 104) are within the Harbour extension of those amended 1878 Regulations.

I

I did not deem advisable to ask the Superintendent whether he had in his archives documents relative to this extension of Harbour limits as he once said his Office old archives had been destroyed at the time of the Revolution; besides as he did not object to my letter objecting to ignorance of the Customs in settling the Ningpo Junks anchorage case (Wenchow despatch No. 3247), it seems he recognises our right to control the Harbour, and I thought just as well not to give a chance to raise the question. It might however perhaps be advisable to ask the British Consul whether he has in his archives any documents concerning Harbour limits ? In any case I think the simplest way to solve this question would be, as I said, to recognize the amended Regulations as now ruling and to this purpose I would like to have definite instructions.

The question of <u>Anchorage of Ningpo Junks</u>, the solution of which by the Supt. and the Governor's special Weiyüan was

found

found satisfactory in your despatch No. 767 threatens to be re-opened, for the Taoyin told me a few days ago that the Ningpo Junk people had again petitioned the Ministry of Communications against the decision!

Yours respectfully,

INSPECTORATE GENERAL OF CUSTOMS,

PEKING, 28th November, 1917.

6 DEC 1917

/O

Dear Mr Tanant,

In the absence of the Inspector General I have to acknowledge the receipt of your S/O letter No. 105 of 19th November, 1917.

Theft of Cargo.

The fraud, though detected at Wenchow, actually was perpetrated, presumably, at Shanghai. What is to prevent the Shanghai Commissioner fining the shipper, if a Chinese, for a false declaration?

Yours truly,

Tanant, Esquire,
WENCHOW.

Inspectorate General of Customs,

PEKING, 29th November, 1917.

Dear Sir,

I am directed by the Inspector General to acknowledge receipt on the 28th Nov. S/O No. 106 dated 22nd Nov.

Yours truly,

W. H. Chapper
Private Secretary.

Tanant, Esquire,

Wenchow.

CUSTOM HOUSE,

S/O No. 107.   Wenchow, 1st December 1917.

SIR,

WENCHOW INDEPENDENT.

News was spread on the 29th that following Ningpo's example Wenchow had proclaimed its independence from the Hangchow Government and the fact was confirmed yesterday by a proclamation posted at the Magistrate's Yamen, signed by the General in command of the Gendarmerie, the Taoyin, the Officer in command of the Battalion of Infantry stationed here since the last few months, and the Chiefs of Maritime Police and local Police Officers. This does not seem to have affected public life which outwardly goes on as usual. However the new government placed guards at the Bank of China so as to prevent the withdrawal of official funds by the various Government Offices, it being feared that the various Officials who are not of this place or province might withdraw their funds and run away. The amount so impressed does not however seem to exceed 30,000 dollars. For the

the present I have experienced no difficulty with our funds. A remittance of 1,000 Tls. was made without difficulty on the 29th and I withdraw quietly another 1,000 Tls. which I am keeping in safe as I must have some funds here while in ordinary incumstances we keep no funds whatever in safe. I thought of wiring to inform you of the change, but Mr. Mao, the old Superintendent whom I saw on the 29th told me it would be no use as the telegram might not be transmitted.

    Yours respectfully,

P.S. I am informed that Mr. Mao fearing to be mulcted of 20,000 dollars quietly left on the 30th. He came to dine quietly with us on the 29th, but on being asked to fix a day for a formal dinner with his successor he said all his evenings were taken, which I now understand! Mr. Hsü officially took charge to-day and called this afternoon.

CUSTOM HOUSE,

S/O No. 108.　　　Wenchow, 4th December 1917.

SIR,

WENCHOW INDEPENDENCE CANCELLED:

　　The free and Sovereign State of Wenchow ceased to exist since yesterday morning when it was reported that upon receipt of a threat from the Hangchow Authorities to despatch a punitive expedition, the declaration of independence had been cancelled. Later on the Manager of the Bank of China called to inform me of the happy event and mentioned that the Bank was still guarded but while previously the guards had laid an embargo on Government funds their function now was simply to protect the Bank in case of rowdyism.

WHEAT: PROHIBITION TO EXPORT PARTIALLY CANCELLED:

　　I mail with this my despatch No. 3261 reporting a relaxation of the prohibition in favour of 8,000 piculs belonging to leading merchants. In this connection I take leave to refer you to letter 114 of of the Chamber of Commerce (Maritime Customs Subject 2, May Summary of Non-Urg. Chinese Correspondence). The Chamber then only asked for permission to export 5,000 piculs the property of the Headman. As the demand was unsuccessful, and this time it was renewed for 15,000 piculs with the result that 8,000 piculs are permitted to be exported; meanwhile I hear from all sides that paddy is freely exported outside my radius and that there is a slight rise in the price of rice due to this illicit exportation. I really do not see any other way to have these prohibitions cancelled, and if necessary regularly established, but by your intervention and demand that the prohibition be established according to Treaty. This local prohibition only profits to local officials. If they have to ask the Governor's permission, matters will be different as the question will become general, and men in search of official positions will see that the prohibition be

regularly

regularly enforced, or else they will petition against delinquents, so as to supersede them - and probably act similarly. But in any case it will be to the ordinary merchants advantage.

    Yours respectfully,

INSPECTORATE GENERAL OF CUSTOMS,

PEKING, 11th December, 1917.

Dear Mr Tanant,

In the absence of the Inspector General I have to acknowledge the receipt of your S/O letter No. 107 of 1st December, 1917.

<u>Independence of Wenchow.</u>

It is to be hoped that there is no question of interfering with the revenue and that there will be no further troubles.

Yours truly,

──nant, Esquire,
──ENCHOW.

CUSTOM HOUSE,

S/O No. 109.   Wenchow, 13th December 1917.

SIR,

DUTY EXEMPTION OF ARTICLES FOR CHIHLI FLOOD RELIEF.

With reference to your despatch No. 778/67,533 instructing to pass free articles of clothing from Lin Hai (臨海) and Huang Yen Hsien (黃巖縣) I beg leave to point out that those places are close to Taichow and that the goods are likely to be sent to Ningpo or even to Shanghai direct by I.W.S.N. Steamer and it seems it would be proper to instruct the Ningpo and Shanghai Customs about their exemption of duty.

POLITICAL.

The situation seems quite normal again. Several Weiyuan were sent from Hangchow to investigate the affairs and one so called Keming-Tang was arrested and taken to Hangchow. It is rumoured that the General, Taoyin, and other officials who put

their

their names to the proclamation of independence were fleeced by those Weiyüan. Another one, a General, accompanied by about 100 men well armed, arrived by I.W.S.N. Steamer from Ningpo a week ago and is still investigating. The General's position is said to be rather shaky. I think I am not far from the truth in ascribing his contribution of 3223 old military garments to the Chihli flood relief to his desire to appease the Hangchow and Peking Authorities.

WHEAT EXPORT OF.

The partial cancellation of the prohibition to export in favour of 8,000 piculs, the property of leading merchants, referred to in my S/O No. 108 and Wenchow despatch No. 3261, has been given effect to. 8 Huchao of 1,000 piculs each were issued by the Magistrate for export to Shanghai, and one of them presented to cover an export of about 650 piculs by junk (Native Customs) to Changchow, Fookien. I refused both exportation and Huchao saying that the Superintendents

Superintendent's despatch did not specify Shanghai, and that a Huchao should accompany each lot; and at last a new Huchao has been issued for the 650 piculs for Fookien. In order to prevent the wheat going abroad I sent the usual "Certificate of Cargo shipped under Bond" to the Superintendent for transmission to the Amoy Superintendent within whose N.C. district the cargo is to be landed. So, this matter is settled, but only partially as only 8,000 piculs can be exported, and this only through privileged firms.

In this connexion I beg to point out that according to Revenue Stamps instructions each Huchao has to be stamped at $1.50 irrespective of number of bags. I think this rather hard considering that it is admitted that Conveyance Certificates for flour are taxed according to the number of bags they cover (vide Circular No. 2292). Will you take up the case and must I report by despatch?

Yours respectfully,

Commissioner.

INSPECTORATE GENERAL OF CUSTOMS,

S/O

PEKING, 14th December, 1917.

Dear Mr Tanant,

I have duly received your S/O letter No. 104 of 12th November, 1917.

Standard Oil Co.'s Tank Installation.

The Customs do not license or touch the matter until they have been officially notified that the Territorial authorities approve of the site.

Yours truly,

--- Tanant, Esquire,
WENCHOW.

Inspectorate General of Customs,

PEKING, 18th December, 1917

Dear Sir,

I am directed by the Inspector
General to acknowledge receipt on the 16th Dec.
S/O No. 108 dated 4th Dec.

Yours truly,

W. H. Chapper
Private Secretary.

Tanant, Esquire,

CUSTOM HOUSE,

S/O No. 110.   Wenchow, 20th Dec. 1917.

SIR,

CUSTOMS AND PORT REGULATIONS.

The receipt of the Statistical Secretary's Memo of 7th December asking to be supplied at once with the copies of Regulations to be republished, obliged me to apply - Wenchow despatch No. 3267 - for a decision about the port's limits referred to in my S/O No. 106. As I said in both S/O and despatch if we are to give up-to-date and accurate Regulations we cannot reprint the error that appeared in the first issue of the book, and in the absence of an official sanction I cannot take on myself to alter those printed Regulations. As I said in my S/O No. 106 it might perhaps be advisable to have recourse to the Consul's archives which were not touched in the 1884 riot. As to the Superintendent's archives Mr. Mao once said they had been

destroyed

destroyed at the time of the Revolution but seeing the difficulty I had to get the text of the missing joint proclamations this statement may be inexact.

THEFT OF CARGO.

In my S/O No. 105 I mentioned a case of theft of cargo presumably on board the China Merchants S.N. Co's S.S. "Kwangchi" between Shanghai and Wenchow, the contents of a box of dyes being replaced by coke or ashes. Mr. Bowra, in your absence, replied: "The fraud though detected at Wenchow, actually was perpetrated, presumably, at Shanghai. What is to prevent the Shanghai Commissioner fining the shipper, if a Chinese, for a false declaration? I transmitted this reply to the Shanghai Commissioner who answered: "It is quite certain that no fraud on the Customs was contemplated or effected, and therefore no fine is possible. It seems to me to be a case where the shipper will probably sue the shipping company for theft by their employees". Such is the case and I do not intend doing anything more, but nevertheless it seems rather strange that the Customs

Customs should disinterest themselves so easily, and I think this disinterestedness is a bad precedent.

GENERAL.

The political situation looks better. The commander of the battalion of Luchün stationed here since a few months, and who was one of the leaders of the independence affair, is transferred back to Ningpo. No decision is yet known concerning our General. Trade unfortunately is suffering and to add to it the "Poochi" who took a cargo of oranges up to Tientsin 2 weeks ago is reported ashore on the Taku Bar. The local exchange of the Shanghai Tael has gone down about $1.50 ever since the independence.

Yours respectfully,

INSPECTORATE GENERAL OF CUSTOMS.

PEKING, 26th December, 1917.

Dear Mr Tanant,

I have duly received your S/O letter No. 109 of 13th December, 1917.

<u>Partial cancellation of prohibition to export wheat.</u>

I think you should point out that the Treaty does not recognise such a state of things as a partial prohibition. If prohibition is raised partially it ipso facto becomes of non-effect.

<u>Revenue stamps for Huchaos.</u>

Carry out instructions.

Yours truly,

nant, Esquire,
NCHOW.

INSPECTORATE GENERAL OF CUSTOMS.

PEKING, 29th December, 1917.

Dear Mr Tanant,

With further reference to your S/O letter No. 109 of 13th December, 1917.

I.G. Despatch No. 778/67,533 (duty exemption of articles for Chihli flood relief): goods in question likely to be sent direct to Ningpo or Shanghai without passing Wenchow.

Shanghai was also instructed.

Yours truly,

nant, Esquire,
WENCHOW.

INSPECTORATE GENERAL OF CUSTOMS.

S/O

PEKING, 31st December, 1917

Dear Mr Tanant,

I have duly received your S/O letter No. 110 of 20th December, 1917.

<u>Theft of cargo on s.s. "Kwangchi".</u>

Captains are allowed to correct their manifests within a specified time and it seems to me that all the Customs have to do in a case of this kind is to see that the manifest is corrected. The theft concerns the ship and not the Customs.

Yours truly,
(signed) F. A. Aglen.

ant, Esquire,
NCHOW.

True Copy:

Private Secretary.

INSPECTORATE GENERAL OF CUSTOMS.

PEKING, 31st December, 1917.

Dear Mr Tanant,

I have duly received your S/O letter No. 110 of 20th December, 1917.

<u>Theft of cargo on s.s. "Kwangchi".</u>

Captains are allowed to correct their manifests within a specified time and it seems to me that all the Customs have to do in a case of this kind is to see that the manifest is corrected. The theft concerns the ship and not the Customs.

Yours truly

—— Tanant, Esquire,
—— WENCHOW.